# The Effective Teaching of
# Physical Education

# THE EFFECTIVE TEACHER SERIES

*General editor: Elizabeth Perrott*

For series list see pages ix–x

*THE EFFECTIVE TEACHER SERIES*

# THE EFFECTIVE TEACHING OF PHYSICAL EDUCATION

*MICK MAWER*

PEARSON
Longman

Harlow, England • London • New York • Boston • San Francisco • Toronto
Sydney • Tokyo • Singapore • Hong Kong • Seoul • Taipei • New Delhi
Cape Town • Madrid • Mexico City • Amsterdam • Munich • Paris • Milan

**Pearson Education Limited**
Edinburgh Gate
Harlow
Essex CM20 2JE
England

and Associated Companies throughout the world

*Visit us on the World Wide Web at:*
http://www.pearsoneduc.com

©Longman Group Limited 1995

First published 1995

ISBN 0 582 095220 PPR

**British Library Cataloguing-in-Publication Data**

A catalogue record for this book is
available from the British Library

**Library of Congress Cataloging-in-Publication Data**

Mawer, Michael.
    The effective teaching of physical education / Mick Mawer.
      p. cm. -- (The Effective teacher series)
    Includes bibliographical references and index.
    ISBN 0-582-09522-0 (paper)
    1. Physical education--Study and teaching. I. Title.
    II. Series.
    GV361.M296 1995
    796'.07--dc20
                                         94-38241
                                           CIP

12 11 10
07 06 05 04 03

Set by 7E in 10pt Times
Printed in Malaysia, PP

# C O N T E N T S

# EDITOR'S PREFACE

This well-established series was inspired by my book on the practice of teaching (*Effective Teaching: a Practical Guide to Improving your Teaching*, Longman, 1982), written for trainee teachers wishing to improve their teaching skills as well as for in-service teachers, especially those engaged in the supervision of trainees. The books in this series have been written with the same readership in mind. However, busy classroom teachers will find that these books also serve their needs as changes in the nature and pattern of education make the in-service training of experienced teachers more essential than in the past.

The rationale behind the series is that professional courses for teachers require the coverage of a wide variety of subjects in a relatively short time so the aim of the series is the production of 'easy to read', practical guides to provide the necessary subject background, supported by references to guide and encourage further reading, together with questions and/or exercises devised to assist application and evaluation.

As specialists in their selected fields, the authors have been chosen for their ability to relate their subjects to the needs of teachers and to stimulate discussion of contemporary issues in education.

The series aims to cover subjects ranging from the theory of education to the teaching of mathematics and from primary school teaching and educational psychology to effective teaching with information technology. It looks at aspects of education as diverse as education and cultural diversity and pupil welfare and counselling. Although some subjects such as the legal context of teaching and the teaching of history are specific to England and Wales, the majority of the subjects such as assessment in education, the effective teaching of statistics and comparative education are international in scope.

*Elizabeth Perrott*

# ACKNOWLEDGEMENTS

We are grateful to the following for permission to reproduce copyright material:

Curriculum and Assessment Authority for Wales, Cardiff, for extracts from *Physical Education in the National Curriculum: Non-Statutory Guidance for Teachers* CCW 1992; Routledge for extract and figure from *A Guide to Teaching Practice* (1989) by L Cohen and L Manion; and material in our Boxes 8, 19 and 20 from *Classroom Teaching Skills* (1984) edited by E C Wragg; School Curriculum and Assessment Authority, London, for extracts from *Physical Education Non Statutory Guidance* NCC 1992; The Rugby Football Union, Twickenham for a figure from *Skills practices for all* (1992); Taylor and Francis for the assessment table in our Box 21, from *Assessment in Physical Education: A Teachers' Guide* by R Carroll (1993); *Physical Education Review* for material in our Box 5 from an article by D Behets 'Teacher enthusiasm and effective teaching in physical education' Spring 1991; The Physical Education Association for material in our Box 23 from an article by A M Laytham (1992) 'Pupil's Self-assessment: Can teachers help?' from the British Journal of Physical Education 23, 1 23–35, also material in our Box 24 from an article by A M Latham and T Lucas (1993) 'Planning assessment and the assessment of planning in games' from the *British Journal of Physical Education* 24, 4, 17–21, and our Figure 13 from 'Practical knowledge and games education at Key Stage 3 (1993) by B Read from the *British Journal of Physical Education* 24, 1, 10–14; Human Kinetics for our Figure 1 (HK Fig. 1-A) from "Towards a Model of Teacher Socialization in Physical Education: The Subjective Warrant, Recruitment and Teacher Education" by H Lawson, *Journal of Teaching in Physical Education*, (Vol. 2, No. 3), p. 6. Copyright 1983 by Journal of Teaching in Physical Education. Reprinted by permission; our Figure 9 (HK Fig. 1) from "A Hypothetical Model of Observing As a Teaching Skill" by K R Barrett, *Journal of Teaching in Physical Education*, (Vol. 3, No. 1), p. 23. Copyright 1983 by Journal of Teaching in Physical Education. Reprinted by permission; our Figure 10 (HK Figure 1) from "Clinical Diagnosis As A Pedagogical Skill" by S J Hoffman. In *Teaching in Physical Education* (p. 37) by T J Templin & J K Olson

(Eds.). Champaign, IL: Human Kinetics Publishers. Copyright 1983 by Human Kinetics Publishers. Reprinted by permission; our Figure 11 (HK Figure 2) from "Clinical Diagnosis As A Pedagogical Skill" by S J Hoffman in Teaching in Physical Education (p. 39) by T J Templin & J K Olson (Eds.). Champaign, IL: Human Kinetics Publishers. Copyright 1983 by Human Kinetics Publishers. Reprinted by permission; material in our Box 10 (HK Table 3) from "Beliefs, Interactive Thoughts and Actions of Physical Education Student Teachers Regarding Pupil Misbehaviors" by J M Fernández-Balboa, *Journal of Teaching in Physical Education*, (Vol. 11, No. 1), p. 69. Copyright 1991 by Human Kinetics Publishers, Inc. Reprinted by permission.

Whilst every effort has been made to trace the owners of copyright material, in a few cases this has proved impossible and we take this opportunity to offer our apologies to any copyright holders whose rights we may have unwittingly infringed.

# *A C K N O W L E D G E M E N T S*

I wish to record a number of acknowledgements.

The first, and most important, is to my wife Annie who has not only demonstrated unfailing support throughout my career, but has been particularly patient and encouraging during the writing of this book.

Secondly, I would like to express my gratitude to those student teachers, newly qualified teachers, advisers and lecturers who willingly gave their time to complete questionnaires distributed as part of the 'Teachers of Physical Education Project'. Their lengthy and honest submissions have contributed substantially to the shape of this book.

Finally, I have appreciated the guidance and encouragement provided by the editor of this series, Professor Elizabeth Perrott.

MAM

# LIST OF ACRONYMS

| | |
|---|---|
| ALT: | Academic Learning Time |
| ALT–PE: | Academic Learning Time – Physical Education |
| BAALPE: | British Association of Advisers and Lecturers in Physical Education |
| BEd: | Bachelor of Education |
| CCW: | Curriculum Council for Wales |
| CUDE: | University of Cambridge Department of Education |
| DES: | Department of Education and Science |
| DFE: | Department for Education |
| EKSD: | End of Key Stage Description |
| HMI: | Her Majesty's Inspectorate |
| HOD: | Head of Department (Physical Education) |
| NCAT: | National Curriculum and Attainment Target |
| NCC: | National Curriculum Council |
| NQT: | Newly Qualified Teacher |
| OFSTED: | Office for Standards in Education |
| PE: | Physical Education |
| PEA: | Physical Education Association |
| PGCE: | Post Graduate Certificate in Education |
| PoS: | Programmes of Study |
| ROA: | Records of Achievement |
| SCAA: | School Curriculum and Assessment Authority |
| SEAC: | Schools Examination and Assessment Council |
| SCOPE: | Standing Conference on Physical Education |
| TEPE: | Teachers of Physical Education Project |

# CHAPTER 1

# Introduction: Becoming a Physical Education teacher

## Why teach PE?

I gained a lot from PE when I was at school and was very much influenced by the PE staff. I want children to at least have a chance of gaining what I have from PE. I wish to teach children the abilities I have. (BEd student teacher)

I enjoyed sport a great deal. I felt that becoming a PE teacher would allow me to pursue my interest as well as being able to pass on my knowledge and skill to others. I personally get a great deal of satisfaction from watching children enjoy sport. (BEd student teacher)

I wanted to work in an outdoor environment and was attracted to some kind of social service. (Male PE teacher – 41 years of age)

Enjoyed sport and wanted to link a career to it. (Male PE teacher – 29 years of age)

Why do people want to teach PE? The above quotations from students in training and experienced teachers of PE taking part in the Teachers of Physical Education (TEPE) Project reflect an overiding interest and enjoyment of sport and a feeling that they wanted to pass on their knowledge, enthusiasm and love of sport to young people. When asked 'Why did you want to become a PE teacher?' the majority of students in teacher training mentioned some aspect of 'working with children' (65%) and 'enjoyment of sport/physical activity' (60%) as their main reasons for embarking on a career in teaching physical education. This is not new. In a study of 50 male and 50 female PE teachers in Hampshire secondary schools by Evans and Williams (1989) the most common reason for entering the PE profession was 'love of sport', and the positive influence that their PE teachers had had on them during their own school careers.

Hendry's (1971) earlier study noted that career choice in physical education related to the possession of high skills ability and a liking of children.

Student teachers in the United States of America appear to have similar reasons for chosing a career in physical education as their UK cousins. In Belka, Lawson and Lipnickey's (1991) study of 55 undergraduates at the beginning of their course of training the majority mentioned wanting to use their 'athletic ability', 'to work with people' and 'to be helpful to others', as the main reasons for embarking on a career in PE teaching.

Dodds and her colleagues (Dodds *et al.*, 1991) also found that service (helping people), continuation (staying associated with sport) and doing work that's fun, were the main occupational decision factors in their study of teacher/coach recruits.

Why students decide upon a career in teaching physical education is the first stage in what Lawson (1983) suggests are the three phases of teacher socialisation into the profession. The first phase occurs prior to initial training and is termed 'anticipatory socialisation' (Dewar, 1989). This phase involves such factors as exposure to PE teachers and participation in the PE curriculum during our own school years as pupils. As a consequence of these experiences we develop perceptions and 'images' of the profession of teaching physical education.

## Images of teaching Physical Education

Lawson (1983) uses the term 'subjective warrant' to describe the perceptions and other information accumulated about a particular professional role: 'The subjective warrant consists of each person's perceptions of the requirements for teacher education and for actual teaching in school.' (p. 6)

It appears that we learn a great deal from the many hours that we spent at school in the gym and on the playing field about what teaching is all about. We may then wish to emulate the attributes and characteristics of our favourite PE teachers and coaches. However, as Lawson (1983) points out, other factors do play a part in the formation of the subjective warrant, and these are shown in Figure 1.

Our teachers and coaches, family members and the opportunity to stay involved in sport and to help others through teaching and coaching, are all factors influencing the choice of a career in physical education. In fact, at least one study has shown that our own experience as pupils at school may well influence our professional practice when we become teachers more so than initial training courses (Atkinson and Delamont, 1985). Schempp (1989) developed this theme by examining the notion originally put forward by Lortie (1975) that an 'apprenticeship by observation' period may exist in which future physical education teachers are influenced by their days being taught PE at school. In his study of 49 student PE teachers, Schempp (1989) concluded that this apprenticeship period as a pupil: '...informs the prospective physical educator of the tasks of teaching, influences assessment strategies for determining the quality of teachers, and helps

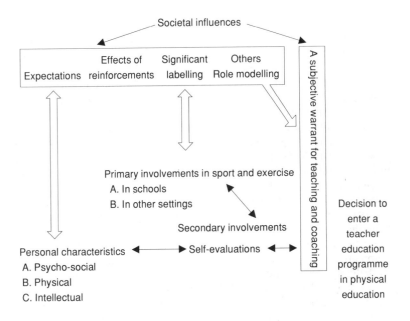

*Figure 1    Factors influencing the Subjective Warrant for a career in teaching Physical Education*
Source: Lawson (1983) p. 6.

shape the analytic orientation towards each teacher's professional work.' (p. 36)

However, Schempp (1989) did not feel that: '...the past would determine the future for PE,' – suggesting that student teachers of PE may not be tempted to emulate the style and approach of their own PE teachers and ignore what they had learned at college:

Those assuming teaching roles are not the same people as those who were students, nor are the schools they enter to teach the same as they left as students. Although tradition stands strong in the process of schooling, time washes anew the circumstances of the educational experience. Teachers will, most certainly, carry with them the lessons learned from their apprenticeship and these lessons will inform their practice as professionals. (Schempp, 1989, p. 36)

The important point to make here for the beginning physical education teacher is to be aware of the dangers of relying too much on one's 'apprenticeship by observation' when preparing to teach. Past experience as a pupil may offer a wealth of knowledge of the personal qualities and 'presence' of teachers, but this would only be valuable if such reflection is critical and leads to the continued personal development of the student teacher in terms of improving professional practice.

Regardless of Schempp's (1989) optimism, there is the danger that the results of such early observation of one's own PE teachers may be so persistent that formal training is unable to alter images and beliefs about teaching already learned. As Graber (1989) and Lortie (1975) have pointed out, in attempting to emulate their favourite teachers, students teachers don't appreciate that they are only imagining what teaching is like. Such a view of teaching is therefore based on intuition and imitation of personalities rather than pedagogical principles. However, whilst taking into account the dangers of an uncritical imitation of one's own PE teachers, it is worth pointing out that student teachers in their early years of training are generally in agreement with other members of the PE profession when identifying the personal qualities of 'good' teachers. Student teachers returning from their first teaching practice are beginning to build up an image of the personal qualities of 'good' teachers based not only on their 'apprenticeship by observation' as pupils, but also their apprenticeship as fledgling teachers working alongside experienced teachers.

As part of the 'Teachers of Physical Education' (TEPE) Project, 87 student teachers were asked: 'What attributes, personality characteristics, interpersonal and professional skills do you think a good PE teacher should have?'

The most frequently mentioned attributes and personality characteristics of a good PE teacher were considered to be: enthusiasm (35.6%), sense of humour (35.6%), approachability (29.9%), patience (21.8%) and the ability to be a good communicator (50.6%) and organiser (43.7%). Other characteristics of good PE teachers mentioned by some respondents included being outgoing, extrovert, fair, open-minded, easy going, the ability to get on well with or relate well to people and pupils, confident, showing consideration for others, a cheerful outlook, lighthearted, sociable, inventive, caring, articulate, assertive and has 'leadership qualities'. The student teachers also felt that good PE teachers were knowledgeable (35.6%) and skilled at sport, were committed to their chosen career, had good discipline, showed consideration for others, had the ability to listen, were aware of pupil differences and understood children. These findings are very similar to the American study of 224 pre-service and experienced teachers of PE by Arrighi and Young (1987). When asked the question, 'What is an effective physical education teacher?', 25% of the total responses referred to such personal qualities as enthusiasm and patience, linked to other characteristics related to skill knowledge, personal skill and personal fitness.

At the SCOPE conference at Nottingham in 1985 (SCOPE 1985) leading physical educationists involved in the initial training of PE teachers in the United Kingdom addressed the concept of 'Teaching

Quality and Physical Education'. In the conference working groups delegates were asked to identify the characteristics of teaching quality in physical education. The groups listed the following personal qualities as being desirable in new recruits to the profession: enthusiasm (overt enthusiasm and the ability to convey it to others), a sense of humour, empathy and sensitivity to others, the ability to relate to others, adaptability/flexibility in thinking, communication skills, cooperative attitude, imagination and initiative, the ability to organise, confidence and an ability to engender confidence, self-motivation, personal 'presence', articulate and good use of voice, capable of self-analysis, commitment and leadership qualities.

Such personal qualities may be an important factor in becoming an effective teacher. For example, the qualities of 'good teachers' as identified by HMI in their paper 'Education Observed' (DES, 1985) included:

...such a personality and character that they are able to command the respect of the pupils, not only by the knowledge of what they teach and their ability to make it interesting but by the respect which they show for the pupils, their genuine interest and curiosity about what pupils say and think and the quality of the professional concern for individuals. It is only where this two-way passage of liking and respect between good teachers and pupils exists, that the educational development of pupils can genuinely flourish. (p. 3)

The Department of Education and Science (DES, 1984) have in fact made certain recommendations to teacher training institutions concerning the personal qualities that those interviewing prospective new recruits to teaching should look out for: 'In assessing the personal qualities of candidates, institutions should look in particular for a sense of responsibility, a robust but balanced outlook, awareness, sensitivity, enthusiasm and facility in communication.' (p. 10)

Therefore, there appears to be considerable agreement between the DES, lecturers in higher education and student teachers in their early years of training, concerning the personal qualities of 'good' teachers of physical education. These personal qualities and 'images' of good teachers are seen by the profession as important basic attributes for the development of an effective teacher of physical education. But it is only a starting point. There are a number of stages on the road to becoming an effective physical education teacher.

## Stages in teacher development

When the question is asked, 'How long does it take to become an effective physical education teacher?', many feel that the process may well start earlier than was originally thought. It appears that our perceptions of the profession of teaching physical education may be formed by our earlier contacts with our family and teachers, as well as the coaches that we meet as pupils at school and as members of our local junior sports club.

According to a number of workers in the field of teacher development in physical education there may be a number of stages in the process of becoming an effective teacher of physical education.

We have already noted what Templin and Schempp (1989) refer to as a 'pre-training period of socialisation' into the profession which may occur prior to initial training, but the first formal stage in becoming a teacher will take place during teacher training. Feiman-Nemser (1983) has suggested three stages beyond the pre-training period in the development of a teacher:

An Induction stage – related to one's experience in training as a student teacher, but also including experiences in the first year of teaching.

A Consolidation stage – where concerns about control and being liked by children common in the induction phase give way to beginning to appreciate how to differentiate learning experiences for different ability levels and being able to identify why some lessons go well and others do not.

'Master teacher' stage – at this stage Feiman-Nemser believes that after several years one begins to orchestrate a variety of teaching skills efficiently, have clearly planned schemes of work, clear lesson objectives, with the majority of lessons taught being effective and satisfying to both teacher and class.

Metzler (1990) has adapted Feiman-Nemser's stages of teacher development to physical education, and includes pre-service, student teaching, induction and veteran stages in his model.

Metzler's 'pre-service' stage includes not only the undergraduate course (if taking the PGCE route), but also what has been discussed earlier as 'anticipatory socialisation' while a pupil at school. However, Metzler does believe that initial formal training marks the onset of this stage as do courses in teaching methods and periods of school experience.

The 'student teaching' stage involves the transition from using the skills learned on the teacher training course and school experience to transferring these skills to the real world of full-time teaching on teaching practice. Metzler (1990) believes that students: '... should have acquired a wide repertoire of effective instructional skills through simulation and lead-up experiences within the pre-service stage. Finding strategies that help transfer those skills from limited contexts to intact classes within a full teaching day is the difficult task for supervisors and teachers in this stage.' (p. 17)

The 'induction' stage is seen by many as being those crucial first few years following initial training when teachers hold a full-time teaching post in schools for the first time. Metzler (1990) believes that during this stage teachers really learn about what it is like to be in the school system: '... they learn about students and the unique characteristics of particular age groups, social groups and community demographics; and they learn about other teachers. Most importantly, teachers learn to formulate ideas and practices related to their instruction that they will likely carry with them throughout their careers.' (p. 19)

Metzler also believes that at this stage teachers learn to cope with professional socialisation, stress and other emotional pressures related to teaching. However, in quoting the work of Zeichner and Tabachnick (1981), Metzler points out that many effective teaching skills can be 'washed out' and lost in the transition from pre-service to student teaching to induction, and therefore progress to the 'veteran' stage of teaching (as it should be characterised by performance rather than passage of time) may be incomplete for many teachers.

Daryl Siedentop's (1991) advice to beginning teachers of physical education is based on his 20 years of research investigating the systematic development of teaching skills at Ohio State University. He envisages five stages in the skill development of PE teachers, but does not relate his stage model to the pre-service, student teaching, induction and master/veteran teacher phases mentioned by previous workers. Siedentop believes that progression in terms of skill development as a teacher may occur quickly if you want to improve and are provided with the appropriate opportunities to practise your teaching skills.

Stage 1 in Siedentop's (1991) model is the 'Initial Discomfort' stage. All student teachers go through this stage of feeling a little self-conscious in front of a class. Words and phrases don't come easily, particularly the effective praising of pupils.

Stage 2 in Siedentop's developmental stages is the learning of a variety of techniques. This is the stage of building a repertoire of different ways to praise and give feedback to pupils, to be enthusiastic and interact more with pupils.

Stage 3 is characterised by 'being able to do more than one thing at a time' – to be able to focus on improving one teaching skill and still be able to work on another aspect of effective teaching.

Stage 4 occurs when the teacher learns to use her teaching skills more appropriately as, for example, with praising a pupil in the right way and at the right time.

These various models of stages of teacher development put forward by American researchers may be valuable in helping PE teachers become aware of the fact that you don't become an effective teacher of PE overnight! Becoming an effective PE teacher requires a professional attitude towards the development of teaching skills and competencies as you progress from being a student teacher in training to your first post in school and throughout a career in teaching. Effective teachers are never satisfied with their teaching. They are constantly seeking to improve and develop, to put their practice under scrutiny, to explore new ideas and to become better teachers. Without this view of teaching as personal and professional development, there is the danger that teaching skills learned during initial training may become 'washed out' in those periods of transition between initial training and first experiences in school, and in that period immediately following taking up the first full-time post in school. Eventually to become a 'master' teacher one needs to establish quickly that important professional skill of constantly being able to reflect on your professional practice and expertise. Many believe that a truly 'master' teacher is a 'reflective' teacher – constantly reflecting on their work throughout their professional lives.

What student teachers and newly qualified teachers (NQTs) experience and learn during their time in the pre-service, student and induction stages of developing their teaching skills, is crucial to their later development as confident teachers. In an attempt to ascertain an impression of the experiences of beginning PE teachers in their early years of teaching, the TEPE Project investigated a number of issues related to being a 'New Teacher of Physical Education'.

# CHAPTER 2

# The new teacher of Physical Education

## Introduction

It really has been a shattering experience, and I have found that I'm tired consistently. However, I really have enjoyed it, and I love going to school everyday. Everyday presents a different challenge and a variety of rewards, making it a great job to have!

Enjoyable, very tiring, times of feeling a bit ineffective, but some real highs!

Being part of a friendly team is essential to how well I feel I have settled down. I feel that the other members of the department were always ready to back me up and also accept or listen to my ideas. I feel that I have been made to feel very welcome and a wanted part of the team which has given me confidence in my teaching.

At times I feel disillusioned due to compromise. On teaching practice you have time to prepare fully and give 100% of your effort. In school this is not the case and at times I feel as if I'm only half doing the job. That, for a new entrant to say, is depressing!

The above comments of newly qualified PE teachers (NQTs) at the end of their first term in teaching, offers a flavour of the range of different individual experiences of newcomers to the profession.

The transition from student teacher to NQT can be a particularly traumatic time. The individual is not only moving from the idealistic world of the teacher training course into the 'real world' of full time teaching, but may also have to move home to live in a different part of the country, leaving friends behind, having to pay off student loans and assume new responsibilities. From the first day of term the NQT is solely responsible for her own classes, will need to meet and discuss pupil progress with parents, and be directly responsible for pupil assessment and reporting. These rapid changes in personal and professional roles may, in some cases, lead to role conflict and anxiety. In many ways the individual is experiencing a new phase of her life, as well as starting a new career. As teacher training becomes more school-based this transition may become less traumatic, but it is still a change from the stage of being a student or 'intern' teacher to what is often termed the second 'induction' phase of becoming a teacher (Lawson, 1989).

Similarly, the student teacher who is about to experience his first contact with the world of teaching may also have feelings of either excitement or anxiety, particularly when placed in front of a class for the first time. The school as an organisation can be very different to the University or College that the student has lived and worked in for the previous two or three years. In comparison with Universities, schools can tend to be more conservative institutions, with their own specific value structures that may reflect their local community. Student teachers or NQTs arriving at a new school with the latest ideas, may find that the school either welcomes 'new thinking', or resents a 'fresh out of college' young teacher giving the impression that the school is 'behind the times'.

As a 'work organisation' the school will attempt to socialise its new members, and this organisational socialisation is intended, according to Lawson (1989): '... to allow new teachers to learn their schools' organisational culture'. (p. 149)

The organisational culture of a school describes the various 'shared ideologies', agreed 'social etiquette', customs and rituals concerning how members of the organisation relate to each other, and what is the appropriate way to behave within the organisation. They do this as a way of coping with and making sense of the environment in which they work. As Lawson (1989) points out, a school's organisational culture is 'largely unwritten', consists of 'deeply embedded assumptions', is usually created by the senior members of the school, and has two main functions: 'It helps the school and it's members meet external environmental demands, and it facilitates the internal integration of diverse school members'. (p. 152)

Whether a newcomer to a school accepts this 'organisational culture' or not, it is important to find out as much about it as possible.

The new teacher in a school, whether student or NQT, may find that the social organisation of the school has invisible organisational boundaries or 'boundary passages'. Initially, a trial period exists in which the new teacher is seen as an outsider, but, gradually, as the teacher becomes accepted and trusted, she crosses this boundary and may be viewed as a 'real teacher'. According to Lawson (1989), three boundaries exist – the inclusionary boundary, the functional boundary and the hierarchical boundary. Ability to cross the inclusionary and functional boundaries may depend on each other. Being initially accepted by experienced teachers (inclusionary boundary), may be dependent on showing that one can control classes and actually teach (functional boundary). The hierarchical boundary separates those individuals that have formal authority and power, such as deputy heads and heads of department, from those who do not.

However, what appears to mark the unique nature of the transition from University student to student teacher, from student teacher to NQT, is their varied experiences of different schools and PE departments, and their associated workplace conditions and organisational culture. Also, as each student teacher or NQT brings with them a range of experiences from their teacher training programme, the induction of new teachers into the teaching profession in physical education might be termed, as Lawson (1989) suggests: '... a culture of variability rather than a culture of professionalism'. (p. 162)

With each beginning teacher bringing such a range of identities and professional orientations to the school, and each school having its own organisational socialisation and culture to add to this, the result is likely to be a professional identity and orientation that is a unique blend of experiences for each new teacher in school. It is therefore felt (Siedentop, 1991), that teacher education programmes should prepare student teachers better for the realities of schools as organisations and 'life in school'.

The purpose of this chapter is to offer the student and new entrant teacher of physical education a slice of life in schools and PE departments from the point of view of the 87 student teachers and 12 newly qualified teachers of PE who took part in the 'Teachers of Physical Education (TEPE) Project'.

They were asked about their first impressions of the school they were due to work in, their concerns and worries, the difficulties they experienced with their first lessons, what they considered to be 'good' and 'bad' lessons and why, what help they received, what they enjoyed or didn't enjoy about their early teaching experiences and how this had changed their views of teaching, and finally, what advice they would give to those following in their footsteps!

## Being a student teacher of PE

Unless the student teacher has already had considerable experience of working with children prior to beginning a course of teacher training, then the first period of teaching practice or school-based training is likely to cause a certain degree of apprehension and anxiety for the average student. This is to be expected, and some would argue that a little anxiety is not a bad thing – it sharpens the mind! However, an over-concern for what is going to happen in the future can be counter-productive, and it is therefore worth considering what aspects of a future teaching practice actually worries student teachers. Being aware of these concerns can help those training student teachers to be prepared to offer appropriate help and guidance in alleviating these concerns, whether they be University tutors or school mentors. For the student teacher, having an insight into the concerns of those that have passed through the system can help them to appreciate that their anxieties are not particularly personal, but affect most student teachers about to embark on their first teaching practice.

What, therefore, are the main concerns of student teachers of PE prior to their first period of teaching practice or school experience? As part of the TEPE Project, 87 student teachers from 4 teacher training institutions were asked this very question, and over 70 different student teacher concerns were identified. These were reduced to the following main areas of concern, with percentage of students mentioning the issue shown in brackets:

● Knowledge (48.3%2)
● Class management and control (39%)
● School concerns and expectations (21.8%)
● Teaching skills (20.7%)
● Acceptance/ relationships with other staff (20.7%)
● Pupil concerns (20.7%)
● Planning and preparation (19.5%)
● Being assessed (9.2%)

As other studies of pre-service PE teachers in the United States and Belgium have shown (Boggess, McBride and Griffey, 1985; Wendt and Bain, 1989; Behets, 1990), student teachers are largely concerned about how they are going to cope or survive in the teaching environment. They are noticeably anxious about their knowledge of the activities to be taught (particularly those they are less familiar with); whether they will be able to control and discipline classes; their ability to plan the right amount of appropriate material to suit their classes; what the school is like (e.g. organisation); what staff will expect of them; their ability to communicate, demonstrate and develop ideas to motivate pupils; and whether they will find staff and pupils ready to accept and cooperate with them. They also, to a lesser extent, appear to worry about being assessed (9.2%), their timetable (5.8%), the support they will get from staff and tutors, the time that will be spent travelling and being nervous and underconfident. In Capel's study of student teachers of PE in the United Kingdom (cited in Capel, 1993) five anxiety causing factors were identified: 'evaluation anxiety', 'pupils and professional concerns anxiety', 'class control anxiety', 'school staff anxiety' and 'teaching practice requirements anxiety'.

In Fuller's (1969) developmental theory of teacher concerns, the first stage involves a greater degree of 'self-concerns'; concerns about one's adequacy and survival as a teacher, about class control, being liked and accepted by pupils and other staff, and about fear of failure. Although Fuller's theory has not been supported by recent studies of PE teachers (Boggess *et al.*, 1985; Behets, 1990), many of the pre-service teacher concerns which are characteristic of Fuller's first stage were apparent in the TEPE Project sample of student teachers.

However, one of the main concerns of student teachers in the TEPE Project related to 'knowledge'. Quite a number of the student teachers were unsure of their knowledge of certain activities they may have to teach and particularly their competency in sports in which they had little experience. Typical of replies were:

Having enough knowledge in all sports to challenge them.

Competency in those sports that I have least experience of.

My weaker sports.

Knowledge, ability to develop enough ideas to maintain motivation levels.

Knowing enough information/practices for each sport.

Officiating skills in unfamiliar sports.

My knowledge in particular areas of the curriculum and being able to demonstrate accurately and effectively what I hoped pupils would mirror initially.

The student teachers were also concerned about their teaching skills and whether they would actually be able to teach:

Will I be able to demonstrate effectively?

Will I be able to put the theory I have learned into practice?

I've never stood up in front of a class of 30 pupils before, will I manage?

Are my communication skills good enough?

Organising large groups of children and making lessons interesting.

– were typical of such concerns.

Being accepted by experienced staff in the school and 'fitting into the department', was also frequently mentioned, and this included concern over the possibility of a 'clash' between the work done in the University and the ideologies of the school PE department: 'The transition from the ideological lectures to the real school environment. Would our new ideas be acceptable to the school?' 'Employing new PE skills in an old traditional department'.

Some of the student teachers were also concerned about whether they would be able to meet the expectations of the PE department and school: 'Not fulfilling my potential and therefore falling short of the professional standards of my department and school'. 'Ability to satisfy department and school expectations'.

Planning and preparation were mentioned by several of the student teachers who felt that they were entering a 'darkened room', having to prepare material for teaching and yet not knowing very much about the pupils or what the school actually wanted them to teach: 'Not knowing exactly what the school wanted, not having observed the professionals at work, and not having seen the children's ability before the first lesson'.

The students were also concerned about 'Being able to plan at an appropriate level for the pupils', 'Making lessons interesting', and 'Running out of material half way through a lesson'.

The second most frequently mentioned series of concerns related to class management, control and discipline, but the student teachers were also concerned about the pupils in the school – what they would 'be like', would they be accepted by them, would they be able to develop a rapport with them, and whether they would have difficulty motivating them. These results are similar to studies of pre-service PE teachers in the United States (Boggess *et al.*, 1985) and Belgium (Behets, 1990), and appear to be characteristic of the 'survival' stage of learning to teach. However, the occasional mention of concerns to do with the task of teaching (planning and instructional materials), and impact concerns (needs of pupils), suggests that although student teachers are largely preoccupied with self-issues, for some students other concerns do play their part during preparation for the first teaching experience.

A number of student teachers expressed concern about 'what the school would be like', whether it was '... a difficult school', how it was organised, what their teaching timetable would be like, and how the school and PE department were coping with the National Curriculum. When the students did actually visit their teaching practice school their 'first impressions' varied considerably. Aspects that first 'struck them' included the school buildings, the behaviour of the pupils and whether they wore school uniform, how friendly and welcoming the staff were, and how well the PE staff 'got on together'.

But, are these student teacher concerns about their future teaching practice school actually real 'worries' or 'anxieties'? In some cases they may not be. They largely appear to represent 'unknowns', and when you feel you are to be evaluated and assessed in relation to your knowledge and professional skill, you don't like being unprepared. Finding out more about the school in advance can alleviate these concerns, and the suggestions in Chapter 5 concerning what to ask and look for on a preliminary school visit, should help put the student teacher's mind at rest on certain issues. Nevertheless, until one becomes involved in the act of teaching, it is very difficult to overcome certain apprehensions. Also, the whole question of whether to get 'stuck in' early in the practice rather than take advantage of observing teachers working with classes (and become familiar with the rules and routines they use), is very much an individual preference.

Some students prefer to take the opportunity to watch experienced professionals at work, others do not. As one student teacher mentioned: 'I started teaching from day one when I knew very little of the school policy and procedure. I would have appreciated more time to observe at the school prior to my main teaching practice'.

When asked if they had received the help and advice needed to overcome their concerns, most of the student teachers reported that staff in their school had been really helpful, offering encouragement, advice on teaching skills and planning, and gave them the chance to gradually 'ease their way in' to teaching: 'I had limited help before embarking on teaching practice – all the help and advice came from the school I taught in. They allowed me to observe lessons in my first week before undertaking the teaching of a whole class'. 'I watched a couple of lessons, asked questions, had a go! – and felt a lot more confident'. One student, however, wanted: 'The freedom to find my own teaching style without having critical eyes cast over me', – and it was noticeable that two student teachers had been pleased that their class teacher had allowed them some 'freedom' during their first lessons:

My head of department made me very welcome and let me make mistakes without himself jumping in and correcting me all the time. I was able to discuss what went wrong with him afterwards, and learned a great deal from him. Because he allowed me to keep going in lessons, I managed to keep hold of the respect of the children.

... he did not make his presence overbearing during my lessons.

A few of the student teachers began to realise that their concerns were really unfounded, and that they soon overcame them as they became more confident:

After a short time it became apparent that any concerns I had were unfounded, and so no real help was needed.

Problems probably relate to confidence, often you know more than you think, especially new ideas.

... after a terrible first week, I approached my TP tutor. After having a long and informal chat about my worries, I realised that these were realistic and fairly normal worries, and most of my problem was trying to be too much like the other PE teachers in terms of professionalism and my expectations of myself were unrealistically high. Also talking to fellow students on my course – found out they were having similar problems.

Sadly, some student teachers needed reassurance and didn't always get it. In many cases a chance to 'talk through' such issues as lesson planning, knowledge of unfamiliar activities, details of the school PE syllabus, the school system of discipline, the organisation and whereabouts of PE equipment, and what pupils had already covered, was all that was needed. Student teachers need time, and school staff need to give them that time. But the students themselves also need to be honest about their concerns and anxieties, and approach staff for help rather than 'bottle it up'. As one student teacher pointed out: 'Initially I did not get the help I needed, but partly because I perhaps did not become as involved as I could. Towards the end the staff were very supportive and response from pupils was excellent'.

Some of the student teachers in the TEPE Project were not concerned about their first teaching practice at all – they were quite simply excited at the prospect and couldn't wait to get started! 'No great concerns about anything but rather a sense of anticipation and excitement at the opportunities and challenges which lay ahead'.

## Student teachers' early lessons

As with any new career there is a lot to learn about teaching, and there are likely to be difficulties to overcome along the way. Teaching is no different from any new job in this respect, except that there are probably more 'unknowns' to have to contend with. Teaching is such a complex activity, that a wide variety of variables can make each individual first encounter with a class of pupils so different. Many feel that this is one of the pleasures of teaching – no two days are the same! However, for the student teacher those first lessons can be quite nerve-racking, and, of course, there is likely to be the odd difficulty. One student teacher simply put this down to being: 'all part of the learning process'. All the same, as someone else once said – 'Forewarned is forearmed!' In other words, it is useful to know what to expect, and the experiences of those who have gone before you are invaluable.

The student teachers taking part in the TEPE Project were asked about the difficulties they had experienced with their first lessons of teaching PE and how they had overcome them.

The aspects of teaching most frequently mentioned were as follows, with percentage of trainees mentioning the issue shown in brackets:

- Organisation and management of lessons (53%) – including specific organisation of equipment (18.8%) and groups (9.4%); also, general lesson organisation; lesson transitions and routines; issuing equipment; getting classes changed and positioning to monitor the class working.
- Lesson delivery (30.6%) – particularly communication skills (16.5%) such as the giving of clear, simple and concise explanations, difficulties with variation in voice tone and

'inappropriate language for the pupils'; timing of lessons (7%) and an occasional mention of not giving enough feedback, lack of flexibility in terms of lesson content and and an inability to 'think on one's feet'.

- Discipline and class control (30.6%) – including keeping control and handling problem pupils (17.7%) and an occasional mention of 'ensuring quiet' and 'gaining class attention before talking'; 'motivating reticent pupils'; 'getting pupils to follow instructions'; 'keeping the "balance" between discipline and class activity'; the difficulties of being seen as 'a student' and the gaining of pupil respect.
- Knowledge (39%) – associated with a lack of confidence in the material being taught and the teaching of unfamiliar activities (9.4%); lack of knowledge of pupil abilities, skill level and previous experience in the activity (9.4%); and an ocasional mention of lack of knowledge of school equipment, facilities and pupil names.
- Planning (24.7%) – difficulties caused by either overplanning and trying to achieve too much in lessons (5.9%); not being sure about the matching of material to pupil ability and skill level (5.9%); and an occasional mention of lack of planning, planning for progression, setting attainable targets and providing more challenging activities for the more able and enthusiastic pupil.
- Personal (10.6%) – several of the student teachers naturally experienced a lack of confidence and a degree of 'nerves' before their first lessons. One trainee felt uncomfortable being observed, and another suffered from occasional loss of voice!

These difficulties experienced by this sample of student teachers of PE are not unusual and could easily be overcome by requesting help and advice from experienced teachers in the school. Most of the student teachers in this study did receive such advice, 11 did not and a small number considered that they could solve their own problems and just 'got on with it' (7%). The remainder either didn't comment or put the answer to their initial problems down to 'experience'.

Organisation and management difficulties were overcome by having the opportunity to watch experienced teachers teach, by finding out about PE department procedures and equipment, routines and rules in advance; by developing 'bridging' organisation for transitions, and by learning to use short, sharp, concise and 'snappy', 'step by step' management of activities, and not over-talking. Practice in organising different numbers of pupils was also mentioned.

Delivery of lessons was improved by learning to simplify lesson content, provide clear and concise explanations and practising voice projection and variation in tone. Timing of lessons was overcome by not over-talking or trying to teach too much and by keeping pupils active during lessons. Getting to know pupil names was improved by using the register and walking around to speak to pupils and ask them their names. The problem of inflexibility was overcome by not being too worried about sticking to the lesson plan if modification during the lesson was appropriate, and the answer to having to 'think on one's feet' was to 'work things out in advance' and having contingency plans.

Being aware of pupil names seemed to help a great deal with control and discipline, but the students also mentioned that this aspect of their teaching was improved by being firmer/stricter with pupils, sitting them down if possible and waiting for, and demanding full attention when they were addressing the class. A knowledge of problem pupils appeared useful in some cases.

It is difficult to plan lessons accurately in the early stages of teaching, and some student teachers overcame the problem of running out of time by learning to keep their explanations 'short, sharp and to the point'. Planning for differentiation and matching the material to pupils' ability levels continued to cause difficulty, although one student 'made lesson plans less detailed' and initially 'taught more basic skills'.

Other staff in the school were helpful to a number of the students who were experiencing a lack of confidence which arose from having to teach activities that they were unfamiliar with, but detailed and thorough planning of such activities appeared to be the main solution. Pupil ability levels were ascertained either by asking staff or as a result of experience with the class.

Overcoming first lesson 'nerves' is not easy, but as one student suggested: '… keep calm, talk slowly and clearly'.

## Reflections on teaching practice and preparing for the first post in school

Certainly the student teachers taking part in the TEPE Project were very aware of what teaching skills they had to develop to improve their professional expertise and and be prepared to take up their first teaching post in schools. They appreciated what had been the factors that had led to 'good' lessons they had taught on teaching practice, and also why lessons had gone 'badly'. When asked after their final teaching practice what teaching and professional skills they now needed to work on for their future development as PE teachers and to help them feel prepared for a full time job in schools, 73.3% mentioned some aspect of 'knowledge' as being the most important. It appeared that the students were not fully confident about their knowledge of certain activities in the PE curriculum, and this is not surprising when one considers the wide range of physical activities that are part of the PE curriculum in schools today.

Feeling competent and having the knowledge and confidence in the activity being taught was also mentioned by 21.8% of the students as contributing to the 'good' lessons they had taught, although additional knowledge of the pupils and their previous experience was also considered to be important.

A number of students (10%) also felt that they needed more knowledge of the National Curriculum requirements for PE, and occasionally students also mentioned GCSE/'A' level work in PE and Sports Studies, catering for special educational needs, new ideas for lessons, officiating games, coaching qualifications and knowledge about how to 'develop a PE curriculum'.

Over half of the trainees (54.7%) felt that they needed to improve their preparation; particularly lesson planning and schemes of work (13.8%), planning for progression (5.7%) and differentiation, use of written resources such as task cards, and developing 'interesting approaches to topics'. In fact, 89.6% of the students had mentioned some aspect of planning and preparation as being the main contributory factor in lessons that had 'gone well' and generally been successful. 'Good' lessons had been 'well prepared', 'interesting', 'challenging' and delivered in a relaxed, enthusiastic and confident manner. Lesson content had been 'appropriate for the pupils' ability and stage of learning', 'progressive', 'well structured', planned for 'maximum activity and participation' and had been 'fun' for the pupils. The opposite had been the case for lessons that had 'gone badly'.

A number of the students (14%) felt that they needed to improve aspects of their delivery of lessons, particulary their communication skills and variation in tone of voice. Teaching skills related to lesson delivery such as clarity of explanations and expectations, lesson timing, and flexibility were also mentioned by 26% of the students as contributing to 'good' lessons they had taught. Also, being well organised had helped lessons run smoothly on teaching practice for 28.7% of the students, whereas poor organisation, such as not being prepared for changes in the weather and facilities suddenly not being available, had been associated with unsatisfactory lessons.

Students also mentioned the need to improve their use of 'a wider range of teaching styles' (16.3%) and their general class organisation (9.3%).

However, regardless of good planning the students were also aware of other factors that could lead to lessons being unsuccessful. This included the time of day the lesson was taught, the facilities, and the size and behaviour of the class. For example, 48% of the students attributed the success of lessons to the response of pupils. Poor pupil attitude, pupil mood, unmotivated pupils and uncooperative pupils were all mentioned as factors leading to unsatisfactory lessons. 'Good' lessons had occurred when pupils were attentive, active, interested, liked the activity being taught, were having fun and enjoying the lesson. Other studies looking at the reasons given by pre-service teachers for the success or lack of success of lessons also identified such issues as 'pupil positive attitude', 'pupil compliance' and 'lack of misbehaviour' as being important factors in the success of lessons (Arrighi and Young, 1987; Placek and Dodds, 1988; Borys and Fishbourne, 1990; Hardy, 1993). It is therefore not surprising that a fifth (20.9%) of the student teachers in the TEPE Project felt that they needed to improve their class management and control.

Successful lessons on teaching practice had also been linked to the student teachers' personal disposition at the time of the lesson. About a quarter of the students (23.3%) mentioned such factors as 'feeling confident in oneself', 'relaxed', 'enthusiastic', being motivated and interested in the activity, and being in the right 'mood' or 'frame of mind'. Lessons had gone badly when when they were tired, did not feel well or felt 'stressed'.

Seven students (8%) felt that they needed to work on their ability to assess pupils and evaluate their teaching skills. However, nine students (10%) stated that they would simply develop their teaching expertise 'through experience', and seven (8%) felt that they did not need any further knowledge, skills or professional training to feel prepared to teach the following term in school! Nevertheless, the vast majority saw their future career being a continuous process of developing and improving their professional skills: 'I feel able to take up a position as a PE teacher, although I recognise that development and training is an ongoing process in a teacher's career and will make use of any opportunities that may arise'.

The majority of student teachers had been a little surprised at the amount of work that had to go into being an effective teacher. When asked if their 'view of the nature of teaching PE had changed since they began their course of professional training', 12.6% felt that there was 'much more to it' in terms of planning, administration and assessment. Others commented that it is 'much harder work' than they had originally realised (10%), and a number had begun to appreciate that they needed a broad base of knowledge in a variety of activities and teaching approaches:

It's a lot more difficult than I originally thought. You don't just play games as most people think – a lot of thought is needed to plan an innovative and successful PE lesson.

It's more than meets the eye if you are to be an effective teacher. You need to be well prepared, enthusiastic and determined to succeed.

A lot of responsibility – you need a sound knowledge base and good preparation and planning.

I did not realise how much was involved. I was unaware of the complexities of teaching in relation to the many things that must be taken into consideration when teaching a class. I did not realise how physically and mentally taxing it would be.

Several students considered that teaching PE had become more 'professional' and 'worthwhile' for pupils, and that there were 'more opportunities for professional development'. But they also felt that these beneficial changes would not occur easily:

My view of the profession has improved. I only hope that with the National Curriculum and exams in PE, other peoples' opinions will also improve.

It is going to be hard to change old traditional teaching methods – in terms of the pupils getting used to change.

Thought it would be easier – lots of paperwork.

That if we manage to teach as we have been trained to the PE lessons should be more worthwhile and enjoyable for all pupils – but how easy will this actually be?

However, a number of student teachers had a fairly positive and optimistic view of the future:

My views have not changed a great deal but the positive experiences of the past twelve months have done a great deal to put me in a positive frame of mind as September approaches.

Much harder work – lot of enjoyment – very rewarding experience.

Difficulty of a new career but also the tremendous enjoyment it can bring.

Regardless of all the difficulties that go with learning the skills of any new job, the student teachers taking part in the TEPE Project all mentioned some aspect of their recent teaching practice that they had enjoyed, and 15% of them enjoyed every aspect of their teaching practice. The most frequently mentioned enjoyable aspect of the teaching practice was related to contact with pupils (79.3%). 'Working with children' (27.6%), and 'developing relationships with children' (26.4%), were mentioned by a number of the trainees, and 'being involved with children in areas I enjoy', 'getting to know pupils individually', 'being asked to watch pupils perform', and 'working with enthusiastic children', were also mentioned. The student teachers also particularly enjoyed seeing pupils learn, progress and enjoy taking part in the lessons (25.3%).

Quite naturally the student teachers enjoyed lessons that were successful, or 'went well' (10%), taking extracurricular activities (26.4%), clubs and teams and working with, and getting to know, other staff in the department and school (13.8%).

The enjoyment of working with children by far outweighed those aspects of teaching practice that student teachers did not enjoy – the pressure to pass the teaching practice, the late nights and hard work that has to be put into the teaching practice file in terms of lesson preparation and analysis (19.6%), the getting up early to travel to the school (8%) and the whole problem of a lack of 'time to fit everything in'. Also mentioned were the occasional 'lack of support and encouragement' from a badly organised and unenthusiastic department, and the individual difficulty with the teaching of certain unfamiliar activities that they did not really feel competent to teach (8%).

In that 23% of the students mentioned aspects of control and management of unmotivated, uncooperative pupils with 'poor attitudes to staff', one gets the impression that the students felt that their positive contacts with pupils by far outweighed the negative. The fact that 79.3% of the student teachers mentioned some aspect of the pleasure of working with children as being the most important aspect of their teaching practice experience is very important. When students return from teaching practice saying that they enjoyed 'seeing pupils' progress', that they enjoyed the 'childrens' reactions when they do well', 'the success of less able pupils', and the overall 'enjoyment of pupils in performing physical activity', then it is good to have so many young teachers approaching their first term as fully-fledged teachers enthusiastic about the most important aspect of teaching – taking pleasure in seeing children learn and enjoying taking part in physical activity.

But, what does that first term of teaching have in store for the newly qualified physical education teacher? As part of the TEPE Project, a preliminary survey of 12 of the student teachers who had agreed to be followed up during their first term of teaching revealed an interesting insight into the experiences of newly qualified teachers (NQTs) immediately after their initial training. Although only a small sample, their comments do offer a 'flavour' of what lies ahead for those about to embark on their first year in schools, as well as providing those whose job it is to monitor the progress of NQTs with an idea of what some NQTs have experienced in their first term of teaching.

## Starting to teach: The first term in teaching

For many newly qualified teachers their first term in teaching is their very first full-time job. There is also an increasing number of 'mature' entrants to the teaching profession; students who have been in the world of work for several years and have decided to embark on a career in teaching in their mid-twenties. However, most student teachers of physical education tend to follow a PGCE after a degree in

Physical Education or Sports Science, or take a teaching degree with qualified teacher status straight from school. For those taking the latter route, the transition from University or College to the real world of work, with it's lifestyle disruptions (e.g. finding a flat, leaving friends, moving to a different part of the country) can be quite traumatic. In addition to this there are the concerns and anxieties about the job itself.

What are newly qualified teachers of PE concerned about prior to starting the autumn term teaching in a new school?

Compared with the student teachers the twelve NQTs taking part in the TEPE project expressed little concern about class management and discipline, but were more apprehensive about meeting, getting to know and being accepted by the pupils and the school, and also how their lessons would be received by both pupils and staff. Capel (1993) also found beginning teachers of PE anxious about 'being evaluated', and particularly how school staff would react to their unsuccessful lessons. Capel's teachers were also anxious about 'getting on with school staff'. As with any new job, meeting one's new colleagues is exciting but also a concern – would they be friendly, would they be ready to 'show me the ropes', will I live up to their expectations? One NQT mentioned that she was concerned about: '... living up to the expectations of staff because of where I was trained, knowing what happens in the everyday running of the school'.

Becoming accustomed to new routines, additional duties (including a tutor group), being unsure about the timetable they would be teaching, the activities to be taught and the overall workload they were to expect were particular areas of concern expressed by the majority of NQTs: 'What activities I would be teaching in the first half-term and associated details related to timetabling – where each activity would take place, numbers, equipment available and standards of pupils. All the planning to get ready and as complete as possible'.

Several young teachers were concerned about planning and having the information to be able to plan. They also were unsure about how the school operated as an organisation, the organisation of PE equipment and pupils, and how the National Curriculum had affected the PE department they were due to work in.

Many of these concerns can be alleviated by visiting the school in the latter stages of the summer term prior to starting to teach at the school. In fact, some schools specifically request that recently appointed NQTs do spend some time in the school at the end of the school year to get to know staff, pupils, have some idea of the timetable they will be teaching, where the equipment is, how the school is organised and have advice on any additional responsibilities they are likely to have. It is therefore worth visiting the school with a checklist of 'questions to ask' so that sufficient information is gathered to be able to spend some of the summer preparing in the knowledge that a little is known about the school and its inhabitants. The suggested set of questions in Chapter 5 may help in the preparation of such a list.

Concerns about being accepted by new colleagues are often unfounded, as over half of the NQTs in the TEPE Project mentioned 'the friendliness of staff' as being one of the main features of their first impression of their new school and PE department: 'Very friendly and supportive school staff. Pupils seemed friendly enough – a chance to make a good start in teaching. Excellent colleagues in PE – very helpful'.

Concerns over the timetable, activities to be taught and whether they would be accepted also often proved to be unfounded: 'Initially I was surprised at the amount of freedom I had to do my own thing. The department was quite responsive to many of the new ideas I used and my own Head of Girls PE was happy to adopt them and follow my line of progression'.

Sadly, not all PE departments gave a good impression to NQTs:

Boys and girls are run as two departments. Very little liaison, poor communication.

The staff are very cliquey and backbiting. The PE department is not at all together. It consists of four individuals working by themselves not as a unit. The department has not moved with the times and needs a radical shake up. None of the department seems to like each other.

However, many negative first impressions can also eventually prove to be inaccurate and, of course, one cannot always step into a new working environment that is harmonious and amicable. But, it is hard for the NQT to enter such a situation, and it is really up to the school and individual departments to offer a smooth and positive transition into the world of teaching for new recruits to the profession.

The first few weeks in the new school, and in particular the first lessons, can be the most exciting yet the most tiring. Not only is the NQT trying hard to understand the organisation of the school and the PE department, finding out the whereabouts of rooms and equipment, but it always seems that everyone else appears to assume that you will just 'slip into the system' and know what to do. Difficulties are bound to exist in these first few weeks, and the twelve NQTs in the TEPE Project experienced a wide range of 'specific difficulties' to do with teaching PE as well as difficulties concerning their 'general teaching duties'.

The transition from student teacher on teaching practice to becoming a fully-fledged teacher does involve taking on a range of additional duties that often takes the NQT by surprise. Being responsible for a tutor group and all it entails, having break, lunch and bus duties, 'covering' lessons when you thought you had a free period to prepare, after school departmental meetings and parents evenings, all add up to a very tiring day when you are still unsure about such things as school and department organisation. A number of NQTs also found learning and remembering pupil names a particular problem.

But many of these difficulties were overcome in one way or another and in most cases the Head of Department or other PE staff would offer support and advice. The following is a sample of how a group of NQTs overcame these general difficulties experienced during the first term of teaching:

Getting to know where equipment was – during my free time I went through the store cupboard and noted down all equipment and where to locate it.

Learning the names of so many pupils so that you didn't have to shout 'YOU' or whatever across the field. Trying to learn a couple of names each lesson.

Pupils trying me out – poor behaviour. I stuck to what I saw as acceptable standards and insisted on these.

One has to accept that the first few weeks in a new job is likely to be exhausting. As one NQT recommended: 'Getting to bed early and rest and recreation was a very important priority'.

It's also easy to feel that you are the only one who is having these problems, and that no one understands or is sympathetic. Those that have been through the transitional process from student to 'proper teacher' are very aware of the difficulties of getting through that first term of teaching, as one PE teacher of eight years experience pointed out:

Basic organisation and preparation on a day to day basis – you all of a sudden find yourself teaching full timetable, having extracurricular activities and a tutor group and all the other responsibilities of being a 'proper' teacher – and it is bloody hard work! Something you cannot possibly be prepared for is the tiredness. I think it is important to ask questions of experienced colleagues and don't be scared of asking for help – it is not a sign of failure and everybody needs a bit of a kick start. Go and watch others teach and poach their ideas until you develop a style of teaching that works for you.

One young NQT who was having a few discipline problems which nobody seemed to notice, found that the support of one particular colleague was invaluable:

As a new teacher you can feel inhibited and reluctant to criticise others – after all, you still have to pass your probationary year! So, I often kept many of my worries to myself, not wanting to make waves. Having an older, established member of staff batting for your team is a bit of a 'cop out', but it certainly helped me through some difficult problems.

Experienced teachers are aware of the difficulties of starting the first term in teaching, and when Heads of PE Departments (HODs) were asked what they felt were the major concerns and difficulties experienced by NQTs during their first term in school, it is not surprising that their answers matched the issues mentioned by the NQTs themselves. As several HODs commented:

There is so much to learn. How the school runs, how to mark the register, how to organise your form – then there is your teaching, reports, meetings, extracurricular activities. Too much to learn and cope with in one term and get right.

Workload – the confusion caused by all the new initiatives which are going on. The feeling that the actual teaching often seems to be secondary to everything else. Learning what the profusion of acronyms mean!

I think the PE side of things is often the least of their worries – there are so many other responsibilities – being a form tutor, ROAs, which all take up a lot of time and add to the pressure, and often experienced staff don't take account of this – they take a lot for granted when in fact a young teacher may be worrying unduly.

It therefore appears that everyone understands how NQTs feel in those first few weeks of teaching, but, what advice would they offer for alleviating the difficulties experienced by many NQTs? Here is a pot pourri of the advice offered by HODs on how to cope with that first term in school:

Don't expect to do or know everything – no one else will expect you to do so (except the pupils). Plan to know names of staff in chunks. Those people you deal with most will be easiest to learn – first concentrate on them in the first two weeks. Then learn three new names a week (putting names to faces). Pupil names can be learned best by repeating their names each time you speak to them. Ask, repeatedly if necessary, for them to tell you their names if you cannot remember them quickly.

Don't panic, don't take on too much. Try to enjoy the actual contact with pupils and as much of the rest as possible. Survive the remainder. Get away from the job, do other things as often as time permits in order to reduce stress and fatigue.

Watch experienced staff – you do not have to copy what they do but watch how they cope with problems, dilemmas, etc. Watch good practice from staff but also mistakes experienced staff make, evaluate and think how you would have coped with that situation. Keep learning all the time. I am!

Take things at a pace you can cope with, be well organised and prepared, don't be shy about asking for help and advice, get to know the assessment procedures of the department (don't leave it until you have to do it), try to relax and above all be professional in your approach – and, try to enjoy it!

Above all, the HODs main piece of advice was that NQTs should always ask for help, and should not: '... be afraid it will be seen as a sign of weakness as there are often short-cuts or strategies which you may not know about – don't struggle on in isolation'.

Newly qualified PE teachers need to feel accepted by their new colleagues and pupils – if they receive a positive and friendly welcome in their new school, it helps them to settle down, as one NQT pointed out:

Being part of a friendly team is essential to how I feel I have settled down. I felt that other members of the department were always ready to back me up and also accept or listen to my ideas. I feel that I have been made to feel very welcome and a wanted part of the team which has given me confidence in my teaching.

## First encounters in the new school

For many NQTs their main area of concern is the prospect of meeting new classes for the first time. In any new job that involves working with people there is likely to be a degree of nervousness, and this was mentioned by a number of the NQTs in the TEPE Project.

Other difficulties experienced during those first lessons of teaching PE included: getting to know names; trying to do too much; being too friendly too soon; organisation of equipment; disciplinary problems; lack of confidence; timing of lessons; lesson progression and generally establishing oneself.

However, in many cases these difficulties were overcome quite easily. In the case of being nervous and lacking confidence: 'I ensured that I was well prepared and became more relaxed with the knowledge'. 'Teaching is all about acting and if you act calm and well organised these problems are usually resolved'. 'Basically I threw myself into lessons!'

Concerns over discipline and establishing oneself with a new class were dealt with in the following way:

Clear rules of what I expected in my lessons were stated in the first lesson and reinforced in subsequent lessons.

Being too friendly too soon. I found it hard to be too firm – it doesn't come naturally to me, but over time you learn strategies to do this.

Disciplinary problems until I knew the school system, and useful to know a little bit about certain pupils before you begin to deal with them.

It was necessary to establish myself and my expectations in terms of behaviour and performance. Obviously when you are new there is a period of sizing each other up. Inevitably you get those who want to test you and see how far they can push you.

The small group of NQTs who had just finished their first term in school were asked what advice they would give to someone about to take their first lesson with a new class in a new school. The most frequently mentioned pieces of advice concerned 'establishing rules, getting class attention, control and discipline', 'being well prepared, clear of lesson objectives, but flexible', 'clear explanations', and 'being well organised in advance of the lesson'. Also mentioned was the importance of 'appearing calm, confident and relaxed even though you might feel nervous', 'helping the children to feel at ease', 'having a sense of humour', 'getting to know names' and 'being yourself and enjoying it'.

These points were reinforced by HODs when they were asked what advice they would give NQTs about to teach their first lesson with a new class, and they all emphasised the importance of 'having class attention and control' including making sure 'they know your ground rules', 'not accepting any misbehaviour', and 'being well organised' as priorities. In fact there does appear to be an agreed 'package' of advice put forward by both the NQTs and HODs concerning the teaching skills and strategies to use in this so called 'survival' phase of learning to teach.

The importance of 'first encounters' with new classes, and the teaching skills that need to be established to make those early lessons run as smoothly as possible, as well as the need to begin to establish a positive atmosphere for learning, are discussed in detail in Chapter 6.

## Becoming aware of effective teaching skills

The newly qualified teachers taking part in the TEPE Project were already becoming aware of the teaching skills and competencies that were needed for lessons to go well, as well as appreciating their shortcomings when lessons had gone badly. According to these young teachers the success or otherwise of a lesson revolved around the issues of lesson preparation, lesson delivery, class control and organisation.

'Good preparation', including the need to have clear objectives and to plan lessons with plenty of activity, variety, appropriate amount of material, and being prepared for all eventualities, was mentioned by 80% of the NQTs. Having depth of knowledge and 'being sure of your material', was also mentioned, and lessons went badly when NQTs felt underconfident about the lesson content or had not prepared thoroughly.

Two-thirds of the teachers commented on the importance of being positive, enthusiastic, relaxed, having a sense of humour and a good rapport with the pupils, if lessons were to go well. 'Good' lessons appeared to be characterised by being started on time, having short precise instructions, activities not lasting too long, flexibility of content, and with tasks flowing neatly one into the other. In 'bad' lessons the teachers felt uncertain, lacked enthusiasm, and were not relaxed because of incomplete lesson plans; consequently such lessons appeared disjointed, and aims were not realised. Good organisation was also seen as a factor leading to successful lessons.

Over a third of the NQTs reported bad behaviour, inattentive pupils, control problems, and generally not dealing quickly enough with inappropriate behaviour as contributing to poor lessons. On the other hand, the attitude, mood and enthusiasm of the class, that they listened and responded enthusiastically to activities that were set and were mainly 'on task' all contributed to 'good' lessons. Different groups of pupils can respond in different ways as one NQT discovered:

I think that when you are a new teacher in a school it is easier to be accepted by Years 7, 8, or 9 than 10, as Year 10 pupils have not grown up with you like they have with other teachers. It takes more time for them to understand you and you them!

In a study of teachers' perceptions of successful teaching by Arrighi and Young (1987), 58% of the American teachers felt that pupil responses, in terms of positive feedback (pupil smiles and makes positive comments), a positive attitude, improved skill, pupil success and participation, were the main signs of success in teaching. Issues related to their personal performance and delivery of lessons (e.g. enthusiasm, knowledge, creative ideas, well planned lessons, positive rapport), were not quite as important, as they were only mentioned by a quarter of the teachers. Although it is difficult to compare this American study with the small sample of NQTs in the TEPE Project, it is noticeable that the more experienced American teachers viewed success in teaching being linked to pupil responses much more than the UK teachers, who saw successful teaching more in terms of their own preparation, personal performance and delivery of lessons.

Those aspects of teaching mentioned by both student teachers and NQTs as being important for the success of lessons are discussed in detail in the remainder of this text, and those teaching skills and competencies that contribute to what teachers and the research literature suggest may contribute to effective teaching are emphasised.

## Starting to teach: Taking the 'rough' with the 'smooth'

After what might appear to be a case of 'surviving' those first lessons as a student teacher and that first term in a new school, what did the NQTs in the TEPE Project say they were enjoying about being a fully fledged PE teacher, and how different was it to being a student teacher? Here is a selection of their comments:

Very different to being a student. In some ways more enjoyable as you can see the progression and your relationships are better because you are with the kids all the time and not just for a few weeks. You also realise how hard it is as a job when you've started to teach a full timetable plus clubs, practices and matches.

Constantly having to be on your toes. The opportunity to have more in-depth relationships with pupils – more advantages.

The probationary year is a lot more realistic and a chance to develop you own styles of teaching and not a case of pleasing teaching supervisors.

In probationary teaching you still need to plan very carefully but you can be more independent, making it, for me, a happier experience and more useful learning process.

The NQTs were particularly enjoying the varied timetable they were teaching, seeing pupils progress and be successful in learning skills, working with school clubs and teams, and the overall positive feedback they were getting from pupils who had enjoyed learning something. For one teacher, teaching PE offered a 'special relationship': 'I really enjoyed the special relationship you seem to have with the children you teach in PE lessons and extracurricular activities. Also, many of the children are very keen on sport and are very willing to give their best effort which is also rewarding.'

But, this set of young PE teachers are not just interested in élite performers, although it is nice to be involved in helping those that come to clubs and team practices to improve their performance. Seeing all pupils progress and enjoy physical activity is important to these young teachers of PE. As one NQT pointed out, she particularly enjoyed: '… catering for Mr and Miss Average. I like helping the less able pupils progress, and planning lessons so that pupils gain in confidence.'

'Seeing pupils progess', 'pupils learning something', 'feeling successful as a teacher' – were the aspects of teaching that the majority of this small group of NQTs had enjoyed during their first term of teaching. I hope that the remainder of this text will help all beginning teachers of PE to show that same concern for their pupils and have a similar enthusiasm for their personal professional development towards becoming an effective teacher, as those students and newly qualified teachers who took part in the TEPE Project. Becoming an effective teacher of PE does not happen overnight or just occur on completion of the first year of teaching as a qualified teacher. It should evolve gradually as a result of professional reflection and a commitment to seek always to improve one's teaching skills and knowledge. As one student teacher offered in the way of advice to colleagues following in his footsteps:

A journey of a thousand miles begins with a single step!

# CHAPTER 3

# Understanding teaching

## What is teaching?

What is teaching? According to James Calderhead (1987) teaching is a complex, professional thinking activity that shares certain characteristics with many other professions such as law, business management and medicine.

Teaching, along with these other professions, possesses a body of specialised formal knowledge. In the case of PE teachers they may have background knowledge in the sports sciences, human movement studies, sports studies or the study of physical education.

Professional activity is also goal oriented in relation to its clients. As doctors intend to solve their patients' medical problems, teachers are oriented towards the education of their pupils and aspire to 'pass on' their knowledge and skills. As one young PE student teacher in the TEPE Project stated: 'I felt that becoming a teacher would allow me to pursue my interest as well as being able to pass on my skill and knowledge to others.'

A third characteristic of professional activities is that they all deal with complex and ambiguous problems, and Calderhead (1987) believes that professionals have to: '… use their expert knowledge to analyse and interpret, make judgements and decisions about them, as they formulate a course of action intended to benefit the client.' (p. 2)

Teaching *is* very complex, and there are so many different issues to take into account when teaching a class. Even in the second year of initial training, student teachers of physical education are beginning to realise that teaching PE is not just 'playing sport':

I did not realise how much work was involved. I was unaware of the complexities of teaching in relation to the many things that must be taken into account when teaching a class. I did not realise how physically and mentally taxing it would be. (Male BEd student)

It's a lot more difficult than I originally thought. You don't just play games as most people seem to think – there is a lot of thought needed to devise an innovative and successful PE lesson. (Male BEd student)

The complexities of teaching, and teaching physical education in particular, has led a number of writers to put forward certain 'analogies' of teaching. For example, Graham (1992) describes teaching PE like being: '... in the eye of a hurricane. Balls, children, and ideas are whirling everywhere with no apparent order – but all demand immediate attention.' (p. 3)

Siedentop (1991) quotes the famous analogy of the teacher as 'Ringmaster', originally created by Smith and Geoffrey (1969) and adapted by Locke (1975) in his article 'The ecology of the gymnasium: What the tourists never see': 'Surrounded by a flow of activity, the ringmaster monitors, controls, and orchestrates, accelerating some acts, terminating others, altering and adjusting progress through the program, always with an eye for the total result.' (p. 36)

Teaching physical education does involve the need to be able to analyse, interpret and make decisions on a stream of rapidly flowing events and, as a young teacher of PE, the sheer speed of events can be quite daunting. The five minute 'clip' of a Year 7 badminton lesson taken by a young PE teacher, Mary, described in Box 1, illustrates the demands that are made on new teachers of PE when confronted by such a rapidly changing teaching environment. It represents 300 seconds of the 16,800 seconds that day that Mary spent teaching PE.

---

**Box 1**
**Three hundred seconds of teaching PE**

Mary has just finished her demonstration of the practice she wants the class to do and proceeds to 'scan' the resulting movement of 30 pupils towards their assigned task. She reminds two pupils of where they should be and her expectations of them, and then poses a series of probing questions to elicit why two girls are discussing that evening's disco rather than attending to the task that has been set. Additional monitoring of the class reveals that three pupils have joined the incorrect group thus causing a breakdown in the practice. Mary then notices a group who are having difficulty making contact with the shuttlecock and, after initially offering encouragement for their efforts gives them an additional demonstration and coaching points related to a modification of the original task. She then stands back to observe the next pupil's skill attempt and closes the teaching cycle with positive and specific feedback. A glance across the hall reveals some excellent work and Mary offers reinforcement to the group mentioning their names. At the far end of the hall a net falls off its stand and Mary moves to adjust the equipment, keeping her back to the end wall and keeping an eye on proceedings throughout the hall. A pupil comes to Mary and points out that: 'None of us can do it Miss!', and Mary moves to observe their efforts and attempt to diagnose their problem. No sooner has she begun to suggest one or two coaching points and demonstrate the skill than a

*continued*

---

**Box 1 continued**

pupil cries out as she goes over on her ankle. Mary helps the pupil to a bench while explaining to the group she has been working with how they might proceed, glances down the hall to see the two pupils performing an alternative task, hitting the shuttlecock into a basketball ring overhanging the court. A sharp reminder of her task expectations brings the pupils back 'on-task' while at the same time another pupil requests a new shuttlecock because: 'Its got caught up in the cricket netting Miss!' . . .

---

This description of a short period of a lesson highlights a fourth feature of a professional activity suggested by Calderhead (1987) – the need to be able to adapt skilful action to its context. A good PE teacher has knowledge of childrens' ability levels and personalities, is aware of different approaches to the activities being taught and has skills related to class management and pupil guidance. However, as may be noted in the 'clip' of Mary's lesson, this professional knowledge has to be closely linked to the practice of teaching to become what Schon (1983) refers to as 'knowledge in action'. Good teachers of PE have a reservoir of this 'knowledge in action' in which their specialised subject knowledge is closely tied in with their professional teaching skills.

But, what are the professional skills and competencies needed to become an effective teacher of physical education? Can they be identified? If they can be identified should we not train all teachers in the use of these skills and thus produce a more effective and professionally skilful profession? This whole notion of focussing on the skills of teaching raises a number of important issues and also a fair degree of passionate argument in the field of teacher effectiveness and pedagogy. Many feel that teaching should be seen as an 'art' rather than a 'science' and to reduce the teaching act to a series of itemised skills and competencies merely to be learned is to destroy it.

Schwab (1969), Stenhouse (1975) and Schon (1987) are supporters of the 'teaching as an art' point of view. Schwab (1969) argues for teaching as a 'practical art', and sees teaching quality as having very little to do with the skilful application of technical knowledge, but more a question of being able to know what to do in a particular situation, to apply one's knowledge ethically and educationally to the real world of practical teaching situations. Good teaching to both Schwab (1969) and Stenhouse (1975) is the capacity to explore and interpret, modify and adjust professional knowledge according to what happens in practice – being a reflective practitioner. Teaching is therefore much more than just technical expertise, as Carr (1989) points out: 'The teacher who lacks this capacity may be technically accountable, but cannot be educationally or morally answerable.' (p. 5)

Schon (1987) believes that we unfortunately have a standard model of professional knowledge that does not fit in with his view of teaching as an art, because such a model is derived from an over-technical view of teaching which he terms a 'technical rationality'. This view suggests that professional knowledge is based on scientific research and the application of theoretical knowledge to 'fixed educational ends'. If such scientific research was based on teacher effectiveness and process-product research, then Tom (1988) might agree with Schon, as he believes that: 'Research on effective teaching does not enlighten us about the technical secrets of teaching, let alone about which subject matter is worthy of being taught.' (p. 50)

Schon (1987) takes the view that a more appropriate model of quality in teaching should include the kind of 'knowing in action' professional knowledge and 'reflection in action' thinking processes that are the basis of the 'art' of teaching when professionals are handling 'divergent' and problematic situations which have a degree of uncertainty, instability and uniqueness.

'Good' teaching to Schon involves the ability to reflect on practice and is similar to Stenhouse's 'teacher as researcher' concept. Such teachers are constantly putting their practice under scrutiny and feel that they have a professional and moral obligation to be constantly improving their professional practice and justify educationally, their work in schools.

Woods (1990), in supporting Clark and Yinger's (1987) view of teaching as an 'art' or 'creative' process, describes how he sees teaching as an intelligent and artful orchestration of knowledge and technique:

The skilful teacher must be instructor, facilitator, critic, friend, parent, controller almost all at the same time, and present a persona to pupils that is one and indivisible, where the seams do not show. Handling these conflicting elements in a constructive way is another example of turning what looks like disadvantage to good account – typical of creative acts. (p. 48)

However, not everyone agrees that teaching is an art. Daryl Siedentop (1991) is not convinced, and in his 'teaching as a science' text *Developing Teaching Skills in Physical Education*, he is quite blunt about his view of the 'teaching as an art' school of thought:

Some people, however, view teaching solely as an art. They believe teaching skills can't be learned – that teachers are born, not made. This view implies that we can discover nothing about teaching that can be passed on to those preparing to teach. Clearly, if teachers are born, not made, then enormous sums of money are being wasted each year on so-called teacher education. (p. 4)

Siedentop takes the view that all artists originally need the basic skills before they can then be creative. They need to master the basic skills in order to develop the more complex skills that will enhance performance. He feels that taking this scientific perspective does not dehumanise the performer. Teachers will have their own personal way of doing things even though they may have mastered similar sets of basic teaching skills.

Hellison and Templin (1991, p. 152), however, take the middle ground: '... teaching is neither pure art nor pure science.'

But, they do go on to add that: '... scientific models are "undercomplicated", that artistry not only exists but is a crucial factor in effective teaching. Although it is by its very nature inexplicable, we believe that it can be conceptualised, at least to a point, and that by so doing, physical education teachers will be able to make at least some small improvements in their artistry.'

Hellison and Templin (1991) believe that as PE teachers we can all improve on our artistry by becoming more aware of the absence or presence of the artistic components that they have identified. These include many of the personal qualities identified by the student teachers in the TEPE Project, such as being enthusiastic and caring, but also other qualities such as empathy, genuineness, persistence and a playful spirit (meaning expressing the fun of an activity). Hellison and Templin consider that intuition, flexibility, creativity and self-reflection are part of the artistry of being a good teacher. They believe that intuition is that ability to: '... predict what is going to work accurately most of the time based on a few clues.' (p. 156)

Flexibility is closely allied to intuition and includes the ability to modify any plans when this is felt to be necessary, whereas creativity is needed to think of alternative ways of doing things.

Even so, as with other writers taking the 'teaching as an art' point of view, Hellison and Templin see the ability of teachers to learn how to reflect on their professional work as the key to quality teaching. They feel that when teachers are reflective they become 'empowered' as they help themselves to become the chief decision makers, problem solvers and evaluators of their own curriculum. But, for teachers to become good at decision making, problem solving and the art of reflective teaching, they believe that teachers need: '... a fat bag of "tricks" – curriculum models, teaching skills, teaching styles, evaluation procedures, and so on....' (p. vii)

This book attempts to offer some of that 'fat bag of tricks' in the form of suggestions from not only the research literature, but also from practising teachers concerning what they feel are the personal qualities, teaching skills and competencies of good teachers of physical education. The book also contains a number of exercises to enable the beginning teacher of PE to develop their self-appraisal skills – an important step on the road to becoming a truly 'reflective practitioner'.

But, what are the personal qualities, teaching skills and professional competencies of effective teachers of physical education? The next chapter attempts to answer this question.

# Effective teaching skills and professional competencies

## What are teaching skills and competencies?

Over recent years there has been a great deal of interest in the need to identify teaching skills and competencies. This interest has developed as a result of a desire to monitor the standard and quality of teaching performance in both initial and in-service training, and in the development of schemes of teacher appraisal in the United Kingdom. Also, considerable research literature has been generated by those interested in teacher effectiveness and this has involved the identification of effective teaching skills, professional competencies and the personal qualities of so-called 'good', or 'effective' teachers.

Attempts to define 'teaching skills' have been made by leading writers in the field including Kyriacou (1991), Calderhead (1986) and Wragg (1984).

Kyriacou (1991) defines essential teaching skills as: '… discrete and coherent activities by teachers which foster pupil learning.' (p. 5)

According to Kyriacou there are three important elements discernable within teaching skills:

1. Knowledge – about subject, pupils, curriculum, etc.
2. Decision making – that occurs before, during and after lessons and is concerned with how best to achieve the educational outcomes intended.
3. Action – overt behaviour by teachers to foster learning.

Kyriacou (1991) also points out that a particular feature of teaching skills is their interactive nature – in other words, how the teacher modifies and changes activities and strategies in the light of the way a lesson is progressing. He believes that, with experience, such interactive decision making becomes: '… routine and only partly conscious, so that the teacher only needs to think consciously about circumstances which are more unexpected, unique or require particular attention and care.' (p. 4)

Calderhead (1986) suggests that certain features help define 'teaching skills': they have a specific goal, they are set in a particular context, they are performed smoothly yet need precision and fine tuning, and above all, they are acquired through training and practice.

Wragg (1984) found it difficult to actually define 'teaching skill', and instead prefers to describe the characteristics of skilful teaching which he feels may: '… win some degree of consensus though not universal agreement.' (p. 6)

Wragg's characteristics of skilful teachers include strategies teachers use that 'facilitates pupils learning of something worthwhile', such as facts, skills, values, attitudes or other desirable outcomes.

He also adds that such strategies or teaching skills should be 'capable of being repeated' and could be 'acknowledged to be a skill by those competent to judge', such as teachers, teacher trainers, advisers and learners.

However, Wragg (1984) does feel that the whole notion of 'teaching skill' is problematic because of the varied nature of the teachers' job:

Pressing the right button on a tape recorder, or writing legibly on the blackboard require but modest competence, and are things most people could learn with only a little practice. Responding to a disruptive adolescent, or knowing how to explain a difficult concept to children of different ages and abilities by choosing the right language, appropriate examples and analogies, and reading the many cues which signal understanding or bewilderment, require years of practice as well as considerable intelligence and insight. (p. 7)

Wragg (1984) appears to acknowledge that a teacher's personal qualities and what one might term 'artistry', may combine with identifiable teaching skills to produce characteristics of good teachers which may be capable of being separated into discrete yet interrelated skills. Such teachers bring that something 'special' to teaching, but an overemphasis on breaking down the teaching act into very small units may destroy it, as Wragg points out: 'When children learn something there is often a magical quality about the excitement of discovery, the warmth of regard between teacher and taught, or the novelty to the learner of what is taking place, and the romanticism seems to be destroyed if teaching is seen as too deliberate, calculated, manipulated or over-analysed.' (p. 7)

Wragg also feels that attempts by competency-based teacher education programmes in the United States were 'misplaced' because they: '… assumed that teaching can be broken down into hundreds and indeed thousands of particles, that trainees could learn each of these, and that they could be certified on the basis of their proven ability to manifest whatever set of competencies had been prescribed'. (p. 7)

However, although the idea of competency-based teaching has not been well supported in the United Kingdom, there have been signs of a movement towards a competency-based interest in assessing quality in teaching, particularly in the appraisal of teachers and in the assessment of student teachers in training. For example, the DFE has raised the issue of teacher competencies in their 'Criteria for the accreditation of Teacher Education' (DFE, 1992) in which they state that: '... the accreditation criteria for initial teacher training courses should require higher education institutions, schools and students to focus on the competences of teaching'. (p. 1)

Also, the Office for Standards in Education (OFSTED, 1993b) in their inspections of initial teacher training courses requires that inspectors evaluate and report on: '... the standard of students' teaching and the range of competences which they bring to their work'. (p. 3)

What then are these professional competencies, and how are they defined?

The DES (DES, 1992a) feel that there are problems with attempting to define professional competencies: 'Defining competences that are precise and capable of assessment without being excessively detailed and over-prescriptive is a complex task.' (p. 4) – and they go on to offer a list of competencies but not a definition.

According to the Collins *English Dictionary* (1986) 'competence' or 'competency' implies: '... the condition of being capable; ability' or, '... the state of being legally competent or qualified.' (p. 173)

Being 'competent' is defined as: '... having skill, knowledge, etc.; capable.' (p. 173)

A 'competent' teacher may therefore be seen as a 'legally qualified and able professional who has the knowledge and skills of a capable teacher as recognised by her fellow professionals.'

What then are considered to be the skills and competencies of capable and effective teachers?

## Teaching skills and competencies of effective teachers

According to the DFE (1992) the competencies expected of newly qualified teachers include those shown in Box 2. Teacher training institutions are expected to arrange for the progressive development of these competencies and monitor them regularly during initial training.

**Box 2**
## Competencies expected of Newly Qualified Teachers

### Subject Knowledge
Newly qualified teachers should be able to demonstrate:

an understanding of the knowledge, concepts and skills of their specialist subjects and of the place of these subjects in the school curriculum;

knowledge and understanding of the National Curriculum and attainment targets (NCATs) and the programmes of study (PoS) in the subjects they are preparing to teach, together with an understanding of the framework of the statutory requirements;

a breadth and depth of subject knowledge extending beyond PoS and examination syllabuses in school.

### Subject Application
Newly qualified teachers should be able to:

produce coherent lesson plans which take account of NCATs and of the school's curriculum policies;

ensure continuity and progression within and between classes and in subjects;

set appropriately demanding expectations for pupils;

employ a range of teaching strategies appropriate to the age, ability and attainment level of pupils;

present subject content in clear language and in a stimulating manner;

contribute to the development of pupils' language and communication skills;

demonstrate ability to select and use appropriate resources, including Information Technology.

### Class Management
Newly qualified teachers should be able to:

decide when teaching the whole class, groups, pairs, or individuals is appropriate for particular learning purposes;

create and maintain a purposeful and orderly environment for the pupils;

devise and use appropriate rewards and sanctions to maintain an effective learning environment;

maintain pupils' interest and motivation.

### Assessment and Recording of Pupils' Progress
Newly qualified teachers should be able to:

identify the current level of attainment of individual pupils using

*continued*

**Box 2 continued**

**Assessment and Recording of Pupils' Progress**
NCATs, statements of attainment and end of key stage statements where applicable;

judge how well each pupil performs against the standard expected of a pupil of that age;

assess and record systematically the progress of individual pupils;

use such assessment in their teaching;

demonstrate that they understand the importance of reporting to pupils on their progress and of marking their work regularly against agreed criteria.

an awareness of individual differences, including social, psychological, developmental and cultural dimensions;

the ability to recognise diversity of talent including that of gifted pupils;

the ability to identify special educational needs or learning difficulties;

a self-critical approach to diagnosing and evaluating pupils' learning, including a recognition of the effects on that learning of teachers' expectations;

a readiness to promote the moral and spiritual well-being of pupils.

**Further Professional Development**
Newly qualified teachers should have acquired in initial training the necessary foundation to develop:
an understanding of the school as an institution and its place within the community;

a working knowledge of their pastoral, contractual, legal and administrative responsibilities as teachers;

an ability to develop effective working relationships with professional colleagues and parents, and to develop their communication skills;

*Source: DFE (1992).*

Kyriacou (1991) identifies what he regards as 'essential teaching skills' that might contribute to successful classroom practice:

(1) Planning and preparation – skills of selecting aims and learning outcomes and the best way of achieving them.
(2) Lesson presentation – skills of successfully involving pupils in the learning experience and instructional skills.

(3) Lesson management – skills of organisation and management and ability to maintain pupil attention and involvement.
(4) Classroom climate – skills of establishing a positive climate and attitude to learning.
(5) Discipline.
(6) Assessing pupils' progress – formative and summative forms.
(7) Reflecting and evaluation.

Kyriacou does also point out that there is: '... clearly an interplay between these seven areas, so that skills exercised in one area may simultaneously contribute to another area.' (p. 9) – and that: '... all the skills involved in lesson preparation, lesson management, classroom climate and discipline, are interactive skills. In other words, exercising these skills involves monitoring, adjusting and responding to what pupils are doing.' (p. 9)

Research work on the development of appraisal systems for teachers tend to agree largely with the lists of teaching skills and competencies put forward by the DFE (1992) and Kyriacou (1991). Suffolk Education Department (1987) produced an appraisal of teaching skills pro-forma based on several of the teaching skills already mentioned:

- Planning and preparation
- Organisation and management
- Teaching skills – e.g. questioning
- Relationships

In their guidance to inspectors for assessing the quality of teaching, OFSTED (1993a) identify the following main aspects of 'quality' teaching:

- Objectives and purpose – e.g. clarity of teachers' objectives for lessons; pupil awareness of objectives.
- Teachers' knowledge and skills – e.g. command of subject; clarity of explanations; quality of questioning.
- Planning and organisation – e.g. suitability of lesson content and activities; range and appropriateness of teaching techniques; effectiveness of lesson planning, classroom organisation and use of resources.
- Meeting individual needs – e.g. effectiveness of challenge, pace and motivation in lessons; matching of pupils' attainments and abilities.
- Assessment – e.g. regular feedback and opportunities for pupils to evaluate their own progress.
- Positive relationships that promote learning.

Therefore, there appears to be a reasonable consensus concerning the general teaching skills and competencies that all teachers should possess to be considered to be competent and effective teachers. Even so, different subject areas may require specific teaching skills and competencies for effective teaching. So, is this the case with physical education?

## The skills and competencies of effective teachers of Physical Education – the professional view

Ted Wragg (1984) made the point that an important quality of a 'teaching skill' is that it is acknowledged to be a skill by those competent to judge. As part of the TEPE Project, 23 Heads of PE Departments and Advisers of PE in Local Education Authorities were asked, 'What do you consider to be the essential teaching skills of an effective teacher of physical education?'

The following teaching skills and competencies were mentioned by all the Advisers and the majority of Heads of PE (HODs):

- Knowledge   – broad based knowledge of subject.
              – content knowledge.
              – knowledge of National Curriculum PE.
              – knowledge of school organisation.
              – knowledge of special events/Sports Day.
- Planning and preparation
              – in relation to National Curriculum programmes of study.
              – safety issues.
              – differentiation of activities according to ability.
- Organisation and management
              – safe use of equipment and resources.
              – class control and discipline.
              – time management.

Also frequently mentioned by each of the professional groups were:

- the importance of teachers using a range of appropriate teaching styles and the ability to 'move in and out of different teaching styles'.
- communication skills – clarity of expression.
              – effective use of voice.
              – ability to demonstrate.
- observational skills   – able to analyse movement.
              – able to recognise skilful performance.
              – know what is meant by quality in performance.
              – ability to assess pupils as a basis for progression.

A number of additional teaching skills, competencies and personal qualities were also mentioned by some of the HODs and advisers. For example, two HODs commented on the importance of 'adaptability' as a teaching skill:

'The ability to improvise, adapt, refine, think on one's feet... '. 'The ability to let the lesson run and yet be in control – to let it develop away from the plan yet to keep the end-product still in sight'.

Adaptability is also closely linked to planning, particularly when preparing work for different abilities. As one adviser pointed out, effective teachers of PE are able to: '... adapt and differentiate work to the needs and aptitudes of a wide range of pupils in all National Curriculum activities'.

The importance of 'interpersonal skills' that help to create a positive and 'enjoyable working environment' was mentioned by a number of teachers and advisers. 'Being a good communicator but not over-friendly with pupils', and having 'negotiation skills', were mentioned by two advisers while the teachers listed the ability 'to praise, encourage, and motivate', and personal qualities such as 'enthusiasm', 'patience' and overall 'presence': 'Enthusiasm ties in with presence (which is very hard to define). Perhaps *the* most important part of the job is enthusing young people about PE'.

According to the advisers, effective teachers have the ability to 'self-reflect', to 'critically evaluate their own work as a basis for development', and to 'review their teaching and its outcomes'. One HOD felt that effective teachers of PE were 'effective enablers and innovators' and 'receptive to new ideas'.

The above are the views of PE advisers and school Heads of PE concerning the teaching skills and competencies of effective teachers of physical education. Five PE lecturers were also asked 'What teaching and professional skills would you expect a new teacher of PE to have prior to taking up their first post in school?', and their views were very similar to those put forward by the advisers and HODs. This is therefore the professional view. To what extent does the research view agree with this professional view?

Although not necessarily conclusive, there is now substantial research literature on the whole issue of 'teacher effectiveness' in general, and a growing body of research evidence related to teacher effectiveness in physical education in particular. First of all, what does the more general research literature looking at subject matter teaching have to offer?

## The skills and competencies of effective teachers – the general research view

The most important and probably most relevant teacher effectiveness research findings concerning subject matter teaching (as opposed to the teaching of physical skills), resulted from studies designed to assess the relationship between process variables (what teachers and pupils do in classrooms), and product or outcome measures (e.g. changes in pupil knowledge, skills, values or dispositions related to instructional goals). In this approach a teacher's patterns of interaction and the associated pupil process variables are correlated with high levels of pupil learning to establish which teacher processes are more effective for pupil learning. This is called process-product research. The next stage is to test these effective teaching behaviours experimentally by training an experimental group of teachers in the effective strategies, and then comparing them in terms of pupil achievement scores with teachers who are not trained in the use of these behaviours. Rosenshine and Stevens (1986) review this form of research and show that not only can teachers learn the effective teaching strategies, but that experimental research results consistently report higher pupil achievement measures in the classes of teachers in experimental groups.

What then are the characteristics of these more effective teachers who appear to elicit higher pupil achievement test results than other teachers?

Good and Brophy (1991) review the process-product, correlational and experimental studies and report the 'most widely replicated findings' concerning the characteristics of effective teachers in their text *Looking in Classrooms*. These findings are shown in Box 3 below.

---

**Box 3**
**The characteristics of effective teachers**

**Active Teaching** — Effective teachers actively teach by demonstrating skills, explaining concepts and assignments/activities, and reviewing when required.

— Effective teachers 'teach' pupils rather than expect them to learn by purely working from curriculum materials.

— Effective teachers do not just stress facts and skills but emphasise concepts and understanding.

**Teaching to Mastery** — Effective teachers offer active instruction on new material and then provide opportunities for pupils to practise and apply what they have learned.

— Effective teachers monitor pupil progress and provide feedback and remedial assistance when required so that pupils eventually achieve mastery.

**Pupil opportunity to learn** — Effective teachers tend to allocate more available pupil learning time and instructional time (Berliner, 1979), and their pupils spend more of this allocated time on learning tasks related to the objectives of the lesson than do pupils of teachers who are 'less focused on instructional goals'.

*continued*

**Box 3 continued**

**Classroom management and organisation** – Effective teachers organise and manage their classrooms more efficiently thus ensuring more time and pupil opportunity to learn.

– Effective teachers quickly establish structured management routines that pupils learn and become accustomed to.

– Effective teachers use positive rather than coercive management styles.

**Curriculum pacing** – Effective teachers progress quickly through the work to be done in appropriate small steps thus minimising pupil frustration and failure and providing greater continuity of progression.

**Teacher expectation/sense of efficacy** – Effective teachers emphasise positive expectations of pupils while at the same time being realistic and setting attainable goals.

– Effective teachers closely monitor pupil progress to ensure pupils are working on the task to be learned.

– Effective teachers use individual instruction and feedback related to each individual pupil's personal level of mastery and understanding, and do not compare pupils with other pupils or class norms.

– Effective teachers use feedback and additional instruction linked to lesson objectives rather than purely evaluate success or failure.

– Effective teachers use diagnosis of pupil learning difficulties when pupils have not understood an explanation or demonstration and follow-up with breaking down the task and reteaching it in a different way or try new curriculum materials.

– Effective teachers encourage pupils to achieve as much as they can and do not protect pupils from failure.

**A supportive learning environment** – Effective teachers are enthusiastic, supportive, and retain a warm, pleasant and enjoyable working/class environment.

**Presentation of information** – Effective teachers communicate lesson objectives, lesson presentations and instructions clearly, enthusiastically and concisely.

**Pupil accountability** – Effective teachers not only rigorously monitor pupil progress, but also hold pupils accountable for their own learning and completion of tasks, and provide opportunities for pupil self-evaluation.

*continued*

---

**Box 3 continued**

**Appropriate tasks**   – Effective teachers set varied and interesting tasks to motivate pupil involvement in learning the task
          – Effective teachers set tasks that are new or challenging enough to constitute meaningful learning experiences, yet easy enough to allow pupils to achieve a high rate of success with reasonable effort.
          – Effective teachers explain work clearly and go over practice examples with pupils before releasing them to work independently.

*Adapted from Good and Brophy (1991) p. 443.*

---

These research findings offering suggestions as to what might be considered to be effective teaching behaviours have been of great value to the teaching profession. All the same, such findings do need to be examined in terms of their limitations, as the image of the effective teacher is far from complete. Good and Brophy (1991) put forward the following criticisms.

Firstly, it has to be noted that many of the recent studies contributing to the generalisations of effective teaching behaviours were conducted with primary age children, and many of the studies specifically investigated pupil achievement in reading and mathematics.

Secondly, the research tended to concentrate on very basic aspects of teaching that might differentiate effective teachers from less effective teachers, and did not really examine those particular aspects of teaching that might describe the most outstanding teachers.

Thirdly, as Good and Brophy (1991) point out, the research:

... relied mostly on standardised tests as the outcome measure, which meant that it focussed on the mastery of relatively isolated knowledge items and skill components without assessing the degree to which pupils had developed understanding of networks of related information or the ability to use this information to think critically, solve problems, or make decisions. In short, the research did not give much attention to teaching for understanding and higher order applications. (p. 448)

Therefore, not only does the research fail to look at 'teaching for understanding' and other 'higher order applications', it has also tended to concentrate on academic skills and knowledge when one might argue that schools may also emphasise the development of other types of knowledge, skills and understanding; such as those related to personal and social education. Teacher effectiveness may therefore have to be judged on the basis of the criteria by which the effectiveness is to be measured. Consequently, different concepts of teacher effectiveness may result, depending on one's objectives for a particular lesson.

A new approach to researching subject matter teaching emerged in the 1980s. In this form of investigation researchers attempted to find out what teachers were trying to accomplish, then they recorded details about classroom processes as they occurred during a unit of work or lesson. Next they assessed learning by using evaluation measures linked to the instructional goals, often by use of interview technique. This particular research on teaching looked at attempts to teach for understanding and a teacher's ability to develop pupils' problem-solving skills. This teaching approach was intended to introduce a conceptual change in pupils, and to develop new knowledge through a process of 'active construction'. (Good and Brophy, 1991, p. 449)

This more recent research on teaching for understanding has also suggested that it is not only teacher presentation of information and modelling that leads to higher pupil achievement gains, the teacher also needs to structure a great deal of discourse related to the content of the lesson. This will entail questioning of pupils and involving them in reflecting, critically analysing, problem solving, and decision making. A variety of different questioning techniques are required, as well as the skill of encouraging pupils to explain and develop their answers, and evaluate their colleagues' answers. Skill in conducting such discourse may also involve teachers in taking advantage of opportunities to elaborate or develop a discussion, particularly when pupils may raise an unexpected issue that is worthy of consideration. Effective teachers are therefore able to plan and use appropriate sequences of questions in developing discourse for teaching for understanding and higher order mental operations. These teaching skills are discussed in Chapter 10.

The research literature related to the characteristics of effective teachers of subject matter teaching is not complete. Also, it is acknowledged that a number of other factors do influence the use of effective teaching strategies. These include pupils' age, pupil socioeconomic status, pupil aptitude or ability level, teachers' lesson objectives and, of course, the subject matter being taught (Rosenshine and Stevens, 1986).

## The skills and competencies of effective teachers of Physical Education – the research view

Compared with most school subjects physical education arrived rather late on the teacher effectiveness scene, particularly in terms of the development of process-product and experimental research. Most of the earlier physical education research in the 1970s relied upon descriptive studies using different observation systems to identify teacher and pupil behaviour in the PE setting. This research helped physical educationists to understand what teachers and pupils were doing in PE lessons but it was unable to offer any suggestions concerning the characteristics of effective teachers.

During the 1980s a number of process-product and experimental studies were conducted in physical education (McLeish, 1981; Yerg, 1981; Pieron, 1982; Yerg and Twardy, 1982; Phillips and Carlisle, 1983; De Knop, 1986; Graham, Soares and Harrington, 1983; Silverman, 1985 and 1988; Rink, Werner, Hohn, Ward and Timmermans, 1986; Paese, 1986; Rink and Werner, 1987; Werner and Rink, 1989; Gustart and Springings, 1989), and additional research examining the work and behaviour of 'expert', 'effective' teachers (Siedentop, 1989), have all provided a degree of information concerning what might be considered to be effective teaching behaviours in physical education. In many cases a 'product' measure of teacher effectiveness related to pupil 'time on task' and pupil 'engagement' in learning was used. The research instrument used to measure pupil time on task was an adapted academic learning time (ALT) measure (Berliner, 1979) known as ALT–PE. A further discussion of the findings of ALT–PE research related to aspects of management appears in Chapter 7 and Metzler (1989) offers a major review of work using this instrument.

In addition to process-product and experimental studies of the teaching of PE there is also a growing research literature that has employed an ecological or ethnographic perspective to the study of teacher effectiveness in PE. While there are arguments concerning the value of this research approach, Lee (1991), in supporting the work of Doyle (1977), considers that: '... effectiveness formulations should include both contextual variables and the meaning teachers and students assign to events and processes during instruction'. (p. 375) Those supporting the value of ecological studies therefore believe that teacher effectiveness research should be as interested in 'how pupils learn from teaching' as 'what kind of teaching causes learning'. Such studies as those by Tousignant and Siedentop (1983), Greenockle, Lee and Lomax (1990), and McBride (1990) are examples of the use of this approach to study teacher effectiveness in physical education.

A number of respected workers in the field of teacher effectiveness in PE have provided reviews of the literature and offer their suggestions regarding what might be considered to be the characteristics of effective teachers of physical education.

Metzler (1990) provides a list of effective teacher/learning process indicators for PE that he considers 'has received some support in the effective teaching/learning literature' (p. 61), and which he feels might provide a list of effective teaching behaviours to be used by supervisors evaluating student teachers. Metzler's list is shown in Box 4.

**Box 4**
**Effective Teaching/Learning Process Indicators for Physical Education**

**Time management** – particularly related to the amount of time pupils are engaged in learning at an appropriate level of difficulty and success.

**Resource management** – affecting pupil time engaged in learning.

**Task relevance and structure** – effective teachers analyse the components of tasks and offer a sequential progression. Task structure involves teachers in designing relevant tasks and maintaining pupil engagement in the task through continuous monitoring of pupil progress.

**Behaviour management and task accountability** – effective teachers plan for preventative management and create a business-like class atmosphere. Effective teachers make task expectations and management procedures clear to pupils with effective communication.

**Engagement and success rates** – effective teachers take account of pupil developmental characteristics when designing learning experiences, and 'match' ability levels to task to ensure appropriate levels of success for pupils.
– effective teachers present material and task requirements so that pupils understand concepts to be learned and what is required of them.

**Instructional cueing** – effective teachers provide appropriate instructional cues to aid learning (verbal, visual, written, audio, demonstration) and clearly communicate accurate, concise and pertinent information in a logical order appropriate to pupils level of learning.

**Performance feedback** – effective teachers provide high rates of both 'task intrinsic feedback' (the task providing its own feedback), augmented feedback (provided by the teacher or other person) and specific feedback.

**Class Climate** – effective teachers create a positive class climate, plan interesting lessons, allow pupils to share in decision making, are enthusiastic and provide pupils with greater opportunities to learn and achieve in lessons.

**Planning** – effective teachers have a clear idea of what they aim to accomplish and how they are going to achieve their lesson objectives efficiently.
– effective teachers reflect on their lessons and in turn modify and adapt later lessons accordingly.

*continued*

---

**Box 4 continued**

**Verbal and non-verbal interaction** – whereas there is no research linking interaction patterns with pupil learning, there is evidence to suggest that more effective teachers have higher rates of interaction which is in turn linked to higher rates of appropriate pupil engagement in learning.

**Use of Questions** – effective teachers use clear, concise questions to establish pupils' understanding of concepts and skills. However, there is little research support related to effective questioning in PE lessons.

**Content development** – effective teachers design learning experiences for pupils that follow a clear sequence and progression which is based on pupil progress and ability.

**Regular evaluation of pupil progress** – effective teachers take into account pupil ability and stage of learning when designing learning experiences and assessing levels of achievement in relation to original instructional goals.

**Establishment of a safe learning environment**

*Source: Metzler, M. (1990) p. 61.*

---

Metzler acknowledges that his final item, 'establishment of a safe learning environment' does not have current empirical support for its role in effective teaching, but he considers that it ought to be a necessary precondition for teaching many activities in PE.

In his review of research on teaching PE, Silverman (1991) lists the following characteristics of effective or experienced teachers of motor skills:

Effective teachers:

- Plan for class management and pupil learning.
- Anticipate situations and make contingency plans.
- Are aware of pupil skill differences and use the information in planning and monitoring.
- Require much information to plan.
- Have a repertoire of teaching styles and know when to use them.
- Provide accurate and focussed explanations and demonstrations.
- Provide adequate time for pupil practice.
- Maximise appropriate pupil practice or engagement.
- Minimise inappropriate pupil practice or engagement.
- Minimise pupil waiting.

These characteristics are derived from comparisons of more and less effective/experienced teachers, studies of teaching methods and correlational studies relating teacher and pupil behaviour to pupil achievement. However, Silverman (1991) does make the point that many of these characteristics are interrelated: 'For instance, planning for management and learning may result in using certain teaching styles that then may influence the ability to provide accurate and focussed explanations and demonstrations and time for practice. This, in turn, will influence whether student appropriate practice is maximised and inappropriate practice and waiting minimised. No one characteristic should be treated in isolation'. (p. 358)

Silverman's (1991) list of characteristics of effective teachers has been criticised for being 'reductionist' by Dodds and Placeck (1991) and: '... too prescriptive without raising appropriate cautions based on specific teaching contexts or situations. The list also focuses on what teachers do, ignoring both specific student outcomes that accrue as a result and intended teacher goals relevant to a given teaching situation'. (p. 367)

Lee (1991) also felt that although Silverman's review may: '... provide some formal base of support for current beliefs regarding what good teaching is, the conclusions derived are not impressive'. (p. 378)

Lee goes on to suggest that Silverman ought to distinguish between experienced and effective teachers and examine certain research methodologies more thoroughly.

However, regardless of these criticisms, Silverman's review does offer us some pointers for identifying the skills of effective teachers of PE, in what is a relatively young and uncertain field of research. In many ways these pointers are in agreement with subject matter research on teacher effectiveness and yet also offer more subject specific guidelines towards what might be suggested as being effective teaching behaviours in PE. Without wishing to appear too simplistic or reductionist, the research literature on teacher effectiveness in physical education (e.g. Phillips and Carlisle, 1983; Rink and Werner, 1987; Siedentop, 1989; Gustart and Springings, 1989) and the views of experts such as Rink (1985), Siedentop (1991), Metzler (1990) and Silverman (1991), seem to suggest the following characteristics and skills of effective teachers of physical education, and that these variables may interact in the overall teaching behaviour of the 'expert' teacher.

## Effective teachers of Physical Education appear to:
PLAN their work more effectively and:

- have a clear idea of what they intend to accomplish and how they will accomplish it;
- analyse and diagnose pupil levels of skill, knowledge and understanding, and are aware of pupil developmental

characteristics in order to be able to design and prescribe appropriate learning experiences to 'match' pupil ability, thus ensuring high levels of success in practice and learning;

- progress work to be done in sequence and in appropriate small steps linked to clear instructional goals, thus minimising frustration and failure and achieving greater continuity of progression;
- provide meaningful, realistic, challenging and appropriate, attainable goals for individual pupil learning and success;
- develop effective sequences of appropriate questions to enable pupils to develop understanding of concepts;
- design effective class management procedures, anticipate situations and have contingency plans prepared in case of unforeseen problems with lesson administration.

**Effective teachers of Physical Education appear to:**
PRESENT new material well and:

- explain new concepts and pupil tasks with clarity and effective communication skills;
- make good use of modeling/demonstrations.

ORGANISE AND MANAGE pupils and learning experiences by:

- planning for preventative management through quickly established management structures, routines, and class rules/contracts, therefore providing more time and opportunity to learn;
- making lesson task expectations clear, monitoring pupil progress and ensuring that pupils are clearly accountable for what they are learning;
- creating a business-like learning environment and class atmosphere;
- effective use of resources.

**Effective teachers of Physical Education are:**
ACTIVE TEACHERS because they spend more time actively involved in teaching pupils and they:

- have highly developed observation skills to be able to diagnose pupil learning difficulties;
- offer task intrinsic and positive, specific, augmented feedback related to lesson objectives;
- demonstrate skills and explain concepts clearly and concisely;
- monitor pupil progress to maximise pupil time for practice, and minimise inappropriate pupil inactivity and waiting;
- sustain lesson momentum;
- utilise more lesson time in the presentation of material and performance feedback.

**Effective teachers appear to provide:**
A POSITIVE, SUPPORTIVE AND WARM LEARNING ENVIRONMENT

- they individualise feedback and guidance for personal levels of mastery and understanding and do not make comparisons between pupils;
- they are enthusiastic, pleasant and positive;
- they plan interesting lessons, allowing pupils to share in decision making;
- they provide pupils with greater time and opportunity to learn;
- they are aware of teacher expectancy effects.

**Effective teachers of Physical Education have a repertoire of:**
TEACHING STYLES and know how and when to use them to facilitate pupil learning and understanding.

**Also, effective teachers of other subjects appear to:**
TEACH FOR UNDERSTANDING by:

- planning appropriate sequences of questions to facilitate pupil understanding of concepts and lesson content;
- the use of a variety of skills and strategies to develop discourse and discussion;
- providing learning experiences and opportunities to apply understanding;
- providing support and task simplification strategies and other forms of 'scaffolding'. (Although it has to be noted that there is at present a lack of research support for this variable in PE.)

A large part of the remainder of this book examines these effective teaching variables in more detail from both a research and a professional point of view.

# CHAPTER 5

# Planning and preparation

### The importance of planning

Her Majesty's Inspectorate have frequently commented on the importance of good planning as an essential feature of effective teaching: 'The lack of explicit long-term course or topic planning, as well as the lack of specific lesson preparation are frequently identified as contributing to work of poor quality.' (DES, 1985, p. 8)

The HMI report *The New Teacher in School* (DES, 1988a) describes what are considered to be 'poor' or 'very poor' lessons in secondary schools as lacking adequate attention to planning: 'The most serious weaknesses were insufficient attention to planning and either a lack of clear objectives or objectives that are misconceived, with the result that pupils often saw no progress in what they were being asked to do'. (p. 22)

In the same report HMI considered that the features of 'good' or 'excellent' lessons that they observed which produced pupil work of a high standard: '... were, first and foremost, thoughtful planning and preparation, in which the choice of content, the use of a range of resources, and a variety of activities and teaching approaches were carefully considered'. (p. 22)

It is therefore not surprising that the DFE (DFE, 1992) expressed the need for newly qualified teachers to be able to: 'produce coherent lesson plans which take account of NCATs and of the school's curriculum policies' (para. 2.3.1), – and when doing so: 'ensure continuity and progression within and between classes and in subjects'. (para. 2.3.2)

Teaching is a professional 'thinking' activity and what is actually done in the classroom is largely dependent upon the teacher's thought processes that have gone on before the lesson. In fact, it was once said that: 'What teachers do is directed in no small measure by what they think'. (National Institute of Education, 1975, p. 1)

Several of the teachers, advisers and lecturers in the TEPE Project recommended that 'thinking through' lessons beforehand was sound advice to all beginning teachers of PE.

Teacher planning and lesson preparation is very much a cognitive process in which, according to Clarke and Peterson (1986), teachers visualise the future, devise goals, instructional methods and procedures, and construct frameworks for future action.

Teaching is a very complex activity and, as with many other professions, involves a considerable degree of decision making, problem solving and 'orchestration' of knowledge and technique (Clark and Yinger, 1987, p. 97). However, many young teachers feel that as long as they have a personal knowledge of a subject or activity there is no reason why they can't teach it. But this 'content' knowledge is not enough to be an effective teacher. In their study of novice teachers, Wilson *et al.* (1987) noted that as these young teachers prepared to teach and experienced teaching lessons, they began to develop a new type of subject matter knowledge that is enriched and enhanced by other types of knowledge: knowledge of the learner, knowledge of the curriculum, knowledge of the context and knowledge of pedagogy which they refer to as 'pedagogical content knowledge'. Shulman (1987) believes that this form of content knowledge reflects a teacher's **ability** to transform: '... the content knowledge he or she possesses into **forms** that are pedagogically powerful and yet adaptive to the variations **in** ability and background presented to the students'. (p. 15)

Planning is therefore an essential feature of pedagogical thinking and reasoning. Planning appears to mediate between a teacher's basic knowledge of the subject being taught and his or her ability to teach the subject effectively, because it brings into play the teacher's general pedagogical content knowledge. This includes knowledge of theories and principles of teaching and learning, knowledge of the learner, and knowledge of the techniques and principles of teaching such as class management. The plan for a lesson, unit or course is the result of a considerable degree of thinking on the part of the teacher.

But, does planning lead to more effective decision making and more effective teaching?

In Clark and Yinger's (1987) review of the subject matter research in this area they concluded that teacher planning: '... does influence opportunity to learn, content coverage, grouping for instruction, and the general focus of classroom processes'. (p. 95)

More specifically, Peterson and Clark (1978) found that teachers who emphasised subject matter in their planning tended to pose more questions; teachers who used objectives in their planning seemed to display more goal setting behaviour; and teachers who referred to pupils when planning appeared to show more concern for pupils when they taught.

Several research workers in physical education have also investigated teacher planning and its effects on teacher behaviour during lessons.

Imwold *et al.* (1984) compared the teaching behaviour of pre-service teachers who planned with those who did not. The results of the study showed that those who planned their work made greater use of equipment and facilities, gave more direction, organised their classes more carefully and precisely, used a greater variety and better progression of activities, timed their lessons better, allowed enough time for reviewing the lesson at the end and the soliciting of pupil comments and questions. Pupils also appeared to be more active and 'on task' in the lessons of teachers who planned.

Byra and Coulon (1994) also noted that in the planned lessons (as opposed to unplanned lessons) of pre-service teachers, pupils spent less time waiting their turn, less time being 'off task' and involved in non-instructional aspects of the activity. In addition, they found that in the 'planned' lessons the teachers' presentations were much clearer, and they provided more frequent specific corrective feedback that was congruent with the skill focus of the lesson, than in 'unplanned lessons'.

More effective teachers in the Phillips and Carlisle (1983) study displayed a greater ability to 'analyse pupil needs' and 'used objectives in planning' than less effective teachers.

Although the research on teacher planning is rather limited and a little inconclusive concerning its effects on pupil learning, there are suggestions that more effective teachers plan their work and thoroughly 'think through' their lessons and units of work. Being well prepared also has a number of other benefits.

Good planning does take a lot of anxiety out of the actual teaching act and teachers consequently feel more confident when they are teaching. In their study of why teachers' plan, Clark and Yinger (1987) noted that planning served three main purposes:

- planning to meet immediate personal needs (e.g. reduce uncertainty and anxiety, to find a sense of direction, confidence and security);
- planning as a means to an end of instruction (e.g. to learn the material, to collect and organise materials, to organise time and activity flow);
- direct uses of plans during instruction (e.g. to organise students, to get an activity started, to aid memory, to provide a framework for instruction and evaluation). (p. 88)

Experienced teachers try to prevent problems by entering the teaching situation with contingency plans if their evaluation of pupil characteristics or responses require alternative tasks, or they anticipate problems that may occur in lesson transitions (Griffey and Housner, 1991). Other studies have shown that planning helps teachers to create an unambiguous teaching environment in which teachers and pupils are clearly aware of management, activity and instructional routines (Emmer *et al.*, 1980; Evertson and Emmer, 1982).

One experienced teacher who took part in the TEPE Project was very aware of the importance of planning in terms of lessons that 'went well' compared with those that didn't: 'Pre-planning is important to having a good lesson. Unexpected problems cause the structure of a lesson to be lost'.

Also, as noted in Chapter 2, 89% of the student teachers and 80% of the NQTs in the project mentioned some aspect of planning as being essential to the success of lessons. So, sound planning is essential, but how do teachers plan their work?

## How do teachers plan their work?

Teachers appear to develop and use different types of plans and several educational researchers have suggested models that describe how teachers do plan.

Considering types of teacher plans, Clark and Yinger (1987) reporting on studies they have conducted into the plans of primary school teachers, noted that they used a variety of plans: yearly, long range, termly, short range, weekly, daily, unit and lesson plans. However, unit planning was mentioned by the teachers as being the most important. They also found that when teachers did plan lessons daily they preferred to do this for the unit as a whole. This approach appeared to enable the teachers not only to consider progression across all daily lessons but also to take into account the overall unit objectives.

But, how do teachers actually plan? What models describe how teachers plan?

For many years Tyler's (1950) linear, rational planning model was advocated as an appropriate approach for teachers to use when planning their teaching. Tyler's model entailed four stages:

(1) specification of objectives,
(2) selection of learning materials,
(3) organisation of learning activities,
(4) specification of evaluation procedures.

In his study of *How Teachers Plan their Courses* in British secondary schools, Taylor (1970) noted that pupil needs, abilities and interests were of priority in planning, and this was followed in order of importance by subject matter, goals and teaching method. A factor analysis of the teachers' responses indicated that, when planning, the teachers tended to think about the following issues in order of importance:

(1) teaching context issues (e.g. resources),
(2) pupil interests,

(3)   aims and objectives,
(4)   evaluation.

Taylor therefore suggested that teacher planning should possibly start with a consideration of the content being taught and important contextual issues (e.g. time, resources, sequencing), and then think about pupil interests, aims and objectives of the course, learning situations, course philosophy, criteria for evaluation, etc., rather than starting with objectives as the Tyler model had done.

Other workers in the field have discovered that teachers may start their planning by thinking about pupil activities and content (Zahorik, 1975), and spend most of their planning time dealing with content and instructional processes (Peterson and Clark, 1978) rather than objectives. Housner (1991) believes that this emphasis on selection and organisation of instructional activities may have something to do with teachers' attempts to simplify and make more predictable what is a very fast moving and unpredictable environment – the classroom! Establishing organisational routines first of all may offer greater predictability.

Research on teacher planning suggests that experienced teachers plan in different ways from novice teachers. Stroot and Morton (1989), in a study of effective primary PE teachers, discovered that some teachers are very dependent on plans whereas others are not. They referred to these two types of teacher as 'plan dependent' and 'plan independent'. The former preferred to have access to lesson plans, to be able to 'glance' continually at them at times during the day for personal comfort and confidence. 'Plan independent' teachers, on the other hand, appear to have a mental image or framework of previous planning and experience of teaching the activity. They were all effective and experienced teachers who had originally drawn up extensive unit and lesson plans, but had internalised these plans through repeatedly teaching them. They were then able to choose from this repertoire of successful teaching plans without needing to specify the methods in writing. They have a wide range of experience and well-tested procedures for asking questions and developing content.

For the beginning teacher it is important to appreciate that experienced teachers may plan in these different ways, and that they may not always pay attention to objectives or evaluation procedures. However, in their discussion of the implications of studies on teacher planning on the training of teachers Borko and Niles (1987) argue that pre-service and inexperienced teachers should still approach planning through the Tyler model of pre-specifying objectives and evaluation procedures, because pre-service teachers do not have the breadth and depth of experience of experienced teachers. Experienced teachers acting as mentors should therefore expect beginning teachers to use different models of planning from those used by experienced teachers.

An objectives model of planning may therefore be advocated as a reasonably sound approach to planning, but, does planning really begin with the pre-specification of course unit and lesson objectives? In the case of the beginning teacher in a new school there is first of all a need to establish a degree of what has been referred to as 'pedagogical content knowledge' – knowledge of the learner, the curriculum and the context of teaching the activity. This will entail gathering the background knowledge needed for planning.

## Background knowledge for planning

What background information and knowledge is needed prior to planning a unit of work?

As part of the TEPE Project, advisers, lecturers and HODs in schools were asked what advice they would give a student teacher about to teach a new class for the first time, or a newly qualified teacher preparing for their first term in a new school. As the following comments show, the collection of a range of background information and knowledge prior to planning is recommended:

Spend time, in advance if necessary or possible, getting to know about – the school, catchment area, ethos of the PE Dept., PE curriculum, schemes of work, storage of equipment, discipline procedures.

Find out as much as possible about the school and the department prior to the first day. Schools usually have booklets with information for new staff and also for parents and pupils. Read the school prospectus and any information which you can obtain from the department about curriculum and policies.

Try to find out as much as possible about the pupils and what previous experience they have had. Plan carefully on this basis and be prepared to adapt the lesson as necessary.

Establish your starting point by talking to previous teachers where appropriate and by making your own observations of ability levels within the group.

Be knowledgeable about the subject, know the progressions in various activities especially the areas of the National Curriculum.

This advice from experienced professionals in physical education suggests the need for knowledge or information in a number of areas prior to planning:

- Knowledge of the National Curriculum for PE.
- Knowledge of the activity to be taught.
- Knowledge of the school context and PE Dept.
- Knowledge of the pupils.
- Knowledge of resources.

Knowledge of the National Curriculum for Physical Education and knowledge of the activity to be taught can be dealt with prior to visiting the school, but the remaining information can only be gathered by visiting the school beforehand. Student teachers preparing for teaching practice naturally have their school visits arranged for them but newly qualified teachers need to make their own arrangements. As one adviser recommended: 'Schools will usually welcome you on a visit before starting to work there, particularly if you offer to help. A great many things can be sorted out by this kind of arrangement. Find out and meet as many of the people who will be able to give you help, support and advice as possible'.

The preliminary visit to your new school is an essential part of your planning and preparation to teach. It is the opportunity to meet school staff including senior management staff (which may include a tutor or mentor who has responsibility for student teachers and newly qualified teachers) and PE department staff.

The information you will need to gather on your preliminary visit will relate to:

- The school context.
- The PE Dept and its work.
- The facilities and resources.
- The pupils.
- Lesson routines.

The following exercise is in the form of a series of questions that will help you to collect the kind of information you will need when making your preliminary visit.

### Exercise 1    The Preliminary Visit

#### The School Context

(1) What is the layout of the school like? (e.g. age of buildings, architectural style, design, single or dual site, position of playing fields/sports hall and gym, whereabouts of headteacher's room, resource centre, etc.)
Drawing a rough plan of the school grounds may be of value.

(2) What is the neighbourhood of the school like? (e.g. urban/rural, locality of parks, rivers, reservoirs, and other places of particular relevance to the teaching of PE)

(3) How many pupils are in the school?
What is the size of the annual intake?
What is the catchment area like?

(4) How is the school pastoral system organised?

Will I have a tutor group? What is done in tutor periods? How often do they meet?

(5) What are the school disciplinary procedures and school rules? What rewards and punishments are used and who administers punishment?

(6) What are the school aims and philosophy? (e.g. traditional or progressive, encouraging competition, forms of groupings, etc.)

(7) What are the school policies concerning equality of opportunity in relation to: special educational needs, gender, and cultural diversity?

(8) What does the school expect of student teachers/new members of staff concerning – time of arrival, free periods, leaving the school premises, attendance at assembly, dress and appearance, etc.

(9) School details – address, name of Headteacher, telephone number, teacher in charge of student teachers or newly qualified staff.

In addition to answers to the above questions it would be valuable to collect copies of the school prospectus and other policy documents related to the topics raised.

## The PE Department and its work

(1) What is the philosophy of the PE Department?

(2) What is the school PE curriculum like and how does it relate to the National Curriculum proposals for PE?

(3) Does the Department have a printed scheme and units of work for different activities, phases, and key stages?

(4) What is the Departmental policy for assessing pupils' work and what are the procedures for recording and reporting pupil progress?

(5) What is the Department extended curriculum like? What extracurricular activites will you be asked to take?

(6) What is the Department policy concerning:
   (a) Special educational needs?
   (b) Equality of opportunity in relation to gender and is PE taught in mixed sex groups?
   (c) Cultural diversity?
   (d) Teaching styles and strategies?

(7) Who are the members of staff in the PE Department? What are their duties and responsibilities?

(8) What is the safety policy of the Department? (e.g. action in the event of an accident, awareness of location of first-aid kit, sick bay/school nurse, documentation after an accident, supervision of extracurricular activities, school trips, etc.)

(9) Is there a 'Special Events' programme for the year? (e.g. dates of special events, tournaments, sports days, swimming galas, health

and fitness week, intramural competitions, regional sporting finals, etc.)

(10) How does the Department liaise with the local community? (e.g. links with local clubs, parental help, etc.)

(11) What are the Department's rules, routines and policy concerning dress for particular activities, showers, non-participation, staff dress, where pupils should wait before and after lessons, etc?

In addition to the above you will need to collect information about your personal timetable and how it fits into the school timetable as a whole. For example, you will need to know:

Details of lessons – time and duration.

Details of classes you will teach – name of class, names of pupils, number in class, activities to be taught.

Details of facilities and rooms available for your lessons and when *not* available (e.g. exams).

Details of equipment available for your lessons.

Details of other teachers' lessons for observation.

Details of free periods and extracurricular duties.

## Facilities and resources

(1) What facilities does the PE Department have at its disposal both onsite and offsite?

(2) What do the facilities that are available for your lessons have in the way of line markings, wall markings, basketball rings and backboards, fixed gymnastic apparatus, grid markings and other field markings.

(3) Are there any safety restrictions in the use of these facilities? (e.g. slippery floor, equipment protruding into the work area, supporting columns in the hall, holes on netball/tennis courts, loose netting surrounding netball or tennis courts, etc.)

(4) What equipment does the Department possess, and in particular, what is available for the teaching of your lessons? (e.g. number of netballs/footballs, markers and cones, agility mats, bibs, rackets, etc.)

(5) What are the arrangements for the use of indoor facilities in the event of bad weather when outdoor facilities cannot be used?

(6) Is an indoor space or classroom available for the teaching of certain aspects of the PE curriculum? (e.g. Health related exercise, GCSE, 'A' level PE)

(7) Is there an indoor space where an overhead projector or video can be used?

What arrangements are there for booking such equipment?

(8) What other resources does the the PE Department have? (e.g. videotapes, curriculum guidelines, textbooks for examined courses, dance music, posters, etc.)

(9)   What resources does the Local Education Authority have? (e.g. videotape library, dance resource centre, outdoor education centre, teachers centre, etc.)

## The Pupils

Information in relation to the following questions may be sought from the Head of PE, class teacher or pupil records of achievement/profiles. You will need this information for each class you will be teaching.

(1)   What have the pupils already experienced in the activity you will be teaching and how did they respond to what was taught?
(2)   What should be expected of the pupils in the activity you will be teaching?
      What are the individual ability levels of pupils in this activity?
(3)   Are there pupils in the class who are particularly able, or have special educational needs, or have medical problems?
      What have other staff done in catering for these pupils?
(4)   Are there any pupils in the class who may become a disciplinary problem?
      What strategies have experienced staff used in the past to solve these problems?
(5)   What would staff with experience of teaching the pupils recommend concerning the way you should approach the planning of the unit of work for this class?

## Lesson Routines

The management routines that the staff use and which the pupils in the school have become accustomed to, can only really be identified by observing them in action. For example, you can ask staff about the procedure for the collection of valuables before a lesson, but only by observing the routines in action can you really begin to appreciate how they operate. Observing a few lessons on your preliminary visit will also enable you to get some idea of the teaching strategies used by staff, and the relationships they have established with their pupils.

Management routines are used before the lesson, during the lesson and after the lesson. Those used before and after the lesson are often referred to as 'housekeeping routines'.

### Before the lesson 'housekeeping' routines

(1)   How does the class teacher organise entry into the changing room? (e.g. do the pupils wait outside until allowed to enter or are they allowed to enter immediately on arrival?)
(2)   What arrangements are made for those who have forgotten their kit?

(3)  Is a register taken? What happens if someone is missing?

(4)  What arrangements are made concerning valuables and the safe keeping of jewellery that has to be removed prior to the lesson?

(5)  Are pupils allowed to put studded boots on in the changing room?

(6)  Does the teacher give any information about the lesson prior to leaving the changing rooms? (e.g. are tasks set inside ready for immediate practice in the work area?)

(7)  Are teams picked and bibs or reversible shirts organised prior to leaving the changing rooms?

(8)  What arrangements are made for the collecting and carrying of equipment to the work area?

(9)  What arrangements are made for preparing equipment for the lesson? (e.g. putting up badminton/volleyball nets)

(10) Does the teacher supervise the last pupil to leave or does he wait until all are changed before taking the pupils out together?

(11) Are the changing rooms locked? Who does this? Will you be able to have a set of keys?

(12) How does the class teacher organise entry into the indoor work area to be used? (e.g. are the pupils told to wait quietly outside?)

*During the lesson routines*

(1)  What routine does the class teacher use to bring the class together?

(2)  What routine does the class teacher use to gain class attention?

(3)  What routine does the class teacher use to organise the class to watch a demonstration?

(4)  What routine does the class teacher use to disperse the pupils to their work areas?

(5)  What routine does the class teacher use for grouping and changing the grouping of pupils?

(6)  What routine is used for organising teams for games?

(7)  What routines are used to define the boundaries of work areas?

(8)  What are the class teacher's 'start' and 'finish' routines for pupil activity?

(9)  What routines are used for the movement of large apparatus during the lesson? (e.g. gymnastic apparatus, badminton/ volleyball nets, netball posts, etc.)

(10) What particular routines are used for the movement of pupils during swimming lessons?

*After the lesson 'housekeeping' routines*

(1)  What routines are used for collecting in, carrying and storing equipment?

(2)  Are studded boots taken off prior to entry to the changing rooms?

(3)  What arrangements are made concerning showers?

(4) What is the routine for returning valuables and jewellery?
(5) What routines are used for the dismissal of the class and movement from the changing rooms?

After completing the above exercise you should now have a wealth of background information to help you in the planning of your schemes of work, units of work and lesson plans, and also feel that you know a little more about the school and how it 'ticks'. However, collecting this information is not always easy. Student teachers may not have enough time allocated for their preliminary visit and school staff may not always be available to answer questions. Others may be offered a reasonable 'observation' period as part of their school-based training, and time for the collection of this background information will not be a problem. If time is at a premium then you need to list priorities. What is the most important information that you need in order to allow you to begin planning? Details of timetable, classes to be taught, activities, facilities and previous experience of the class that you may consider to be of particular importance. You could always collect the remaining information on other visits, possibly during the period between the end of the college-based phase and the end of the school term.

As a student or newly qualified teacher you will be given your timetable and probably be asked to prepare units of work for the particular activities that you will be teaching. However, the department may have already produced detailed schemes and units of work for you to work from.

Your timetable should include certain information about the age of pupils you will be teaching, whether single or mixed sex groups, number of pupils per class, and the activity to be taught. It may also include details of organisation, facilities and equipment, and assessment procedures. If it doesn't include this information then you will need to ask about these details as indicated in Exercise 1.

You may be somewhat dissatisfied with the timetable that you receive, whether it be related to the groups, the activities to be taught or the facilities and time available for the lesson. As far as school timetables are concerned, nothing is perfect. There will always be difficulties in relation to allocation of time and working spaces because there is so much to put into a school timetable. It is therefore worthwhile having some idea of the difficulties confronting staff who have a particular responsibility for planning the school timetable.

When each Head of Department in a school has had the opportunity to respond to and discuss the timetable that the Director of Studies or Deputy Head has produced, it is highly unlikely that she will come out of the meeting totally satisfied with the result. The kind of factors that put constraints on the Physical Education timetable are as follows:

- Time allocation for physical education varies from school to school. Some may have physical education timetabled in double lessons of 70/100 minutes, others may have 'doubles' for outdoor games lessons and 'singles' for indoor lessons of 35/50 minutes. Single periods can result in very little time available because of changing before and after the lesson. Therefore, planning for single lessons needs a great deal of thought concerning what can be achieved in the time available. Many PE staff often complain about double periods being too long for the teaching of certain activities, and often 'split' the time to cover the teaching of two different activities. This may sometimes include an indoor and an outdoor activity. .

- Large schools with split sites may have additional timetabling difficulties because of the movement of staff from one building to another.

- Some schools have to transport pupils to 'offsite' facilities for physical education lessons and travelling time can cut into available activity time. If facilities are not owned by the school, equipment may not always be available as anticipated, and contingency plans need to be built into lesson planning to avoid being left with a totally disrupted lesson.

- Schools with dual use facilities have their advantages and disadvantages. Having to dovetail the use of such facilities into a programme of provision for the general public needs careful planning and checking of equipment before the school day starts. An adult club using the equipment and facilities the previous evening may have damaged something or left a store cupboard in a mess, thus causing problems for pupils at the beginning of a lesson and loss of valuable teaching time.

- Weather conditions can naturally constrain many activities in physical education. The need to accommodate twice as many pupils into an indoor space because half of a teaching group are unable to work outside necessitates special arrangements. It is worth finding out what the department policy is for these situations and whether there is a need to plan alternative indoor lessons for a section of an indoor space, or the changing rooms, or a classroom. Even indoor spaces can become unsafe and out of use when it rains because certain types of sports hall flooring can become very slippery when rain water has been dripping from the roof. In one sports hall I have worked in, low temperatures caused condensation dripping from the ceiling to freeze on contact with the floor and produce dozens of icy patches over the basketball court!

- Some indoor space allocations make the planning of particular activities rather difficult. In one school that I have visited the school assembly hall is allocated for the teaching of indoor games and it has four large columns within ten metres of each other supporting the roof. The teaching of any physical activity in such a space would need very careful planning for safety reasons, but ball games (which the the department taught in this space) necessitated particular care. Safety problems related to indoor space design or the storage of tables and chairs for lunch, may totally inhibit certain activities and make the planning of others difficult because of the need to restrict certain movements and possibly have pupils static for periods of time.

• The marking out of teaching spaces on playing fields or hard play areas is often restricted by the 'contract' the Local Education Authority has with subcontractors in the area. You may need to have contingency plans for marking out your own teaching spaces with marker cones using existing pitch lines.

It is important that student or newly qualified teachers are aware of all the factors and constraints that may affect their planning of units of work. These constraints can influence the setting of objectives for a particular unit of work, the teaching strategies or styles to be used, pupil groupings, lesson progressions and safety precautions. The unit of work will have to include contingency plans for disruptions caused by inclement weather or the school examination timetable.

Information about the pupils' previous experience of the activity and their levels of achievement is particularly important and every effort should be made to ascertain this information from the class teacher or Head of Department.

## The foundations of sound planning: Subject knowledge and 'instructional alignment'

You should now have the background information needed to sit down and begin planning your work. However, before starting it is important to have in the back of your mind an important planning concept originally put forward by Cohen (1987) and reinforced by Siedentop (1991) – that is the concept of 'instructional alignment'. Instructional alignment means that for more effective pupil learning there needs to be a 'match' between intended outcomes, instructional processes and instructional assessment. In other words, to achieve instructional alignment you need to plan in such a way that the tasks you set your pupils match your original goals or objectives, and that your assessment of learning or achievement matches your objectives and your instruction.

Cohen (1987) believes that to be able to plan for instructional alignment effectively the teacher needs to have a sound knowledge of the activity they are about to teach, a point made earlier in this chapter.

Whether you are a student teacher or NQT your initial degree course should have provided you with this knowledge of the activities you will be asked to teach in school and, except for a short discussion of the importance of task analysis later in this chapter, it is beyond the scope of this text to provide such basic subject knowledge. It was noticeable that one of the major areas of concern mentioned by student teachers in the TEPE Project related to their lack of knowledge of certain physical activities that they were less familiar with. It is therefore important that beginning teachers do attempt to make the effort to fill gaps in their knowledge of physical activities taught in the school PE curriculum. This can be done either by further reading or actually taking part in the activity by playing or practising with the college or local club. The Physical Education curriculum is now very broad and some would argue that it is impossible to be an 'expert' in all sports. However, although it may be possible to be more of a 'specialist' in a very large PE department, in smaller departments you do have to be a 'Jack of all trades' and turn your hand to a wide range of activities because that is the pupils' entitlement. When you become a member of a new department as a newly qualified teacher, school-based or Local Authority based in-service training may be available to help you to 'plug' gaps in your knowledge. Alternatively the local Sports Council or sports governing body may offer courses in the activities you need help with, or you could attend one of various Physical Education summer or Easter schools. Developing a broad expertise beyond initial training is really up to you.

## Planning by objectives

The objectives approach is widely regarded as an essential feature of educational planning. Her Majesty's Inspectorate (DES, 1985) have been quite clear about this: 'The value of clear objectives for each lesson, and the need for pupils to understand these objectives, are often demonstrated. Where pupils understand the teacher's objectives for a lesson, and know why they are doing what they are doing, they are able to participate more actively and intelligently.' (p. 9)

Also, in their guidance to Inspectors for assessing the quality of teaching, OFSTED (1993a) identify 'clarity of teachers' objectives for lessons' as a judgement recording statement.

In the HMI survey of 1987 (DES, 1988a), one of the reasons for the lessons taught by newly qualified teachers to be 'unsatisfactory' was that: '... the teachers had often failed to consider the purpose of the lesson and had not established clear objectives ...'. (p. 3, para. 1.11)

Thinking about and expressing what you want pupils to achieve in schemes of work, units of work and lessons, brings structure and purpose to your planning. Experienced teachers are very aware of this.

When asked what advice they would give to a newly qualified teacher on the question of planning schemes of work, HODs taking part in the TEPE Project made the following comments: 'Very important to have a basic idea of what you want to achieve or rather would like to achieve in a given period, and that things progress logically from lesson to lesson'. 'Break down tasks into clear objectives'.

Planning by objectives is therefore seen as being important but, what are objectives?

I'm sure there are a lot of student teachers and practising teachers who have wrestled with the issue of aims and objectives and, having read the literature, given up in confusion because of the interchangeable use of a variety of terms such as aims, goals, intended outcomes and objectives. In addition to this, in the National Curriculum objectives are actually referred to as 'Attainment Targets'.

For the student teacher or NQT Cohen and Manion's (1989) text offers a very useful account of the definitions and characteristics of aims and objectives, as well as providing advice on the writing of objectives. They refer to an 'aim' as: '... a general expression of intent, and the degree of generality contained in the statement may vary from the very general in the case of long term aims, to the much less general in the case of the short term aims'. (p. 29)

The aims of the National Curriculum, as outlined in the 1988 Education Reform Act (NCC, 1990), states that schools should provide a broad and balanced curriculum which:

- promotes the spiritual, moral, cultural, mental and physical development of pupils at the school and of society
- prepares pupils for the opportunities, responsibilities and experiences of adult life. (p. 1)

To Cohen and Manion (1989) an objective: '... is characterised by greater precision and specificity'. (p. 29)

Some objectives can be very specific yet others less so. The objectives of the National Curriculum are specified in greater detail in the form of particular attainment targets which are stated as being (DES, 1991): 'Objectives for each foundation subject, setting out the knowledge, skills and understanding that pupils of different abilities and maturities are expected to develop within that subject area'. (p. 89)

There is one attainment target for Physical Education and it is the sum total of all the 'end of key stage descriptions'. An 'end of key stage description' describes 'the types and range of performance that the majority of pupils should characteristically demonstrate by the end of the key stage' (SCAA, 1994a, p. 11). End of key stage descriptions are therefore more specific objectives. Key stage introductory statements and activity specific statements within the PoS are even more specific objectives for the activity being taught, and lesson objectives will tend to be more specific than activity specific statements.

The time it may take to achieve an objective will naturally depend on the specificity of the objective. More general, global aims or objectives like the National Curriculum attainment target for physical education, will need considerable time to be achieved, but in the case of more specific lesson objectives one might expect observable learning outcomes much sooner.

Examples of general aims and more specific objectives for physical education may be found in the National Curriculum documents for physical education.

The aims of physical education according to the earlier National Curriculum document (NCC, 1992) included the following statements:

Physical Education contributes to the overall education of young people by helping them to lead full and valuable lives through enjoying a purposeful physical activity. It can:

- develop physical competence;
- teach pupils, through experience, to know about and value the benefits of participation in physical activity while at school and throughout life;
- develop an appreciation of skilful and creative performances across the areas of activity.' (B1, para. 1.1.)

An example of the more general end of key stage descriptions for Key Stage 3 includes (SCAA, 1994b):

Pupils devise strategies and tactics for appropriate activities, and plan or compose more complex sequences of movements. They adapt and refine existing skills and apply these to new situations. (p. 11)

The National Curriculum document adds to the above end of key stage description more specific introductory and activity specific key stage statements. For example, in games:

Pupils should be taught: to extend the skills and principles learned in earlier years to develop techniques, tactics and strategies applicable to a variety of games ... [and] ... the rules, laws and scoring systems specific to different games. (p. 6)

The Curriculum Council for Wales (CCW, 1992) prefer to use the term 'learning outcomes' instead of objectives in the planning of units of work. An example of such a learning outcome is that pupils: 'Can recognise the effect of physical activity on the body'. (p. 37)

How do these aims and objectives fit into the planning of schemes/units of work and individual lessons?

Cohen and Manion (1989) offer a simple model (Figure 2) that shows the interrelationship between these elements of planning.

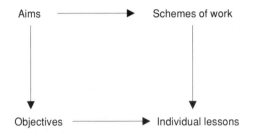

*Figure 2 Elements of planning*
Source: Cohen and Manion (1989) p. 31.

Objectives or learning outcomes are of more immediate use to the teacher when planning a scheme/unit of work than the more general aims because they tend to give more specific guidance regarding content, teaching strategies and evaluation or assessment. However, objectives do differ in terms of the specificity with which they state the behaviour they expect the learner to display. When an objective actually identifies the behaviour that the learner is expected to achieve, and this behaviour or learning can easily be measured, then such an objective is referred to as a 'behavioural objective'.

Other objectives are more open-ended and do not specify measurable pupil achievement or behavioural outcomes – these are referred to as non-behavioural objectives and it is more difficult to assess whether or not such objectives have been achieved. Being a more process-oriented rather than a product-oriented curriculum the National Curriculum for Physical Education is largely made up of non-behavioural objectives.

The reader is referred to the texts by Kirk (1988) and Cohen and Manion (1989) for a more detailed discussion of the different types of objectives that may be used in curriculum planning.

Planning of the school PE curriculum occurs at three levels:

(1) Schemes of Work,
(2) Units of Work,
(3) Lesson Plans.

## Planning schemes and units of work

Each department in a school ought to have a 'curriculum statement' for physical education which should describe the areas of activity to be offered for each key stage, and include resource requirements, procedures for assessment, record keeping and reporting, and opportunities for pupil choice of activity. Within this statement there ought to be a scheme of work for each area of activity.

Schemes of work are written documents describing the work that has been planned for a particular activity over a set period of time, such as for example, a key stage or a year. According to the National Curriculum Council (NCC, 1992), schemes of work should be derived from the National Curriculum programmes of study and end of key stage descriptions. They should represent a set of coherently planned programmes of learning experiences that pupils are entitled to under National Curriculum Orders. The scheme should state the knowledge and skills to be learned and the processes to be experienced for that particular area of activity. It also provides a 'frame of reference' for all teachers working in the department, and should ensure continuity of learning experiences for pupils across all phases and key stages.

Student teachers and NQTs are unlikely to be immediately involved in the writing of schemes of work, although NQTs might be asked at some stage to 'share' or contribute to the collaborative task of reviewing and rewriting schemes. It is therefore worth appreciating the issues that have to be considered when drawing up a scheme, and these are outlined in the Curriculum Council for Wales document (CCW, 1992) and shown in Figure 3.

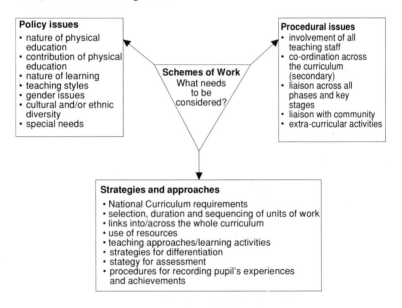

**Policy issues**
- nature of physical education
- contribution of physical education
- nature of learning
- teaching styles
- gender issues
- cultural and/or ethnic diversity
- special needs

**Schemes of Work**
What needs to be considered?

**Procedural issues**
- involvement of all teaching staff
- co-ordination across the curriculum (secondary)
- liaison across all phases and key stages
- liaison with community
- extra-curricular activities

**Strategies and approaches**
- National Curriculum requirements
- selection, duration and sequencing of units of work
- links into/across the whole curriculum
- use of resources
- teaching approaches/learning activities
- strategies for differentiation
- stategy for assessment
- procedures for recording pupil's experiences and achievements

*Figure 3   Issues to be considered when developing Schemes of Work*
*Source: Curriculum Council for Wales (1992) p. 23.*

Whereas the scheme of work represents long term planning, the unit of work describes the medium term planning, such as a half-term or six-week unit. A unit of work is a set of lessons within a particular activity area working towards a certain theme or topic. The number of units or lessons will vary according to the area of activity. Figure 4 illustrates how a scheme of work for gymnastics may be broken down into five units of work, each unit having up to six lessons devoted to it.

Certain activity areas lend themselves to being planned to occur intermittently throughout the key stage; examples being outdoor and adventurous activities and health-related exercise. Such activity areas can be planned as a timetabled unit but can also be planned to occur as a cross-curricular input, as with health-related exercise (linked with Health Education and Personal and Social Education), or dance (linked with Drama and Music), or in the form of a residential experience in the case of outdoor and adventurous activities.

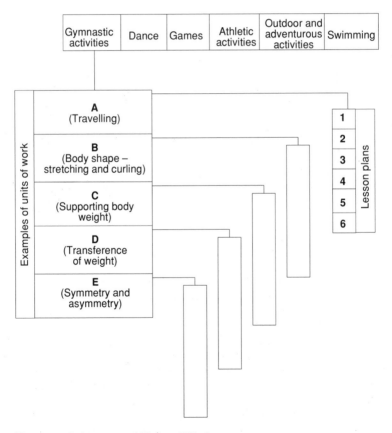

*Figure 4    Schemes and Units of Work*
*Source: National Curriculum Council (1992) (p. C2).*

When planning units of work the National Curriculum Council (1992) recommended that particular requirements are met within the programmes of study. These are called 'general requirements' for all Key Stages 1–4, and key stage activity specific requirements. For example, one of the general requirements for all key stages is that:

1. To promote physical activity and healthy lifestyles, pupils should be taught:

   (a)  to be physically active;
   (b)  to adopt the best possible posture and the appropriate use of the body;
   (c)  to engage in activities that develop cardiovascular health, flexibility, muscular strength and endurance;
   (d)  the increasing need for personal hygiene in relation to vigorous physical activity. (SCAA, 1994b, p. 2)

An example of a key stage activity specific requirement for Key Stage 3 gymnastics includes:

Pupils should be taught to refine and increase their range of gymnastic actions, involving balancing skills, including the ability to move fluently into and out of a balance. (SCAA, 1994b, p. 6)

However, when planning units of work, the introductory paragraphs at each key stage need also to be considered as these 'establish the scope, character and objectives of physical education at each key stage' (SCAA, 1994a, p. ii). An example is that pupils should be taught: 'the role of exercise establishing and maintaining health.' (SCAA, 1994b, p. 6)

It is important initially to ascertain the pupils' previous experience in the activity prior to planning the unit, and then unit planning should involve consideration of the following issues:

(1)  **Objectives**
     What do you want the pupils to learn?
     What are your overall objectives and intended learning outcomes for the unit?
     How do these objectives relate to pupils' previous experience?
     What cross-curricular themes, dimensions and competencies will you also be working towards?

(2)  **Learning activities**
     What learning activities do you intend to provide in order to achieve these objectives and intended learning outcomes?
     How will you provide for coherence and sequencing of content, progression and continuity, differentiation and flexibility in your planning?

(3)  **Teaching approaches**
     What teaching approaches do you intend to use, and how do they relate to your objectives for the unit as a whole?

(4) **Resources**
   What resources, facilities and equipment are required, and how much time is available for the unit?
(5) **Management routines**
   How will the learning activities be managed and organised? (e.g. grouping of pupils)
(6) **Assessment**
   How will the content of the unit be assessed?
   How will assesment of pupil learning outcomes be built into the overall planning of the unit?

These issues will now be explored in a little more detail.

## 1. Objectives and intended learning outcomes

When planning units of work, objectives and intended learning outcomes need to be clearly defined, assessable, and related to National Curriculum programmes of study and end of key stage descriptions.

Examples of unit objectives or 'intentions' for a unit of work for Year 7 gymnastics prepared by teachers for the Curriculum Council for Wales National Curriculum non-statutory guidance for physical education included the following:

To develop the range of actions involving travelling by stepping, rolling, sliding and wheeling; To develop smooth progression from one action to the next; To increase the range of and refine balancing skills; To improve the quality in body performance including extension, body tension and clarity of body shape. (CCW, 1992, p. 43)

The teachers' intended learning outcomes for the unit included, for example, for pupils to be able to: '... link movements smoothly both on the floor and on apparatus; ... work safely alone and with others'. (p. 43)

## 2. Learning activities: Progression and sequencing of content

In order to achieve the 'instructional alignment' mentioned earlier in the chapter, in which clear unit objectives are stated, a progression of activity leading towards the objectives is planned, and assessment of pupil performance is related to the original objectives; then it is important that the progression and sequencing of learning activities are well thought out.

Siedentop (1991) recommends that after establishing unit objectives, planning of the unit is developed by: '... working backwards from the final performance description to where the unit begins'. (p. 289)

The instructional design process Siedentop recommends for this is task analysis – procedural task analysis and hierarchical task analysis.

Procedural task analysis entails breaking down a particular skill or unit of performance into a 'chain of events'. In the lay up shot in basketball a procedural analysis might reveal the following chain of events:

Run and dribble – last stride and gathering of the ball into two hands – take off and reach to place the ball on the backboard.

As a result of such a procedural analysis, Siedentop believes that individual elements in the chain can be learned independently and then put together to form a chain. This is the basis of the 'part' method of planning learning, so common in the teaching of swimming and certain gymnastic movements over the years. When using this approach it has always been appreciated that putting together the components of the skill can be a problem, success often being due to whether the components in the chain are performed in an integrated way, and whether the teacher has been able to identify the points at which the components should be linked together into a smooth movement. However, although research is not conclusive, part practice does appear to be effective (depending on the nature of the skill being taught, the capability of the learner and the organisation of the practice) in that it may reduce the information load on the performer, offer more realistic and attainable goals and may allow for more intensive practice on the 'critical or more difficult elements of the task' (Chamberlain and Lee, 1993, p. 231).

A procedural task analysis can also apply to a team movement within a game, such as quick break in basketball, and the sequence of skills leading from a dig and a set to a spike in volleyball.

However, many feel that the breaking down of skills into too many parts may lead to an over-emphasis on the 'parts' to the exclusion of learning the whole. Regardless, analysis of the skill to be taught is an important process to go through prior to planning the development of a skill over a unit of work.

Siedentop's (1991) hierarchical task analysis can also be of benefit when planning the development of content over a unit of work. In this approach the teacher starts by looking at the final performance and works backwards in sequence. The learner is then taught the skill through a series of steps in a 'progressive part' approach. Many athletic events and gymnastic movements have been taught in this way over the years. Siedentop offers the swivel hips movement on the trampoline as an example of a hierarchical task analysis, and this is shown in Box 5.

The planning of progression does appear to be one of the major difficulties facing physical education teachers when planning their work, as the National Curriculum Council (1992) point out: '... making individual tasks in physical education progressive is one of the biggest problems that faces teachers'. (p. D1)

**Box 5**
**Hierarchical Task Analysis: The Swivel Hips movement on the trampoline**

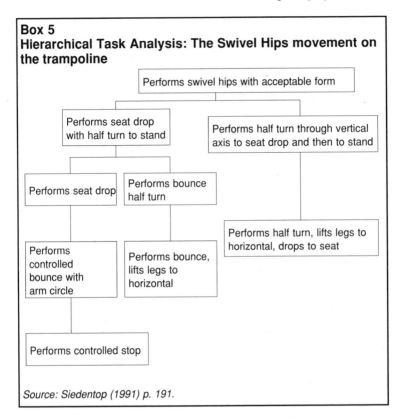

Source: Siedentop (1991) p. 191.

One solution to this problem and considered to be one of the skills of effective teachers by an adviser in the TEPE Project is: 'Analysis of skills – to provide relevant progression and assessment'.

The ability to analyse an activity and design appropriate progression is very dependent on one's knowledge of the activity being taught. If, as a student teacher or NQT, you find yourself taking an activity that you are not particularly familiar with, then, as mentioned earlier, it is essential that you not only improve your knowledge of the activity by reading and consulting video material, but that you also seek advice from experienced colleagues.

Ability to analyse the activity to be taught is therefore one of the answers to sequencing of content over a unit of work. However, there is the danger that all the teacher then thinks about is the activity, and consequently the unit of work may become activity-oriented. The development of a unit of work should also take cross-curricular issues (e.g. health education, personal and social education) into account, as well as other more process-oriented aspects of the unit of work such as independence of learning, and the development of pupils' ability to plan and evaluate each others' work.

The National Curriculum Council provide some advice concerning progression related to both the 'process' of physical education and how progression exists within the National Curriculum end of key stage descriptions. The 'process' of physical education within the National Curriculum entails the development and progression of knowledge, skills and understanding through an interrelated process involving planning, performing, and evaluating – with the emphasis on performing. Examples of some of the descriptors used in the National Curriculum Order for each of these three strands may be seen in Box 6.

---

**Box 6**
**The Process of Physical Education**

| Planning | Performing | Evaluating |
|----------|-----------|------------|
| Exploring | Practising | *Evaluating in the early stages* include: |
| Composing | Participating | Describing |
| Designing | Repeating | Recognising |
| Preparing | Refining | *leading to:* |
| Creating | Adapting | Comparing and contrasting |
| | Improving | Analysing and interpreting |
| | Improvising | *and finally to:* |
| | | Making judgements |
| | | Reviewing |

*Source: NCC (1992) (para. D1.2) and SCAA (1994b).*

---

For each of the three strands of planning, performing and evaluating, four elements of progression are put forward (NCC, 1992) – difficulty, quality, independence and interaction. Each of these should be developed according to the age, ability and previous experience of the pupil.

When planning a unit of work there are a number of different ways of building progressive difficulty into an activity or task.

First of all the **complexity** of an activity may be increased by:

- moving from simple, single movements such as jumps and rolls in gymnastics to the development of sequences involving combinations of movements;
- moving from concrete ideas to more abstract ideas as in the expression of feelings, ideas in movement following the development of the basic actions of travelling, turning, jumping, gesture and stillness;
- moving from simple techniques in, for example, athletics, to the more advanced techniques of throwing and jumping;

- moving from a basic knowledge of particular activities to more advanced knowledge and the ability to analyse and improve performance.

Secondly, the decision-making requirement of an activity may be increased by:

- requiring pupils to solve a particular problem (e.g. 3 v 2 attack versus defence in basketball);
- providing less space or time in which to perform a particular games skill (e.g. by increasing opposition in a games skill, 3 v 1, 3 v 2, 3 v 3);
- by restricting the type of movement/skill to be used (e.g. all passes below head height in basketball).

Thirdly, the requirements of a particular task may be made more difficult by:

- asking for a greater variety or different ways of responding to the task as set (e.g. gymnastics);
- reducing the size of a target;
- increasing the number taking part in games and the size of teams.

It is acknowledged (NCC, 1992) that the issue of **quality** of performance as an aspect of progression is affected by physical development and maturation, particularly at puberty. However, it is also appreciated that additional demands need to be made on pupils to improve the quality of their work, and teachers need to take account of this in their planning by setting tasks that require (NCC, 1992, para. 1.9):

- better poise;
- improved form and tension (e.g. gymnastics/dance);
- better hand/eye coordination (e.g. striking games);
- increased control of the body (e.g. swimming stroke);
- increased knowledge and understanding of the mechanical principles of activities.

Planning of the physical education curriculum should also take into account the need to help pupils to become more **independent** in terms of taking greater responsibility for their actions, planning and evaluating tasks, and showing initiative. This may be seen in the way pupils make increasing use of the community sports provision either through partnerships or otherwise, or the way they take responsibility in forming groups for an activity, or in planning, performing and evaluating their own activity programmes. This might include pupils planning their own warm up in athletics, progressing to showing each other their warm up routine, and finally evaluating each others warm up routine. One of the OFSTED (1993a) criteria used by Inspectors assessing the quality of teaching in PE includes '... use of well designed tasks to enable pupils to plan an activity, perform it successfully and evaluate that performance with clear criteria, including its effect on health'.

The notion of independence is linked to an additional aspect of progression related to the development of **interaction** skills. When pupils reach Key Stages 3 and 4 they should gradually be expected to interact in larger groups and 'lead' certain parts of physical education lessons such as the warm up or cool down, in devising tasks, and evaluating each others work. In being held responsible for forming their own groups, working cooperatively or competitively, sharing working spaces and resources, giving feedback and help to others, and evaluating their own performance, pupils will gradually be developing their interaction skills. An example of progression in terms of interaction might include a group 'planning their own baton change in athletics', in which they 'observe and comment on each others style and performance'. At Key Stage 4 in dance pupils should be taught:

(c) to design and evaluate aspects of production for their own compositions;
(d) to evaluate aspects of dance, including choreography, performance, cultural and historical contexts and production. (SCAA, 1994b, p. 9)

*Differentiation*

It is interesting to note that in their descriptions of 'good' and 'excellent' lessons taught by probationary teachers in secondary schools, Her Majesty's Inspectorate (DES, 1988a) pointed out that even in these lessons there were occasional weaknesses. One of these weaknesses was: '... difficulty in differentiating the work so as to match the different levels of ability among pupils'. (p. 22)

Also, the OFSTED (1993c) survey of *The New Teacher in School* reported that: '... a lack of adequate differentiation was a feature of many lessons observed'. (p. 24)

These issues of 'meeting individual pupil needs' and 'matching of work to pupils' attainments and abilities' are identified as criteria that OFSTED Inspectors are to use when assessing the quality of teaching in schools. (OFSTED 1993a)

But it is not just NQTs that have difficulty in planning for differentiation, as one HOD in the TEPE Project pointed out when asked what advice he would give a student teacher or NQT regarding the topic of planning to differentiate activities for different abilities: 'Very difficult – most difficult art in PE teaching'.

However, both he and several HODs did make a number of suggestions:

Teacher H
- Get to know your students;
- think about the activity you are teaching and how it can be broken up to accommodate varying abilities;
- observe experienced teachers in action;
- think about the end product and within that framework have a progression that all abilities can drop into and achieve from the weakest to the most competent.

Teacher E
- Keep in mind the following to set different challenges:
- vary number of goes allowed/time taken;
- alter type of equipment used/size of practice/play area;
- alter game area (e.g. different net heights);
- vary conditions imposed (e.g. number/type of passes allowed in a game);
- vary scoring conditions;
- look at difficulties of movement/skills involved and increase complexity;
- set different planning/evaluation expectations;
- have in mind 'expansion' activities (e.g. gymnastic sequence, raise level of performance);
- how many differentiated tasks are possible for the individual/group?

Teacher F
- Be aware of flexible learning opportunities and setting of groups;
- consult previous teachers of that particular class.

Several of these suggestions are incorporated in the National Curriculum Council document (NCC, 1992) of non-statutory guidance in which they suggest several ways of planning for differentiation:

- appropriate pupil groupings (e.g. by ability, group or individual activities);
- appropriate equipment for different levels of ability (e.g. different size/weight of ball, varying target size/height, varying distances from target);
- appropriate tasks – differentiation may be achieved by offering a range of more difficult tasks in which the pupil may choose at which point to enter the learning situation, or in which different individuals or groups may have different roles or responsibilities. Pupils should have the opportunity to experience these different roles.

    – differentiation may also be achieved by setting tasks which are appropriate for pupils by varying time allocation or pace of task to suit different levels of ability.

- appropriate tasks differentiated by outcome – in which the teacher may set tasks that are appropriate for the pupil's starting level, or pupils might answer the task as set according to their level of ability. In gymnastics, for example, an able pupil may produce excellent limb extension in a balanced stretched shape, while others may not be able to demonstrate the same level of extension while balancing.

The Curriculum Council for Wales (CCW, 1992) offer an example of how tasks might be differentiated for gymnastics at Key Stage 2 and 3, and these are shown in Box 7.

---

**Box 7**
**Examples of Differentiated tasks in Gymnastics at Key Stage 2 and 3**

| KS 2 Perform more complex sequences. | Individual sequence in which weight must be taken on four different body parts, one of which must be upside down. | 1. large body surfaces; 2. stable bases e.g. two feet one hand; 3. unstable bases e.g. two hands; 4 inverted e.g bunny hop or shoulder stand or handstand. | more challenging balances; clear shapes/better body awareness; variety of balances; greater control. |
|---|---|---|---|
| KS 3 Perform longer sequences of movement. | Use variety of apparatus with different surfaces to show symmetrical/asym-metrical body positions. | 1. using low, wide, stable surfaces; 2. using a variety of surfaces including high, narrow and unstable apparatus. | clear body shapes; variation of symmetrical and asymmetrical shapes; greater control; greater body awareness; better quality with variety of levels and pathways. |

*Source: Curriculum Council for Wales (1992) p. 35.*

Planning for differentiation is a difficult task for the student teacher or NQT in a new school because they are not aware of the ability levels of their pupils. In such a case it is important to consult the Head of Department or previous teacher of the class, as one HOD in the TEPE Project pointed out: 'Establish your starting point by talking to previous teachers and by making your own observations of ability levels within the group'.

To begin with you may need to plan material that is suited to the class as a whole. However, it would help if you also thought about a particular activity or practice that might be adapted to suit pupils of higher or lower ability, so that you can later adapt and change the activity during the lesson as you notice that some pupils are becoming frustrated because they are failing, or bored if the activity is too easy. Developing this ability to be adaptable and flexible in your planning is one of the first signs of becoming an effective teacher. In fact, advice from several HODs for student teachers and NQTs on the topic of planning included:

Don't be afraid to adapt if it seems that the group is coping well/poorly.

Be flexible – things will never go to plan.

Make sure it is suitable for the group and be prepared to modify.

Be prepared to modify your thinking if it doesn't work out. Be flexible and able to change the lesson and have contingency plans for bad weather if you are doing an outside lesson.

In planning your unit of work it is therefore worthwhile having alternative lessons or contingency plans up your sleeve in the event of inclement weather, smaller numbers than expected, or a wider variation in standard of ability than you anticipated. A trainee teacher with little experience of responding to quickly changing circumstances that can occur in any school needs to 'think through' and prepare for all possible eventualities. In the early stages of teaching, flexiblity and adaptability are the results of thorough planning!

## 3. Teaching approaches

The whole question of teaching strategies and styles will be dealt with in detail in Chapters 8, 9 and 10, but it is worth pointing out at this stage that the teaching approaches to be used in the unit of work and the reasons for using them need to be carefully considered and written into the initial planning. These teaching approaches and strategies should relate to the specific objectives for the unit, the programmes of study activity requirements, and the knowledge, skills and understanding that is intended the pupils should learn and experience.

As discussed later in Chapter 8, the use of a range of teaching approaches may be required to be able to achieve National Curriculum end of key stage descriptions and PoS activity specific requirements. The Curriculum Council for Wales (CCW, 1992) emphasise this point:

Traditional teaching methods in PE have relied previously upon pupil response to teacher instruction. This direct teaching method, however, does not work in all situations when pupils, for example, might be required to make decisions, to take initiative, to create or to solve problems, or to reproduce a motor skill. Similarly, as pupils move through Key Stage 3 and Key Stage 4 in particular, they will need to be encouraged to become more self-reliant and achieve greater independence in their mode of working. If pupils are to learn effectively teachers will need to practise a range of teaching approaches and employ varied forms of organisation. (p. 50)

Therefore, in planning the unit of work, one needs to be sure which teaching approaches and teaching techniques will be appropriate for the achievement of unit objectives.

## 4. Resources

The ease with which pupils learn a particular skill may in some way be determined by the space available for practice. The size of the working space may inhibit or restrict the development of a skill. For example, having to teach gymnastics to a large group of pupils in a small gym may, because of safety considerations, limit the pupils' opportunities to develop and improve certain gymnastic skills. Having just one long jump pit for a class of 24 pupils may involve the teacher in planning a lesson involving the use of different types of group work in order to keep the pupils active and interested. Physical education teachers have to be very resourceful individuals, and need to design working spaces from what is available in order to provide the optimum level of interest, challenge and success at pupils' levels of ability. The teaching 'grid' is a commonly used work area for the teaching of games both indoors and outside. These 10–15 metre squares can easily be converted into larger work areas, channels or pitches/courts depending on the activity. Where grids are not marked out, coloured markers or cones may be used with the existing lines of pitches or court markings in sports halls.

Equipment may need modifying for particular lessons, and the availability of lightweight hockey balls, sponge short tennis balls, short-handled rackets and hockey sticks may make the difference between early success and failure in learning a new skill.

The ratio of items of equipment to number of pupils may also need to be considered at this stage of planning as it can affect all later planning of lessons.

## 5. Managerial routines

It may be necessary to consider what specific managerial rules and routines are necessary for the particular activity being taught. In gymnastics, rules and routines for lifting, carrying and moving equipment, and waiting for permission to use apparatus, will all need establishing from the very first lesson. Similar safety rules and routines will apply to units of work in swimming and athletics. When equipment is limited there may need to be routines for sharing or working in groups. For example, in the teaching of badminton, groups of six to eight may need to use one court area. In weight training with free weights, a barbell set may need to be shared by a group of four.

Planning 'transitions' and establishing 'bridging routines' between activities may prevent time being wasted in lessons. Similarly, efficient movement of apparatus at the beginning and end of lessons preserves valuable learning time. A typical example might be the movement of gymnastic apparatus in which groups practise the safe taking out and putting away of the same items of apparatus. During a badminton course, groups may be responsible for a particular court, and be asked to take out and put away the net and posts before and after each lesson. Management routines are dealt with in more detail in Chapter 6.

## 6. Assessment

As assessment is very much an integral part of the teaching/learning process, the effective teacher builds assessment procedures into the planning of activities and learning experiences. Opportunities for assessment of learning outcomes may be indicated in the planning alongside the details of activities to be taught. In this way the teacher is able to appreciate which learning experiences match which unit objectives, and at the same time be aware of the need to collect evidence of attainment or the extent of achievement related to the particular objectives in question. Procedures for collecting this evidence of attainment may also be built into the planning of schemes and units of work. As Chapter 11 is devoted to the whole question of assessment, details of the principles and procedures of assessment will not be dealt with at this stage.

### Planning lessons

A thoroughly well thought out unit of work makes the planning of individual lessons much easier. In fact, research by Clark and Yinger (1987) found that unit planning appeared to be the most important aspect of planning for teachers. Teachers often preferred to work either from the unit every day (rather than have individual lesson plans), or had planned all the lessons for the unit as a whole in advance. It appears that teachers were then able to visualise unit progression more easily as they worked their way through the unit. However, having confidence in the delivery of lessons only happens as a result of meticulous planning, particularly in the early stages of teaching. As teachers become more experienced their planning is less detailed, and they use more of a 'mental map' of an intended lesson and it's objectives. But, they **do** plan, as Siedentop (1991) explains: 'Effective teachers plan! No matter what method they use to teach or how independent they become of actual physical lesson plans, they all carefully consider objectives and activities, progressions, equipment and space needs, safety and managerial issues and evaluation'. (p. 185)

What should be included in a lesson plan?

This will vary according to the activity being taught, and it is likely that there are as many approaches to lesson planning as there are teacher education institutions – there is no agreed format to lesson planning! However, most professionals involved in the teaching of PE would agree that a lesson plan should include the following (which may be laid out in the format shown on page 87):

(1)  Background information related to:

- class name, age and number of pupils, duration of lesson, activity to be taught, date;
- previous experience of the class, noting any details of individual or group ability levels and previous teachers' suggestions for differentiation of activities;
- facilities available;
- equipment required.

(2)  Lesson objectives.

Specific lesson objectives describing what the pupils are to learn in relation to the unit objectives, with possible additional reference made to National Curriculum end of Key Stage descriptions, programmes of study and cross curricular issues.

(3)  Lesson phases and content.

This may be placed in a vertical column for lesson phases and one for content/tasks. Depending on the activity to be taught, lesson phases may include:

- a first phase which may be a warm up or introductory activity.
- a second phase of development which may include:

**Example Outline Lesson Plan**

Activity:

Previous Experience:

Learning Objectives: *
                     *
                     *

Date:

Class

Facility:

N.C. End of Key Stage Descriptions:

Cross-Curricular Themes/Competences:

Lesson Duration:

Number of Pupils:

Equipment:

| Lesson Phase | Contents/Tasks | Teaching Points/Questions | Organisation/Safety |
|---|---|---|---|
| Pre-lesson transition | | | |
| Phase 1/Introductory Activity | | | |
| Transition | | | |
| Phase 2 | | | |
| Transition | | | |
| Phase 3 | | | |
| Transition | | | |
| Phase 4 | | | |
| Concluding Activity | | | |
| Post-lesson transition | | | |

- skill development;
- exploration and development of movement ideas;
- awareness of movement/knowledge/concepts;
- establishing the context for later learning.
- a third phase of development extending the second stage of development into:
  - a dance or game;
  - applying knowledge/concepts learned;
  - learning skills identified in an earlier context (e.g. a game);
  - applying movements learned in a new context (e.g. gymnastics floorwork to apparatus work);
- additional phases of development or repetition of a previous phase depending on activity, length of lesson or teaching style;
- concluding activity which may take the form of a review, cooling down or calming down.

Lesson content and progression will also vary according to the teaching strategy or style being used. The resulting lesson plan may therefore have a number of different phases, components and aspects of development.

It is also useful to indicate in the lesson plan the estimated time allocation for each component/activity in the lesson. Inexperienced teachers often underestimate the time it will take to complete lesson components, and find themselves with little time for important later aspects of the lesson.

The main content column may include details of how each task will be communicated to the pupils, including teacher exposition, explanation, demonstration (pupil or teacher), and teaching approach to be used.

(4)   Teaching points/Questions

A third column in the lesson plan might include the teaching points you will be looking for when you observe pupils performing and which will guide your diagnosis and correction of pupil performance faults and difficulties. Listing teaching points is therefore a useful reminder of the components of successful performance.

When using a question and answer teaching approach this section may include notes on the type of questions to be asked and possibly include a description of the anticipated pupil responses.

(5)   Organisational details and safety

'Thinking through' and writing out the organisational details of a lesson is essential in the early stages of teaching. These details may be put in a fourth column of the lesson plan entitled 'Organisation/Safety' or 'sandwiched' between lesson phases and activities. The organisation column can include details of how the class will be organised for activities, both in terms of the use of working spaces, or how groups will be organised for particular practices, activities or games. A diagram of the organisation showing the movement of pupils for the activity and how each group will be positioned within the working space can help you to visualise the organisational details of the activity. Aspects of safety should also be mentioned in this column.

Organisational details that occur at a particular time in the sequence of a lesson may be written out in a thin sandwich stretching across the lesson plan. Lesson transitions and 'bridging routines', pre-lesson and post- lesson organisation of equipment and groups can be outlined in these thin 'sandwiches'. Writing out lesson transitions/routines is particularly important in the early stages of teaching as they act as an *aide-memoire* to the novice teacher concerning the actual 'mechanics' of organising groups and equipment. With experience, these transitions/routines become second nature and can be dispensed with when planning.

## Evaluation of lessons

An important aspect of your planning for teaching is a consideration of how you will evaluate your teaching performance and planning decisions. The objectives, learning activities, teaching approaches and structure of future lessons will be dependent on the results of your evaluations of pupil responses and the appropriateness of material taught in previous lessons. Consequently, any planned unit of work should be modified in the light of unit and lesson evaluations. Without a well thought out and structured self-reflection strategy, it is easy to drift aimlessly into a limited form of reflection based purely on aspects of teaching that cross your mind at a particular moment in time. A well-structured self-reflection strategy worked out in advance ensures that all aspects of your teaching performance are reflected upon during the unit of work.

Self-reflection may be general and 'all embracing', or it can be designed to 'zoom in' on particular teaching skills, such as use of praise, questioning or the giving of specific feedback to pupils. This text includes a number of 'exercises' that are designed to focus on specific aspects of teaching, and these can be used by a colleague 'observer' who may offer a less biased view of your teaching. A more general form of self-reflection might involve attempting to answer some, or all, of the following questions on completion of a lesson:

To what extent were lesson objectives achieved?

To what extent were the activities appropriate for the age and ability of pupils?

How successful were attempts to differentiate activities during the lesson?

How many pupils had difficulty learning the tasks set?

Which pupils?

How many pupils found the tasks set too easy? Which pupils?

How will you modify your learning activities and objectives in the light of answers to the above questions?

How effective were the teaching approaches used? Were they appropriate for the objectives for the lesson, the pupils and the activities being taught? If not, how will you modify your teaching aproaches in the light of answers to the above questions?

Did the lesson run smoothly without any undue waste of time or is there a need to improve upon certain management routines? What aspects of class management might benefit from the introduction of a routine?

What aspects of the lesson caused most time to be wasted?

Were presentations and explanations clear and concise?

Did the class always understand your explanations? If not, how could this be improved?

This is only a selection of the type of questions one might ask when reflecting on a lesson. As you work through this book a variety of ideas for self-appraisal and observer appraisal are offered. It doesn't matter what approach you use as long as you have a positive attitude towards putting your practice and expertise under scrutiny. Only then will your planning of pupil learning experiences be effective, and you become a truly reflective practitioner!

# Creating an effective learning environment

## Introduction

Being well prepared certainly gives a young teacher the confidence of knowing exactly what they are going to do and how they are going to do it. But, according to the majority of student teachers taking part in the TEPE Project, the most frequently mentioned 'concern' prior to taking a new class for the first time, related to class control and management. Also, both student teachers and NQTs frequently mentioned class control, class management and organisation as the main difficulties they experienced during their early lessons. Concerns about disruptive behaviour and pupil compliance appear to be the main preoccupations of many beginning teachers. Some student teachers enter the classroom with confidence expecting pupils to do everything that is laid out in the lesson plan. They expect pupils to listen attentively to what they are told, move quickly between activities and work hard at the set task. This is a dangerous assumption.

Of all the teaching skills seen as essential for an effective teacher of physical education 'good discipline', 'organisational skills', 'class control' and 'class management' were most frequently mentioned by HOD's and PE lecturers. Also, when student teachers and NQTs were asked 'What advice would you give a student or newly qualified PE teacher taking a class for the first time?', class management, control and organisational issues were most frequently mentioned. Yet, it is these aspects of teaching that have also been identified by many HODs as being the major omissions or weaknesses of teachers' initial training.

But, creating an effective learning environment is not just about class control and discipline, it is largely about *management*. It would be inappropriate to consider that managing pupils is purely about dealing with misbehaviour – it is really about avoiding misbehaviour and establishing a positive atmosphere for learning through what Good and Brophy (1991) term 'proactive problem prevention', and, establishing what Siedentop (1991) refers to as the 'managerial task system'. The whole question of discipline and coping with problems will be dealt with in the next chapter. In this chapter we are concerned with preventative class management as a key factor in creating an effective learning environment. Preventative class management should allow the teacher to get on with the business of teaching without having to attend constantly to managerial details. In this way pupils 'know where they stand', what is expected of them and are offered the opportunity to act responsibly. All the same, you don't have to be seen as a disciplinarian to create an effective learning environment. Findings from numerous studies of effective teachers have shown that teachers who plan their class management through the use of rules, routines and procedures as a means of establishing and maintaining an effective learning environment are more successful than those who emphasise being a disciplinarian or 'authority' figure (Brophy, 1983; Doyle, 1986; Emmer, 1987; Evertson, 1987; Gettinger, 1988). This is not to say that one should not be seen as a figure of authority when persuading pupils to conform to rules and routines but, as Good and Brophy (1991) point out: '... these rules and procedures are not ends in themselves but means for organising the classroom as an environment that supports teaching and learning. Thus classroom management is closely associated with and should be designed to support instruction, which is why schools were established in the first place'. (p. 194)

Therefore, planning and 'thinking through' your management routines, procedures and transitions is as important as planning the content of your lesson if you want to establish an effective learning environment and avoid a carefully planned lesson falling apart because of lack of attention to management detail. It may in fact be wise in the initial stages to write out your management plans, particularly routines and transitions, as recommended in the previous chapter.

However, creating an effective learning environment is also about being respected by pupils. A sign of respect is that pupils want to please the teacher by producing good work. Therefore, the attitude and personal qualities of the teacher are crucial in establishing this unique blend of 'positive firmness' that is the basis of successful management.

This chapter examines this notion of 'positive firmness' and the principles of planning for preventative classroom management that may help to create an effective learning environment during those crucial early lessons.

## Planning for preventative class management

Preventative class management begins before you enter the school – it is planned in advance. Studies of effective teachers by Brophy and Good (1986) with classroom teachers, and Fink and Siedentop (1989) with primary school specialist PE teachers, confirm the importance of establishing rules, routines and procedures in the first lessons with a new class. These need to be 'thought through' thoroughly at the same time as the content of lessons are planned. 'Off the cuff' solutions to problems that arise don't work in most situations.

What then are the rules, routines and procedures in the context of class management?

Siedentop (1991) believes that rules and routines are the foundation of the 'managerial task system' which is a set of structures that are unambiguous and clearly defined, and which set the limits of behaviour and the expectations the teacher has for the pupils. It sets the boundaries of behaviour and expectations and, if well established during early lessons, it may allow the teacher to teach rather than have to spend time continually laying down expectations for behaviour.

A 'rule' defines general expectations of acceptable and unacceptable behaviour that will cover different situations. For example, expecting pupils to be quiet and attentive when the teacher is talking is an important 'rule' for young teachers to lay down.

According to Siedentop (1991) a 'routine' is: '... a procedure for performing specific behaviours within a class, behaviours that tend to recur frequently and, unless structured, can potentially disrupt or delay the pace of a lesson'. (p. 83)

The most commonly used routine in the Fink and Siedentop (1989) study of effective primary PE specialist teachers was the 'attention/quick' routine in which teachers used a specific signal, such as a clap of the hands, for pupils to attend to the teacher. This routine would be described, practised and reinforced on frequent occasions at the beginning of and throughout the school year.

In the Wragg and Wood (1984a) study of teachers' first encounters with their classes, the frequency of use of 11 classroom rules established in September are shown in Box 8.

---

**Box 8**
**Frequency of occurrence out of 313 lessons of eleven classroom rules**

| Rule | | No. of lessons |
|---|---|---|
| (1) | No talking when teacher is talking. | 131 |
| (2) | No disruptive noises. | 125 |
| (3) | Rules for entering, leaving, moving in class. | 109 |
| (4) | No interference with work of others. | 99 |
| (5) | Work must be completed in a specified way. | 84 |
| (6) | Pupils must raise hand to answer not shout out. | 55 |
| (7) | Pupils must make a positive effort in their work. | 49 |
| (8) | Pupils must not challenge the authority of the teacher. | 47 |
| (9) | Respect should be shown for property and equipment. | 38 |
| (10) | Rules to do with safety. | 26 |
| (11) | Pupils must ask if they don't understand. | 8 |

*Source: Wragg and Wood (1984a) p. 67.*

In the Fink and Siedentop (1989) study of effective primary PE teachers' rules related to acting safely, participating fully, using equipment properly, being dressed appropriately and paying attention to the teacher were described on the first day before any activity began. However, they were not actually described as 'rules' or their compliance considered to be 'rule following'. They were largely treated as being 'the way to behave' and the teacher's expectations were made clear. Although one teacher in the study did indicate to pupils what the consequences of breaking a rule would be, the teachers appeared to be able to maintain appropriate pupil behaviour without relying on the use of formal consequences for breaking rules.

Siedentop (1991) believes that rules in physical education tend to relate to the following aspects of pupil behaviour:

- Safety – using equipment safely in relation to self and fellow pupils. Examples: not to enter the gym until told to; not to get out apparatus until told; lifting and carrying equipment.
- Respect for others – teacher and fellow pupil. Examples: don't talk when teacher is talking; encourage fellow pupils.
- Respect for the learning environment – equipment and facilities. Examples: keeping store cupboards tidy; taking boots off before entering changing rooms; don't kick basketballs or volleyballs; don't pick up shuttlecocks with badminton racket head.
- Support the learning of others – in terms of careful use of space, taking turns, guiding a fellow pupil in a reciprocal teaching situation, and feeding a ball/shuttlecock in a cooperative practice situation.
- Try hard – using learning time well by: concentrating hard when practising a skill as suggested by the teacher, not fooling around or doing something the teacher has not asked you to do (e.g. when asked to practise passing a basketball, not to practise shooting!).

Establishing class routines is particularly important in the teaching of physical education because they save learning time that could easily be wasted because of disruptions to the flow of lessons. But, as with rules, they need planning in advance.

In the Fink and Siedentop (1989) study of effective primary specialist teachers of PE a number of routines were established by the teachers early in the school year. These included:

- Preliminary routines – entering the gym/hall; warming up; pupils method of gaining teacher's attention; teacher's method of gaining pupil attention and request for quiet.

- Transitional management routines – pupil dispersal; pupil 'gathering' together (to a designated area) equipment (how to get equipment out, put equipment away, and ways of handling equipment); organising pupils into pairs; lining up and returning to a central base.
- Instructional management routines – starting an activity; defining boundaries of the class work space; defining boundaries of individual work space; retrieval of equipment (e.g. ball, shuttlecock, etc.) that may have invaded other pupils' work area.
- Housekeeping routines or general knowledge of school procedures – such as: fire drill; dress; collection of valuables; grading/ assessment; going for a drink; accidents.
- Closure routines – finish or end of activity routines and leaving the work space (gym or field) routines.

The Fink and Siedentop study concentrated on primary school specialist PE teachers and, as far as the author is aware there has been no in-depth study of rules and routines used by secondary PE teachers. It was noticeable that student teachers in the TEPE Project often had difficulty in their early lessons with organisational routines, possibly because they had not established the structure of these routines early enough. When asked what difficulties they had experienced with their first lessons of teaching PE and how they overcame these difficulties, student teachers made the following comments:

Student A – Difficulty: 'Organisational problems – making the transition between phases of the lessons such as individual work to small group work to whole class game'. Solution: 'I needed to prepare my lessons better bearing in mind class numbers'.

Student B – Difficulty: 'Moving from one task to the next'.

Solution: 'I used the previous task to arrange the next one and developed by bridging (transition) organisation'.

Heads of PE departments were also asked what advice they would give a student teacher or NQT on the topics of 'organisation and management of classes and groups', 'class control', and 'the organisation and management of equipment'. Typical advice on procedures and routines were as follows:

Have groups near to you and sitting/stationary when giving instructions.

Always arrive and be ready before the class.

Ensure pupils are listening to instructions.

Make sure equipment needed for each lesson is organised and ready for use and safe. Ensure pupils know how to use equipment correctly and safely.

Make sure size of groups fit in with practices so that everyone is kept busy.

Do a head count so that you can be thinking how to organise games.

## Developing rules and routines

Developing routines is really just like teaching any other skill or movement in PE. Pupils need to know what is expected of them, so the routine needs to be explained, demonstrated and then practised. After that, regular prompting, praise for compliance or reprimand if necessary for non-compliance, is necessary to keep the routine in the minds of the pupils.

The development of rules is slightly different, although there is often an overlap between what one might consider a rule and what is a routine. Pupils should naturally be praised for adhering to rules but rules may also need to have consequences, and these should be clearly explained to pupils and consistently enforced. Siedentop (1991) offers the following guidelines for developing class rules:

(1)   Rules should be short and directly to the point.
(2)   Rules should be communicated in language or symbols appropriate to the age levels of the pupils.
(3)   No more than five or eight rules can both communicate important categories of behaviour and be remembered by pupils.
(4)   When possible, state rules positively, but make sure that both positive and negative examples are provided.
(5)   Make sure class rules are consistent with school rules.
(6)   Relate consistent consequences to rules.
(7)   Don't create rules you cannot or are not willing to enforce. (p. 86)

When developing rules it is important that pupils understand and are aware of why a rule should exist. Rules relating to care of equipment are justified for its efficient functioning and the need to have a sufficient number to prevent pupils having to wait a turn. Safety rules are justified because of danger to self and others.

Stating clear examples of rule compliance is essential. Rules need to be mentioned regularly and not only at times when a rule has been broken. Sowing 'seeds' in the minds of pupils at regular intervals is the key to positive preventative management.

Cohen and Manion (1989) believe that rules should be kept to a minimum, and that the criteria for compiling this minimum list are relevance, meaningfulness and the need to be positive.

To be relevant, rules may vary according to the objectives and content of a lesson. Therefore, rules concerning immediate use of equipment may be different in badminton lessons compared with gymnastics lessons. Consequently, some rules may be seen to be content specific.

To be meaningful rules should relate logically to the task and not be arbitrarily imposed by the teacher.

To be positive a rule needs to be positively expressed, and be something to achieve rather than to avoid. For example, one might say 'Discuss your views more quietly – you are talking too loud', rather than, 'Don't make such a noise'.

Certain specific situations may involve a degree of negotiation between teacher and pupil concerning rules, and these may change with time, be dispensed with, or even renegotiated depending on the circumstances.

As far as rule description is concerned, flexibility may be the key to good classroom management as Cohen and Manion (1989) point out: 'Good classroom management involves clear rules where rules are needed, avoiding unnecessary ones, eliminating punitive ones, reviewing them periodically, and changing or dropping them when appropriate. Additionally, greater flexibility may be introduced by having recourse to more informal arrangements, frequently arrived at by negotiation and bargaining'. (pp. 218–19)

Talking to experienced teachers about the rules and routines they use, and watching them teach, can give you some idea of the rules and routines that work for them, and also what the pupils you are about to teach are accustomed to. In addition there might be general school and department rules which you will need to be aware of. Exercise 1 in Chapter 5 suggested some observation tasks that might help you become more aware of the rules and routines used by teachers. Having collected this information you will need to plan your own rules and routines prior to teaching a new class for the first time. Exercise 2 below is designed to help you identify the categories of rules and routines that you may need to consider in your planning. The next section examines how these rules and routines may be introduced and developed.


## Exercise 2   Rules and Routines

Indicate under each heading the rule or routine you intend to establish with your new classes, and for which particular activities.

### RULES

(1)  Safety rules – general

(2)  Safety rules – activity specific

(3)  Respect for equipment and facilities

(4)  Respect for other pupils

(5)  Respect for teacher rules

(6)  Helping other pupil rules (e.g. don't talk when teacher is talking)

(7)  Attitude to work rules (e.g. try hard, doing the task as set)

## ROUTINES

(1)  Preliminary routines

- Entering/leaving changing rooms and work area

- Warming up

- Teacher gaining pupil attention

- Pupil gaining teacher attention

(2)  Transitional management routines

- Pupil dispersal (e.g. to work area)

- Pupil gathering together (e.g. for demonstrations)

- Equipment movement (e.g. taking out and putting away)

- Group work (e.g. movement into pairs, teams, etc.)

(3)  Instructional management routines

- Starting activities

- Defining boundaries of work area (whole group)

- Defining boundaries of work area (individual, small group)

- Retrieving equipment (e.g. if shuttlecock lands outside work area)

(4)  Housekeeping routines

- Non participant (e.g. forgot kit, injured, etc.)

- Collecting valuables

- Record keeping

- Accident

(5) Closure routines

- Finishing the activity

- Leaving work space (e.g. gym or field)

The question of how one develops these rules and routines was neatly summed up by one NQT who was attempting to establish her personal 'presence': '... clear rules of what I expected in my lesson were stated in my first lesson and reinforced in subsequent lessons'.

There is no doubt that rules and routines established in those first encounters with classes can set the tone for the whole year, saving valuable learning time and much nervous energy.

## First encounters

The development of rules and routines begins with the very first contacts with a new class and then need to be reinforced at regular intervals. Student teachers observing experienced teachers controlling classes during the initial stages of teaching practice often do not appreciate the rule and routine development which has been introduced early in the school year.

In their study of first encounters of experienced and student teachers in UK secondary schools, Wragg and Wood (1984a) noted marked differences between experienced and student teachers in a number of aspects of teaching. The experienced teachers had very clear ideas of what they were going to do concerning the management of the class before the beginning of the autumn term, and their intentions were largely achieved when they were observed by the researchers in September. On the whole, experienced teachers:

... seemed clear in their minds before the year begins how they would conduct themselves. What they described in interview was by and large fulfilled when they were observed in September. Most sought to establish some kind of dominant presence, usually though not always chose to make up their mind about children from their own experience rather than from scrutiny of pupils' records, tempered any initial harshness with humour, and conveyed to their class that they were firmly in charge, using their eyes, movement and gesture to enhance what they were trying to do. There was a strong moral dimension to some of their classroom rules, and they strove to establish these substantionally in the very first lesson. (p. 77)

It appeared that student teachers were not so clear about their rules, or what they were intended to do with their classes. They tended to believe that 'rules would become evident as the need arose' (p. 77), yet they appreciated that they had to be careful about personal relationships and being too friendly. Experienced teachers, on the other hand, were seen as being more business-like, confident, warm and friendly than student teachers, and were more careful about learning pupil's names. However, Wragg and Wood (1984a) did note that the differences between experienced teachers and student teachers did not persist throughout the first term. The PGCE students in the study lost their 'rawness' and hesitation as the term progressed.

A number of additional issues concerning first encounters arose from the Wragg and Wood study that were also reinforced by students, teachers, lecturers and advisers in the TEPE Project. These included the importance of:

* Information prior to meeting a class,
* 'Thinking through' the first lessons (e.g. content, rules and routines),
* lesson openings (e.g. introduction),
* personal relationships (e.g. mood, manner and image),
* pupil accountability.

Consideration of a number of points related to these issues may help the student teacher or NQT to 'think through' those first encounters with new classes.

### Information prior to meeting a new class

Experienced teachers in the Wragg and Wood (1984a) study felt it was important to have information concerning a pupil's medical background (e.g. deafness, epilepsy), but preferred not to have any additional information that might prejudice their view of a pupil. They would rather check a pupil's records later in the term in order to 'throw some light' on their experiences with pupils.

The PGCE student teachers in the study were quite anxious about the need to have some knowledge of pupil background, such as their individual needs, tendency to disrupt, etc. The BEd students, having had the benefit of at least one teaching practice, preferred to have information about materials, resources, facilities, school organisation, standards of work, punishment, discipline, and rules/routines used by staff.

Getting to know as much as you can about the classes you are going to teach has been recommended elsewhere in this book, and this advice is supported by teachers, advisers, and lecturers taking part in the TEPE Project:

... watch the group you will be teaching in order to get to know them with regard to both abilities and individual personalities. (Head of PE)

Try to find out as much as possible about the pupils and what previous experience they have had. (PE Adviser)

Make sure that you have gained as much information as possible about the group and their previous work. (PE Lecturer)

## 'Thinking through' the first lesson

Experienced teachers in the Wragg and Wood (1984a) study used the first lesson with a new class to establish rules and routines. The content of their early lessons was generally simple and secondary to the laying down of 'ground rules' for behaviour. Creating a relaxed personal 'presence' in the first lesson yet being 'in charge' is important, but so is thorough preparation, as several teachers, students teachers and advisers in the TEPE Project pointed out:

Appear confident (even if you don't feel it!). Be prepared (i.e. equipment), have a flexible lesson plan, lay down your ground rules and make sure you enforce them. (PGCE student)

Try and relax – get organisation and control right. Get children active as soon as possible and give simple instructions. (PGCE student)

Do not try to be too adventurous on task demands. Concentrate on organisation and control. (PGCE student)

Prepare enough/more than necessary – take in notes if you need to. Assert yourself in the class, be approachable but not overfamiliar, set standards and routines for pupils, and be confident. (Advisory teacher)

Go in and make your presence felt and known. Do something which will make an immediate and lasting impression on the pupils. Grasp their attention/imagination/respect the first time you have contact with them. Devise a strategy to achieve this. Let them know who is in charge. (Head of PE)

First of all establish ground rules for a high standard of behaviour, appearance and expectations of pupils, then concentrate on content of lessons and improving standards. (Head of PE)

Don't try to do too much, keep it fairly simple but well planned and well thought out. Be organised and get your discipline right. (Head of PE)

## Lesson openings

Wragg and Wood (1984a) noted that both experienced and BEd student teachers tended to introduce themselves in their first lesson, and the experienced teachers were present before the pupils arrived.

Experienced teachers secured attention by using their voice, but made use of a particular posture such as hands on hips, waiting without expression or a smile, and rapid scanning of the class with their eyes.

Compared with the self-conscious manner of the PGCE students the experienced teachers displayed a 'centre stage', 'larger than life' image, were confident, with elaborate mannerisms and careful articulation. Advice from teachers, student teachers and advisers taking part in the TEPE Project included the following:

Go in with confidence and self-assurance even if you don't feel it! Don't be frightened to smile. Keep control by whatever means, show them you mean business, you are their teacher, you want to teach them and you want them to enjoy it! (Head of PE)

Be calm and well organised. A quiet approach encourages a quiet response from pupils. Show enthusiasm for the subject and the lesson. (PE Adviser)

Initially be firm to establish control. Introduce yourself – use a few names but don't be overfamiliar. Get the class working quickly as activity will be the quickest way of breaking the ice, developing relationships and ensuring discipline. (Head of PE)

Don't 'dither', be direct, clear and precise in instruction. Know what you want and how you are going to achieve it. (Head of PE)

However, it is interesting to point out that in the Wragg and Wood (1984b) study of pupils' appraisals of teaching, although first impressions were crucial:

Those who wish to make a firm start and establish control should recognise that, whilst pupils can see the need for and even expect such a beginning, if they are over bossy, fail to temper their authority with humanity, they may never secure a positive working relationship with their class. (p. 95)

## Personal relationships and interpersonal skills

In the Wragg and Wood (1984b) study of pupil impressions of teachers, it appeared that pupils preferred teachers who were firm but fair, were consistent, stimulating, interested in individuals and had a sense of humour.

Whereas experienced teachers establish their presence, rules and routines early in the school year, student teachers entering the school half-way through the year have to balance the tightrope between laying down rules and routines, establishing their presence, and developing positive relationships with classes. Creating this balance whilst at the same time not being overfamiliar can be difficult. The following is a sample of the advice offered by teachers, advisers and lecturers taking part in the TEPE Project:

Don't try to be their big friend – it doesn't pay. They must know where the line is drawn. (Head of PE)

Assert yourself in the class – be approachable but not overfamiliar. (Advisory teacher for PE)

Keep your distance – but be sincere and warm with pupils and move on to practices quickly. (Lecturer)

Always be positive – use voice clearly and make sure that the pupils understand what is expected of them. Try to learn a couple of names and start building a relationship with the group. (Newly qualified teacher)

Although it is important to be 'in charge' in those first encounters with a new class, Wragg and Wood (1984a) did identify a number of different ways that experienced teachers were also able to develop positive relationships with their classes. Experienced teachers frequently praised and encouraged pupils for effort and good work, they were attentive to individual children, they were prepared to apologise when they made mistakes, they offered to help pupils with their work, and they were particularly quick to learn pupils' names and use them. These points were reinforced by teachers and advisers taking part in the TEPE Project:

Relate! Praise, commend, set high expectations and deal with issues quietly and not confrontational, and learn a few names. (PE Adviser)

Show a genuine interest in the pupils and get to know as many names as possible as quickly as possible. Teachers develop different strategies for doing this, and it is really important. If the school has record cards it might even be possible to know some of the names of a new class before meeting them for the first time. The children will usually be quite impressed by this. (PE Adviser)

Quickly try to get to know some names – pick out someone from their conversations – ask them a question by name! The pupils will be amazed that you know them. (Newly qualified teacher)

The whole question of developing relationships with pupils and maintaining a positive learning environment will be dealt with in more detail in Chapter 7.

## Pupil accountability

For pupils to learn they need to be engaged fully in the task as set by the teacher. Yet, evidence from one study (Tousignant, 1982) suggests that in physical education pupils may be tempted to 'modify' tasks to suit themselves, or become what Siedentop (1991) refers to as a 'competent bystander'. In the former case pupils may be seen to be actively doing something, but on closer examination appear not to be performing the task as set, and therefore not learning. In the latter case, pupils who are always 'good', in that they are always quick to respond to rules and routines, may avoid participation in a way that the teacher does not immediately notice. They do this by avoiding taking turns, attaching themselves to a good performer to avoid the action, or they only perform when the teacher is watching or is in the proximity. In these cases the pupil has 'negotiated' the boundaries of the task the teacher has set. To avoid this negotiation of task boundaries it is essential that the teacher not only clearly introduces the requirements of the task, but also states the task boundaries and the accountability system that will be imposed. Tasks need to be absolutely explicit and unambiguous, the way tasks are to be performed clearly defined, the performance that is to be expected outlined, and the standards by which pupils are to judge their own and others performance made clear.

Pupils need to be made accountable and responsible for learning the task as set, and to work hard to achieve an appropriate level of learning. In the Tousignant (1982) study it was noticeable that certain pupils would modify the task set by the teacher according to the level of success they had achieved in the task. If the task was too easy, pupils would either misbehave or modify the task to make it more challenging. If the task was too hard, pupils would 'bystand' or not participate, or, alternatively, they would perform a totally unrelated or easier task to show that they were actually working. This sort of problem arises when the teacher has not differentiated the activity to suit the ability levels of the pupils, and as a result they become bored if the task is too easy, or frustrated if the task is too difficult. Whatever, the result is that pupils are not involved in learning.

Sometimes teachers are quite happy to let such deviant behaviour continue provided pupils are actually active. They will turn a blind eye to pupils' modification of tasks provided pupils do not misbehave and are seen to be physically active. This is the syndrome of 'busy, happy and good' noted by Placek (1983) in her study of how experienced and student teachers viewed success in teaching. Teachers tended to equate success in teaching with keeping pupils 'busy' (participating), 'happy' (enjoying themselves) and 'good' (doing as the teacher directs), with pupil 'learning' being of secondary concern.

The effective teacher ensures that pupils are concentrating on the task set by not only making it clear what pupils are to do and what is expected of them, but also by carefully monitoring what they are doing. Effective teachers are constantly 'scanning' the class while they are working. Even when they are helping a group of pupils, effective teachers have one eye on what is going on throughout the work area. Such teachers are what Kounin (1970) calls 'with-it' – they are aware of all that is happening in the class – they have eyes in the back of their heads! Pupils who are not working on the set task are reminded of what is expected of them, and any task modification or misbehaviour is 'nipped in the bud', so to speak.

These teaching skills of 'with-it-ness' and scanning are essential for monitoring the learning environment and will be dealt with in more detail in Chapter 7. But, explanations of task demands and making pupils accountable for their work do need planning in advance. Hardy (1992), for example, noted that as the majority of incidents of misbehaviour (58%) occurred during class instruction or when pupils had been sent to work on a set task (25%), it may be that a lack of clarity when explaining tasks might be a major cause of pupil misbehaviour. Therefore, when you write out your lesson plan, be sure that what pupils are being asked to do is made explicit and unambiguous, and that performance standards are made clear. The way you present a task to pupils does need very careful thought, and this will be considered in detail in Chapter 9.

Creating an effective learning environment is also about creating a positive climate for learning, because pupils are more likely to work happily on a task and be interested in learning if a positive climate exists to begin with.

## Creating a positive climate for learning

A positive learning atmosphere can influence the motivation of pupils and their attitude to learning, so, what constitutes a positive climate for learning and how might it be created? One HOD in the TEPE Project offered the following advice to beginning teachers:

Every student has to feel important and has a contribution to make. Don't be sarcastic, be positive in your approach. Be approachable but firm. Make the pupils feel that what is being done with them is not done to them. Also
   – have a sense of humour;
   – always be well organised;
   – have additional information on the activities available for the students;
   – be enthusiastic about your subject;
   – don't try and 'con' them, show off, be honest and be yourself;
   – be a good role model for the students;
   – be prepared to give time to the students.

These comments also reflect the view of a number of authors who have reviewed the teacher effectiveness literature and believe that effective teachers: '... are sensitive to the climate of the class and constantly attempt to improve it. Improvement can come from being more friendly, accepting student opinions, planning for interesting lessons, sharing decision making with students, showing enthusiasm, and providing students with real opportunities to learn and achieve in physical education'. (Metzler, 1990, pp. 65–6)

'... maintain pleasant, friendly classrooms and are perceived as enthusiastic, supportive instructors'. (Good and Brophy, 1991, p. 443)

Also, Kyriacou (1991) believes that the type of classroom generally considered as best for facilitating pupil learning is one that: '... is described as being purposeful, task oriented, relaxed, warm and supportive and has a sense of order'. (p. 65)

Therefore, in terms of teaching skills, creating a purposeful and business-like working climate means that the teacher should not only be well organised and well prepared, but start lessons on time, keep lessons running smoothly and monitor pupils' work and progress. Such a teacher has the mutual respect of pupils who see the teacher as competent, a clear and committed communicator, a good manager, a person whose authority is respected, and who has a good 'rapport' with pupils. A teacher's 'rapport' with pupils arises from a relaxed and warm, supportive manner, in which the teacher shows he cares for individuals and their progress, is able to share the pupils' interests and feelings, and is also a good role model in terms of behaviour and dress. Developing a good 'rapport' with a class involves being honest, knowing your pupils well and being a good 'listener', showing respect for pupils and acknowledging their efforts, and, as they get to know you and respect you, possibly allowing them to be more involved in decision making as far as lesson content is concerned. However, as frequently pointed out by PE teachers in the TEPE Project, the student teacher or NQT with a new class has to beware of being 'too friendly' to begin with, and until the teacher has the pupils' respect, allowing them to be more involved in negotiation of lesson content may have to wait. It is possible for a class to misinterpret friendliness and freedom as a sign of weakness, and the wise new teacher should tread carefully in their efforts to build a 'rapport' with their classes.

A positive learning environment is also one in which the pupils are motivated to learn. According to Good and Brophy (1991) three conditions need to exist for pupils to motivated to learn:

- a supportive learning environment in which the teacher is patient and encourages pupils' efforts;
- a task that is clear, at an appropriate level of difficulty and in which they might achieve high levels of success with reasonable effort;
- a task that is challenging, interesting, meaningful, and worthwhile, such that pupils can see the reasons for learning the activity.

These conditions have obvious implications for planning lessons and units of work, and in particular the need to differentiate tasks for the pupils' level of ability or learning.

More detailed accounts of the implications of motivational theory are dealt with elsewhere (Biddle, 1991), and therefore will not be covered in detail in this text. However, the effective teacher of PE should be aware of the implications of attribution theory (Biddle, 1991, 1993), achievement psychology (Biddle and Fox, 1988) and the effects that motivational systems may have on pupil participation and interest in physical activity (Fox and Biddle, 1988; Biddle and Goudas, 1993). It was noticeable that in one study by White and Coakley (1986) in South-east England, not only was physical competence a vital ingredient in continuing to take an interest in physical activity, but that negative memories of school PE such as boredom, lack of choice, feeling stupid and incompetent, and the negative evaluation of peers could lead to being totally 'put off' all physical activity. Girls in particular associated physical education experiences with embarrassment and discomfort, mainly because of the need to take showers, changing and PE kit requirements. According to Fox and Biddle (1989), the most effective PE programmes create more opportunities for success, create the right kind of success (not just performance-oriented but also participation-oriented), create the desire or intrinsic motivation to participate (because pupils understand the 'why', 'what' and 'how' of participation) and create the 'know how' (goal setting, self-evaluation techniques) for maintaining participation in physical activity. Biddle and Fox (1988) believe that the effective PE teacher is one who encourages 'self-motivation and decision making' in young people, and who promotes continued participation at all levels of ability through: '... a mastery orientation to skill learning and fitness, where children are taught to develop personal improvement strategies... ' (p. 185)

In short, the effective teacher of PE is likely to motivate pupils by being aware of pupil needs, preparing interesting, meaningful lessons with learning experiences that are challenging, realistically attainable and which offer pupils a high chance of success. Such a positive learning environment is supported by a teacher who, according to one HOD in the TEPE Project: 'Encourages and rewards success, ensures pupils appreciate each other's efforts, makes success accessible to all, sets out activities that will lead to positive effort and enjoyment – and makes lessons fun!'

However, there are traps that teachers can indirectly fall into that may result in some pupils not receiving the kind of teacher support that is necessary for creating a positive attitude to learning. These are the dangers of 'teacher expectancy' effects: teacher behaviour resulting from the inferences that a teacher makes about a pupil's possible achievement or behaviour based on her knowledge of that pupil, and the resulting effects this may have in terms of pupil achievement in response to the teacher's expectations. One of these effects has been termed 'the self-fulfilling prophecy'.

The self-fulfilling prophecy effect, referred to as the 'Pygmalion Effect' by Rosenthal and Jacobson (1968), is said to occur when a teacher's incorrect expectations of a pupil leads to teacher behaviour that causes the expectation to be realised. Unfortunately, later attempts to replicate Rosenthal and Jacobson's study at Oak Elementary School were unsuccessful, although researchers have continued to attempt to make sense of the complex processes that appear to be involved in teacher expectancy effects.

In physical education the work of Martinek (1989, 1991) and his colleagues (Martinek and Johnson, 1979; Martinek and Karper, 1984; Martinek, Crowe and Rejeski, 1982) have shown that there may be an association between teacher expectations and certain types of teacher behaviour, and in some cases pupil performance and affective behaviours. The specific teacher behaviours related to low teacher expectations are reviewed by Martinek (1991) and shown in Box 9.

---

### Box 9
### Teacher behaviours related to low teacher expectations in Physical Education

- Teachers tend to give less praise and more criticism to low expectancy (LEX) students;
- Teachers asked less analytic questions and provided fewer response opportunities to LEX students;
- Teachers gave LEX students less evaluative comments to their responses;
- Unanswered questions were rephrased or repeated less for LEX students;
- Fewer dyadic contacts were directed to LEX students;
- Less information on content-related behaviours was directed towards LEX students;
- Acceptance and use of student ideas and actions were less for the LEX students;
- LEX students initiated fewer interactions with their teachers;
- LEX students were given more technical feedback.

*Adapted from: Martinek (1991) p. 66.*

---

Why do teacher expectancy effects occur?

Martinek (1991) has suggested a model to explain the complexity of expectancy effects in PE and this is shown in Figure 5 below.

The model puts forward the view that:
(1) Teachers may form expectations of their pupils from perceptions of pupils as a result of cues picked up related to such pupil characteristics as gender, physical attractiveness and skill.

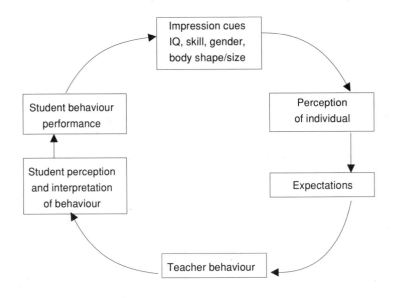

*Figure 5   Martinek's teacher expectancy model for Physical Education*
Source: Martinek (1991) p. 61.

(2) As a result of these perceptions the teacher may form expectations regarding the future performance of the pupil, and these expectations may affect the quantity and quality of the teacher's interactions with the pupil.
(3) The pupil may then perceive and interpret these interactions and perform in a way that is consistent with the teacher's expectations.

If a teacher communicates negative expectations to a pupil over a period of time, the pupil may develop a feeling of helplessness. This may be particularly the case when a pupil perceives that however hard he tries he will receive the same response from the teacher. Martinek (1988) has shown that low expectancy pupils exhibit signs of learned helplessness when they are constantly being reprimanded by the teacher. When teachers undermine the efforts of pupils who are trying to improve their skill, this may result in such pupils avoiding new challenges because similar efforts have met with failure in the past. Martinek (1991) calls this the 'What's the use complex', as shown in Figure 6 below.

Good and Brophy (1991) suggest that some teachers may be more susceptible to expectancy effects, especially negative effects that may influence pupil achievement. The 'over-reactor' teacher, for example,

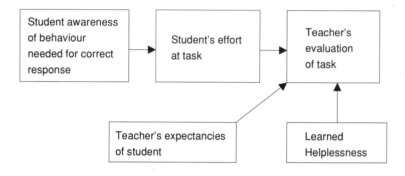

*Figure 6   The 'What's the Use' complex model*
Source: Martinek (1991) p. 72.

may develop rigid, stereotyped perceptions of pupils based on records and 'first impressions', and consequently treats pupils as stereotypes rather than individuals, with resulting negative expectancy effects. Proactive teachers tend to have positive expectations of their pupils because they are aware of appropriate goal setting for the class as a whole, as well as for individual pupils. Reactive teachers are between these two extremes and, although they have expectations of pupils, they do not take them too seriously and adjust them according to their developing knowledge of pupils.

The effective teacher will therefore avoid falling into the 'trap' of having low expectations of certain pupils, particularly low achievers. How can this be done? How can negative expectancy effects be avoided and a positive learning environment retained? The teacher effectiveness literature (Martinek, 1991; Good and Brophy, 1991) suggests the following:

- keep expectations appropriate, flexible, current, and in perspective – stress present performance rather than past history;
- have positive, realistic expectations of pupils and set clear and realistic goals;

- avoid comparing pupils with other pupils and stress the pupil's present level of understanding and mastery;
- provide feedback and instruction that pupils will need to meet the objectives set for them;
- diagnose pupil learning difficulties and break down tasks into smaller units;
- stimulate all pupils to achieve;
- make a special effort to show interest and sympathy in the efforts of low achievers by accepting the pupil's contribution, offering the pupil opportunities to make a contribution to the activity and look for ways of using the pupil's ideas.

The effective teacher will be fully aware of the dangers of expectancy effects, and when 'thinking through' a future lesson will have prepared appropriate material for all pupils in the class to be able to achieve success and a boost to their self-esteem. Physical education teachers have to be particularly aware of preparing appropriate material for pupils with special needs, and for mixed-gender groups, as the creation of a positive learning environment for such groups requires considerable thought and attention to detail.

In the case of teaching children with special educational needs, Groves (1979), Jowsey (1992), BAALPE (1989a), Brown and Jones (1989), Brown (1986), and special issues of the *British Journal of Physical Education* (e.g. 1987; 1990; 1993) offer the reader detailed practical advice, as does Talbot (1990, 1993), Thomas (1991), Scraton (1993), and Turvey and Laws (1988) on the issue of the teaching of mixed gender groups and equality of opportunity. These issues will not, therefore, be dealt with in detail in this text.

# CHAPTER 7

# Maintaining an effective learning environment

## Introduction

As noted in Chapter 6, creating and maintaining an effective learning environment is about thorough preparation and management, particularly preventative class management. The effective teacher will have planned carefully to establish an effective learning environment from the beginning of the school year by introducing rules, routines and procedures, and by outlining clear expectations for behaviour. Effective teachers are effective managers who think through their first encounters with a new class, and make pupils accountable and responsible for their work and behaviour. The keys to good management and the maintenance of an effective learning environment is therefore the use of techniques that elicit pupil cooperation and involvement and prevent problems emerging.

According to a number of sources (Good and Brophy, 1991; Wragg, 1984), teachers who are effective classroom managers tend to be more successful than those who try to be authority figures or disciplinarians. It is generally agreed that the ultimate aim is to develop a managerial system that requires pupils to be involved in a degree of self-management, that creates responsible class members, thus allowing the teacher to attend to teaching and learning issues rather than management. This sounds alright in theory, but how does it work in practice? What are the skills and techniques that effective teachers use to maintain an effective learning environment? This is an issue of particular concern to student teachers and NQTs starting off in a new school. Forty per cent of the student teachers of PE in the TEPE Project mentioned 'control', 'discipline' and 'class management' as their main areas of concern prior to teaching practice, and similar results have been obtained by other studies (Boggess *et al.*, 1985; McBride *et al.*, 1986). The student teachers in Placek's (1983) study most frequently attributed examples of non-successful teaching to managerial and disciplinary concerns. Also, of the 12 NQTs followed up in their first year of teaching PE as part of the TEPE Project, 6 expressed various degrees of concern about 'maintaining the appropriate degree of control' in their teaching.

In addition to thorough preparation and clarity of presentation, to be able to maintain an effective learning environment the teacher of PE may need to develop skills related to the following aspects of teaching:

- Class monitoring skills and minimising off task behaviour;
- Maintaining a positive class climate and reinforcement of appropriate behaviour;
- Dealing with inappropriate behaviour.

## *Class monitoring skills and minimising off-task behaviour*

If the teacher has made it absolutely clear to pupils what is expected of them during the lesson then there is a reasonable chance that they will work on the task the teacher has set. However, as mentioned in Chapter 6, pupils may negotiate the boundaries of the task, modify the task or just 'bystand' as Tousignant and Brunelle (1982) discovered. It is therefore essential that the teacher monitors what pupils are doing immediately after setting work by constantly 'scanning' the class for compliance. Effective teachers always know what is going on in the work area. Kounin (1970) refers to this being 'with-it', having 'eyes in the back of the head'. Marland (1975) coined the phrase 'the lighthouse effect' to describe how effective teachers monitor all corners of their classroom. These 'scanning' and 'with-it' skills are essential for monitoring the learning environment, and ensuring that pupils are adhering to the teachers' expectations and are accountable for their work.

What are the finer skills of class monitoring? Effective class monitoring is about movement, positioning, having a 'wide angled vision' of the class, and knowing what to look for.

The way the teacher moves around the class is crucial to effective monitoring. At all times the teacher should be able to see the whole class and not have pupils working behind her. This will entail moving around the periphery, but always facing the whole class so that a wide angle of vision can be used.

Establishing a wide angle of vision involves avoiding concentrating on a few pupils that you may be helping at a particular point in time, or focussing on the pupils who are in your particular line of vision. Being alert to what is happening in the whole class and still able to interact with a small group of pupils is what Kounin (1970) refers to as 'overlapping' – being able to do two things at once without affecting the smooth flow of the lesson.

In addition to looking for immediate compliance in terms of pupils' work, and scanning the class for particular learning difficulties, the teacher should also be looking for good work and behaviour and reinforcing it.

Effective class monitoring is therefore an important skill in preventative class management and keeping pupils on-task. In Kounin's (1970) study the three main skills of 'with-itness', 'overlapping' and 'desist clarity' (the ability to give specific feedback about behaviour), were characteristic of effective managers and teachers who had few discipline problems.

As life in classrooms and in the gym is so complex with so much happening at once, it is not surprising that student teachers have initial difficulty displaying 'with-itness' and 'overlapping' skills. Whereas experienced teachers are able to quickly pick up subtle cues and signals that inform them of what is happening in the class, student teachers are generally too preoccupied with lesson content and the organisation of pupils and equipment to be fully alert when monitoring the class. In fact, one PE lecturer in the TEPE Project mentioned that one of the most common faults observed on teaching practice was: 'A general lack of awareness – not aware of pupils fidgeting or doing other things'.

One way of improving this skill is to make a conscious attempt to 'scan' the whole class every couple of minutes to see if there are any particular problems. The beginner teacher can easily become so enthusiastic and engrossed in individual guidance with a pupil having learning difficulties that they are oblivious to what other pupils are doing. It is also easy to fall into the 'busy, happy and good' syndrome (Placek, 1983) discussed in Chapter 6, and allow pupils to be 'off-task' provided they are active and enjoying themselves.

Keeping pupils 'on-task' refers to the time they are actually learning the task as set by the teacher, and has its origins in the concept of Academic Learning Time (ALT) identified by those working in the California Beginner Teacher Evaluation Study (Denham and Lieberman, 1980). ALT very simply refers to (Fisher *et al.*, 1980): '... the amount of time a student spends on an academic task he/she can perform with high success. The more ALT a student accumulates, the more the student is learning'. (p. 8)

Researchers considered this variable to be an important intervening variable acting as the mediating link between teacher behaviour and pupil achievement. Teachers with high ALT scores for their pupils during lessons were considered to be more effective teachers because they gave their pupils more opportunity to learn. An observation instrument known as 'ALT–PE' was used by physical educationists to study learning time in PE lessons, and they were alarmed by the seemingly low amount of lesson time that pupils actually spent being physically active practising and learning the movements set by the teacher. Studies showed that approximately 10–20% of lesson time 'could be viewed as contributing to learning outcomes' (Metzler, 1989), and pupils appeared to be actively engaged in physically learning appropriate skills and movements for little more than 20–30%

of lesson time (Tousignant and Brunelle, 1982; Dodds, Rife and Metzler, 1982; Grant, 1990), with possibly less than 15% of this time engaged at an appropriate level of difficulty (Godbout, Brunelle and Tousignant, 1987; Shute *et al.*, 1982). It was also noted across the different studies that 25% or less of class time is spent in explanation/demonstration or receiving information, and approximately one-third of class time is spent 'waiting' (Godbout *et al.*, 1987; Shute *et al.*, 1982; Silverman, 1991). It is important to compare these results with those studies that suggest that more experienced teachers of PE provide higher pupil engaged, practice or activity time (Paese, 1986; Phillips and Carlisle, 1983; Pieron, 1982), less pupil waiting time (Graham, Soares and Harrington, 1983), and produced greater pupil achievement (Gustart and Springings, 1989). In fact, Silverman (1991) goes as far as to say: 'Overwhelming evidence indicates that the amount of time students spend practising (either measured by time or the number of practice trials) at an appropriate or successful level is positively related to student achievement and that inappropriate or unsuccessful practice is negatively related to achievement'. (p. 356)

However, Silverman does add that the quality of student engagement in learning is more important than the total practice time, and others agree (Ashy, Lee and Landin, 1988). Some believe that time itself is an empty concept (Wragg, 1993). In other words, although the amount of time pupils are engaged in practising or learning the task introduced by the teacher is important for pupil learning, the two issues of appropriate task difficulty (for pupil stage of learning) and the quality and suitability of pupil engagement (whether the pupil is actually practising and interested in the task as set), appear to be equally important. Therefore, one needs to scrutinise carefully the activity itself, how it is differentiated for pupil ability levels, and not only the time engaged in the activity.

If you are interested in finding out about the level of 'time on task' of your pupils, try Exercise 3 with the help of an observer. This is not always possible but is a valuable aspect of a school staff development programme or departmental evaluation or appraisal policy.

*Exercise 3  Pupil Watching: Looking at time on task*
*Guidelines for a lesson observer*

You will need a pad, time line sheet, stop-watch and pencil. A blank time line sheet is shown on page 117. Read the following ground rules carefully so that you are clear about the type of behaviour that each category refers to, and then watch a particular pupil for a period of time (e.g. 1 minute, 5 minutes, etc.) and indicate in the time line box opposite the appropriate category of behaviour with the time in seconds that the pupil was engaged in that particular behaviour.

Alternatively a tally may be placed in the box to indicate that the behaviour occurred. The vertical columns of the time line sheet are used to represent a particular period in time, and therefore each recording needs to be placed in a different column in order to view the sequence of pupil behaviour through the lesson. An example of timed recordings is shown on the time line sheet in Figure 7 on page 119.

## Categories of pupil behaviour

The following are brief descriptions and examples of each category of pupil behaviour.

(1) Pupil response – appropriate.
   The pupil is actively engaged in performing the task exactly as set by the teacher.
(2) Pupil response – inappropriate.
   The pupil is moving but his movement is *obviously* not related to the task as set by the teacher. For example, if the teacher has asked for stretched shapes in gymnastics the pupil may respond by rolling in a curled shape on the floor. If the teacher has asked for a push pass in hockey and the pupil is wildly attempting to strike the ball with a high back lift. These responses would be considered inappropriate in response to the task set by the teacher.
(3) Pupil response – deviant.
   The pupil is not performing the task as set and is engaged in illicit chatter, wandering around doing nothing in particular, or interfering with the work of other pupils.
(4) Pupil inactivity – waiting turn.
   In this category the pupil is quite clearly having to wait for their turn. Examples might include a skills practice in files or relays, where there is insufficient equipment for a continuously active practice, or where a practice has not been adapted well enough to ensure maximum activity.
(5) Pupil inactivity – teacher guidance or organisation.
   In this category the pupil is sitting or standing listening to the teacher either explain the task to be learned, demonstrate the task (by teacher or pupil) or when the teacher is organising pupils into teams, groups or arranging the movement of equipment.

Notes:

• When a new 'target' pupil is being observed indicate the change of pupil with a double line through a vertical time column as shown in Figure 7.
• Use the 'comments' space at the bottom of the schedule to clarify any observations made. This is a particularly important part of the

## PUPIL WATCHING – LOOKING AT TIME ON TASK

Teacher's name _____

Observer's name _____

Date _____

Class _____

Time _____

Brief description of lesson _____

Objectives of lesson _____

| | | | | | | | | | | | | | | | | | | | | | | Totals |
|---|---|---|---|---|---|---|---|---|---|---|---|---|---|---|---|---|---|---|---|---|---|---|---|
| Pupil response – appropriate | | | | | | | | | | | | | | | | | | | | | | | |
| Pupil response – inappropriate | | | | | | | | | | | | | | | | | | | | | | | |
| Pupil response – deviant | | | | | | | | | | | | | | | | | | | | | | | |
| Pupil inactivity – waiting turn | | | | | | | | | | | | | | | | | | | | | | | |
| Pupil inactivity – teacher guidance/organisation | | | | | | | | | | | | | | | | | | | | | | | |
| Pupil response – appropriate | | | | | | | | | | | | | | | | | | | | | | | |
| Pupil response – inappropriate | | | | | | | | | | | | | | | | | | | | | | | |
| Pupil response – deviant | | | | | | | | | | | | | | | | | | | | | | | |
| Pupil inactivity – waiting turn | | | | | | | | | | | | | | | | | | | | | | | |
| Pupil inactivity – teacher guidance/organisation | | | | | | | | | | | | | | | | | | | | | | | |

Observer's comments:

observation because such comments add more meaning to the time line figures recorded. For example, a lengthy explanation of the safety issues related to a particular practice may need qualifying by the comment: 'Important safety issues needed to be explained.'

### Interpreting 'pupil watching' data – short tennis lesson

Taking the example of a completed time line coding sheet shown in Figure 7, the pupils are inactive for the first 70 seconds of the lesson as the teacher explains and demonstrates the task. The first pupil to be observed responds appropriately and practises the task as set by the teacher. The teacher then presents a new task (the backhand stroke to be practised against the Sports Hall wall) and the observer follows a new 'target' pupil. This pupil (according to the observer), finds the task too difficult and, after initially spending 40 seconds attempting the task, proceeds to modify the task (instead of practising the backhand stroke he begins hitting the ball up into the basketball net). The pupil then attempts to disrupt others by kicking their ball away whenever it comes near. However, the proximity of the teacher ensures that this pupil did attempt the set task for the final 15 seconds of the practice period.

Vigilant class monitoring would have helped this teacher to see that the second pupil was frustrated by his lack of success in a task that was possibly too difficult for him, and he should have offered individual guidance with particular reference to footwork and body position, or a modified task with a better chance of success (e.g. further practise of forehand stroke to enable the pupil to establish footwork and correct contact with the ball). Of the 115 seconds devoted to this period of learning this pupil only spent 55 seconds engaged in the task as set, and this engagement was possibly not at an appropriate level of difficulty. The 'ALT–PE' score for this pupil (if using the ALT–PE schedule devised by Siedentop, Tousignant and Parker, 1982) might have been very low because the pupil had not been learning a skill at the appropriate level of difficulty for his stage of learning.

Observers comments: Target pupil 2 was obviously having difficulty with the backhand stroke and I think his frustration caused him to mess about by hitting the ball into the basketball net and disrupting others by kicking their ball away.

There are obvious implications of the work on time on task for the planning of lessons, the presentation of new material and class management. Lessons need to be planned in such a way that learning experiences are within the capabilities of the learner yet are also challenging and provide maximum activity for all pupils in the class.

| | | | | | | | |
|---|---|---|---|---|---|---|---|
| Pupil response – appropriate | | 190 | | 40 | | | 15 |
| Pupil response – inappropriate | | | | | 40 | | |
| Pupil response – deviant | | | | | | 20 | |
| Pupil inactivity – waiting turn | | | | | | | |
| Pupil inactivity – teacher guidance and organisation | 70 | | 50 | | | | |

*Figure 7   Pupil Watching – Example coding sheet using timed recordings for a short tennis lesson*

Teacher presentations need to be clear and concise with pupils in no doubt about the teacher's expectations. Class management needs to be 'snappy' with the minimum amount of time spent on organisation of equipment and pupils, providing, of course, that safety factors are clearly explained.

What then, are the implications of this short review of time on task research for class monitoring skills and keeping pupils 'on task'?

As shown in the example 'pupil watching' coding sheet in Figure 7, vigilant class monitoring by the teacher should identify those pupils who are either having difficulty with the task (and may need guidance or a modified task) or are not using the learning time profitably. A number of techniques are used by experienced teachers to bring pupils back 'on-task'. These techniques relate to the following four aspects of class monitoring:

- Momentum and flow;
- Keeping pupils 'on their toes';
- Being aware of pupil's changing needs;
- Class movement and proximity.

Teachers keep the momentum and flow of the lesson going by not allowing distractions to disrupt the flow of the lesson, and by being aware of pupils' changing needs. According to Kounin's (1970) research, effective classroom managers were not only 'with-it' and always knew what was going on, but they also used 'signal continuity' to keep pupils 'on-task'. Signal continuity implies that the effective teacher is able to use techniques to keep pupils 'on their toes' that do not cause disruption to the lesson. They might ignore minor cases of inattention but will naturally deal with more sustained inattention before it escalates. They may also avoid lengthy reprimands and over-reaction that can affect lesson continuity.

Effective classroom managers use techniques such as eye contact, questions and proximity to keep pupils attentive and working on the set task, thus retaining lesson momentum. Moving close to pupils can be sufficient to bring pupils back 'on-task' and lead to the completion of work. A probing question such as: 'Haven't you started yet John?'; may also have the effect of reminding pupils that they are accountable for getting on with the task, and at the same time reinforce your expectations of behaviour and work. This can create what Kounin and Gump (1958) referred to as the 'ripple effect', as other pupils realise that you expect work to have started immediately.

Keeping pupils 'on their toes' can also be done in a positive way. Giving supportive and informative positive feedback can motivate pupils to continue to work hard and, at the same time, give the impression that you are constantly monitoring their progress. Occasional use of positive feedback from a distance may not only be an incentive for the pupil performing, but may also act as a reminder to others of what they should be doing. However, it is important to appreciate that not all pupils like their performance and positive attitude to work to be made public, so a careful mixture of appropriate praise and public feedback needs to be used.

As the majority of PE teachers in the TEPE Project mentioned, getting to know pupils' names and using them is particularly important when giving feedback, praise, reprimands and when posing questions. In the early stages of teaching in a new school, learning names can be difficult. One way of overcoming this is to always ask a pupil's name when giving guidance, posing a question, asking a pupil to move a piece of equipment, or when organising pupils into groups.

Being aware of pupils' changing needs is also a crucial factor in keeping them 'on task'. A 'with-it' teacher knows when interest in a particular activity is waning, either because the activity has been going on for too long or because it is not appropriate for pupil needs. Also, it may be that the lesson is moving too quickly or too slowly for the pupils, and they are becoming tired or bored. The effective teacher is aware of these factors and either adapts the lesson plan accordingly or differentiates activities for particular groups of pupils. This is not an easy task for the student teacher or NQT because it necessitates knowing the class well. However, student teachers may fall into the trap of being 'lesson plan driven', and push through an activity or series of practices just to get through the prepared lesson plan rather than adapt to the responses of the pupils. Although it is important to plan lessons well, the effective teacher is also adaptable to changing pupil needs.

Variety and challenge are also important features of good planning to keep pupils 'on task'. According to Doyle (1986) and Brophy and Good (1986), effective classroom managers provide tasks that pupils are capable of doing successfully, yet are varied and challenging enough to sustain motivation.

The effectiveness of vigilant class monitoring and effective differentiation of content were emphasised in the study by Hastie and Saunders (1990) of secondary school PE lessons. It appeared that pupils were significantly more off-task in non-monitored situations compared with 100% task engagement with closely monitored tasks. It was also noticeable that there was more likelihood of pupils staying on-task if they enjoyed the activity, and when there was a close match between their level of ability and the demands of the task. However, even when there was not a good activity/ability match, vigilant monitoring was able to prevent deviant pupil behaviour.

## Maintaining a positive class climate and reinforcement of appropriate behaviour

The 'with-it' teacher not only carefully monitors pupil work and progress with a view to keeping pupils 'on task', but he is also looking for every opportunity to help pupils with their learning by giving appropriate guidance and feedback, and reinforcing good work and behaviour.

Pupils that are motivated to learn because they find the work challenging and interesting, who respect and enjoy working with their teacher, are less likely to misbehave or be 'off-task'. Therefore, maintaining a positive class climate and learning environment is an important aspect of preventative class management – happy, interested, successful and contented pupils will want to learn and please their teacher. However, pupils will only want to learn if they feel positive about themselves in relation to the activity. If an activity or learning experience does not foster pupil self-esteem, self-confidence and self-respect, then they will vote with their feet – or misbehave! Unfortunately, in the past, schools, and particularly PE departments, have not fostered the self-esteem of all pupils, and a large number have experienced failure, both in the formal and the 'hidden' curriculum. The effective teacher of physical education is therefore very aware of how she can maintain a positive learning environment through the development of pupil self-esteem. She will attempt to do this by planning appropriate material for individual pupil needs and capabilities, and in the way she treats pupils and shows that she is interested in their progress and welfare.

Teaching for positive pupil self-esteem is therefore important but, what actually is self-esteem?

Lawrence (1989) sees self-esteem as an individual's evaluation of the discrepancy between his self-image and his ideal self, and the extent to which he cares about that discrepancy. In his research Lawrence noted that teachers, through the teaching approaches they use and their individual contacts with pupils, were able to enhance the self-esteem of their pupils, and, in turn, develop a positive climate for learning. He also found that teachers with a personally high self-esteem, who accept pupils for what they are and what they are capable of doing, who are genuine and have empathy for their pupils, are more likely to raise the self-esteem of their pupils. But the way the teacher treats her pupils is a particularly important factor. For example, effective teachers who seek to raise the self-esteem of their pupils will attempt to communicate with pupils in such a way that:

- they are seen as enthusiastic, relaxed, supportive, encouraging;
- they show that they value, respect and acknowledge the efforts of their pupils by use of praise and positive specific feedback;
- their non-verbal behaviour, such as body posture and physical proximity, eye contact, tone of speech, and use of other gestures such as smiling, head nods, etc., reflect warmth and a supportive, caring disposition.

Also, pupil self-esteem is enhanced when the teacher:

- knows pupils well and attempts to share pupil interests and feelings;
- is prepared to 'give them time' and is a good 'listener';
- accepts pupil opinions, ideas and lesson contributions, offers pupil's opportunities to make contributions to lessons, and attempts to share decision making with pupils;
- stresses pupil present performance rather than dwelling on past performances;
- has positive expectations of pupils.

The effective teacher is particularly aware of the need to raise the self-esteem of low-achieving pupils and will endeavour to stimulate **all** pupils to achieve regardless of ability, gender, etc. In other words, the effective teacher is very conscious of the dangers of teacher expectancy and bias effects discussed in Chapter 6.

The way teachers respond to pupil errors in performance is also an important factor in the development of pupil self-esteem. As discussed in Chapter 6, initial interactions with pupils need to be sympathetic and encouraging, and the evaluation of pupil performance and the associated provision of feedback and guidance that follows should not be a critical evaluation, but should focus on individual improvement and effort rather than a comparison with other members of the group.

This emphasis on fostering pupil self-esteem and awareness of its role in the maintenance of a positive class climate is associated with the humanistic approach to teaching and learning originally applied to education by Maslow (1970) and Rogers (1983), and to physical education through the work of Hellison (1985). Such approaches emphasize the positive, and they visualise the teacher's role as a facilitator for learning in which pupils are offered more opportunity to be involved in their own learning. As a result, it is expected that pupils might be more positive about themselves and what they are learning, and therefore less likely to misbehave or be 'off-task'. As Hellison and Templin (1991) point out, such personal and social development models for teaching and learning help pupils: '... to feel better about themselves, deal with fairness, co-operation and take responsibility for their own actions – all of which can reduce discipline and motivation problems while promoting positive human qualities'. (p. 127)

Maintaining a positive learning atmosphere is also concerned with the identification and reinforcement of appropriate behaviour. Earlier studies have suggested that PE teachers may tend to be a little negative in their interactions with pupils, with certain studies showing limited evidence of a more positive teaching approach as far as positive and negative feedback is concerned (Cheffers and Mancini, 1978; Pieron, 1983; Mawer and Brown, 1983). In Fernandez-Balboa's (1991) study of PE teachers' thoughts and reactions to pupil misbehaviour, it appeared that the student teachers in the study showed little sign of realising the importance of using positive reinforcement for appropriate behaviour.

Effective teachers not only state rules and procedures clearly beforehand, and then constantly remind pupils of what is expected of them, but they are also looking for opportunities to reinforce desirable behaviour. They do so without overdoing praise or making it too public, for fear of creating a negative effect in the case of certain individuals. The effective use of praise is dealt with in more detail in Chapter 9.

This positive behavioural approach in which teachers are encouraged to consider the reasons for pupil behaviour and then offer positive reinforcement and encouragement for certain defined pupil behaviours, has been developed by Wheldall and Merrett (1989) and is discussed in greater detail later in this chapter.

Regardless of whether the teacher makes every effort to be positive, planning pupils' work carefully and appropriately for different ability levels, and taking account of all the other issues raised so far in this chapter, there will still be occasions when inappropriate behaviour will have to be dealt with.

## Dealing with inappropriate behaviour

Dealing with inappropriate behaviour is often referred to as 'discipline', 'keeping control' or 'desists' (Kounin, 1970), and it is seen by many teachers as one of **the** essential teaching skills; a point reinforced by the teachers, lecturers and advisers in the TEPE Project. It is also the topic of a major government report, the Elton Report (DES, 1989b), and an area of particular concern to student teachers. Of the student teachers taking part in the TEPE Project, 40% mentioned aspects of control and discipline as one of their 'concerns', and 60% of HODs mentioned aspects of control and discipline as being the major concerns and difficulties experienced by student teachers and NQTs. HODs saw the establishment of control and discipline as essential starting points for the student teacher, with safety being of paramount importance:

Control and discipline are crucial. It should underpin everything you do. With me discipline and control come first. Once established you can get on with teaching and enjoyment, without discipline and control there can be only chaos and potential danger.

Pupils need to know where the boundaries are – important for safety!

Concentrate on getting discipline first – let the class know exactly what your expectations are. Don't accept any rude or anti-social behaviour towards either yourself or members of the group.

The well-organised, well-prepared teacher has a good chance of avoiding control problems – but not totally! Even in the most carefully planned lessons misbehaviour may occur. Therefore, the effective teacher has a planned discipline strategy with short-term and long-term goals.

Short-term targets are to cut down inappropriate behaviour and disruption, and reinforce good behaviour. In the long-term, however, one should be aiming towards pupils being responsible for their own behaviour, and developing positive attitudes towards their learning and towards other members of group. This requires a very carefully planned and progressive approach, and advocates of this strategy make it clear that desirable outcomes do not appear overnight!

The initial short-term target is to deal with inappropriate behaviour. But, what sort of misbehaviour are we talking about and why does it occur? Understanding the nature of misbehaviour is an important first step on the road to handling problems effectively. According to the Elton Report (DES, 1989b) and the work of Wragg and Dooley (1984), most pupil misbehaviour is mainly minor but irritating, and can be dealt with by the skilful teacher who has well-established rules, routines and procedures. Examples of such misbehaviour include:

- excessively noisy talk;
- non-verbal behaviour not appropriate to the task;
- talking out of turn;
- irrelevant talk;
- not paying attention to the teacher;
- not getting on with work;
- inappropriate movement;
- arriving late for lessons.

However, if a teacher allows these forms of misbehaviour to 'snowball', then more serious types of inappropriate behaviour may occur, such as bad language, cheek, disobedience, verbal and physical aggression, and insulting behaviour to other pupils and the teacher.

What types of misbehaviour occur in PE lessons? In an American study Fernandez-Balboa (1991) observed 15 student teachers teaching three to five lessons each and identified the types and frequencies of misbehaviour shown in Box 10.

---

**Box 10**
**Types, frequencies and percentages of misbehaviours in Physical Education experienced by USA student teachers**

| Types | Frequency | % |
|---|---|---|
| Individual misbehaviours | 268 | 86.1 |
|   Off task | 122 | 39.2 |
|     – equipment related | 83 | 26.6 |
|     – not equipment related | 39 | 12.5 |
|   Non participation | 72 | 23.1 |
|     – not showing full effort | 16 | 5.1 |
|     – showing no effort at all | 56 | 18.0 |
|   Aggressive | 74 | 23.7 |
|     – towards other pupils | 54 | 17.3 |
|     – towards student teacher | 8 | 2.5 |
|     – impersonal | 12 | 3.8 |
| Group misbehaviours | 43 | 13.8 |
|   – off task | 23 | 7.3 |
|   – non participation | 16 | 5.1 |
|   – other | 4 | 1.2 |

*Source: Fernandez-Balboa (1991) p. 69.*

So why do pupils misbehave? This is a difficult question to answer because each individual pupil brings with them to a lesson a wide range of different emotional, social, physical and maturational issues that can influence their behaviour. Home and peer group circumstances can sometimes cause young people to react in unexpected ways, and sometimes this may challenge the authority of the teacher. In one study of the causes of misbehaviour in comprehensive schools cited by Cohen and Manion (1989), an unsettled home environment (49%), peer pressure (35%), and pupil psychological or emotional instability (29%), were mentioned by teachers as being particularly important. Also, lack of interest in the subject (30%), general disenchantment with school (30%), inability to do the work (21%) and lack of self-esteem (13%), were rated by teachers as influential factors in pupil misbehaviour (Dierenfield, 1982).

As one young newly qualified PE teacher in the TEPE Project mentioned when asked why lessons sometimes went badly: 'There are so many things that can affect the outcome of a lesson. You have 20–30 people bringing their own personal baggage with them to a lesson. There is no doubt that they will have varied expectations and intentions.'

However, the majority of misbehaviour may be caused by problems arising from the content of the lesson or a combination of the lesson content and social and emotional problems all occurring together. If the activities offered are too easy or too difficult for the pupils, they may become bored or frustrated because of a lack of success or challenge. Constant failure can lead to a loss of self-esteem, which in turn may lead the individual to look for alternative forms of behaviour to boost their self-esteem within the peer group; the result possibly being anti-social behaviour or behaviour that challenges the authority of the teacher and leads to a confrontation. In Fernandez-Balboa's (1991) study, 23% of pupil misbehaviour in PE lessons was considered to be related to boredom, 20.3% due to 'lack of interest in physical education', and 19.8% caused by the personal characteristics of the pupil, such as aggressiveness or hyperactivity. Additional pupil-related causes of misbehaviour in this study were: gender (boys) – 16%; tendency to test the teacher – 7.4%; tendency to socialise – 6.5%.

One HOD in the TEPE Project mentioned that student teachers and NQTs are more likely to have control problems because of pupil disenchantment with the physical education curriculum: 'There is a growing tendency for girls in particular to be disenchanted with PE and lack home support which goes with this disaffection. Try, therefore, to examine carefully what you are teaching – is it appropriate?'

Whatever the initial cause of the inappropriate behaviour, the skilful teacher will be aware of the many different possible reasons for pupil misbehaviour, and deal with it accordingly. However, 'dealing with it accordingly' is not so easy for the student teacher or NQT because they do not have the benefit of knowing the pupil's background or the strategies that are likely to work in certain cases of misbehaviour with certain pupils. HODs in the TEPE Project offer the following advice:

Watch experienced staff. You don't have to copy, but watch how they cope with problems, dilemmas, etc.

Ask for advice from other members of staff about strategies they use for specific groups and individuals.

Get the support of experienced teachers in cases of really difficult students – there are often strategies which avoid confrontations.

Don't be afraid of saying you have a problem – don't think that older staff have the answer with difficult pupils and it is just you! Nobody has the answer – we all try as best we can and everybody will give you helpful suggestions.

Evidence from the Fernandez-Balboa (1991) study suggests that student teachers are in danger of believing that there is nothing they can do to prevent pupil misbehaviours from happening, and this inhibited them from seeking and implementing appropriate strategies to deal with it, or prevent it. The author also concluded that students put little thought into what might have caused the misbehaviour or how it could be avoided and they based their reaction to misbehaviour largely on the ways in which their former teachers acted in similar situations. Consequently, their strategies were mainly reactive rather than proactive, and largely ineffective. Fernandez-Balboa therefore suggested that student teachers need 'specific feedback about suggested actions' and practice in using them to help them to anticipate and solve problems. He also recommended that students needed help with motivational and instructional approaches to improve pupil non-participation.

Suggestions for dealing with minor misbehaviour problems vary in the literature from the Good and Brophy (1991) advice that teachers should: '... not intervene every time they notice a problem, because such behaviour may be more disruptive than the problem itself. In such a situation it is better to delay action or simply ignore the problem'. (p. 231) ... to the advice of Cohen and Manion (1989) that student teachers need to be careful about overlooking minor misbehaviour because it: '... could easily be misconstrued by pupils as either weakness or lack of awareness'. (p. 220)

One strategy is to 'save your big guns'! Much minor misbehaviour (if not affecting pupil safety) can be dealt with by 'eye contact', 'physical proximity', 'gesture' (e.g. a frown), or a 'probing question'. Such action avoids disrupting the flow of the lesson or drawing other pupil's attention to the misbehaviour. One HOD suggested that a more positive reaction can work in some cases: 'A smile and a beautiful remark to some little horror can completely disarm them for the whole lesson, they think you're wonderful even though you want to shout at them, and this could go well. Above all, don't let them wind you up!'

Prolonged and disruptive behaviour should be stopped immediately, unless the teacher feels that further information is needed by investigating the situation. There are two ways of doing this. First of all the teacher should insist on the behaviour ceasing but may also follow this up by indicating alternative behaviour or making reference to the work going on. In the Leverhulme Primary Project (Wragg, 1993), the most common teacher responses to such behaviour were 'orders to cease', the 'naming of pupils', and 'reprimand'. However, one of the most successful strategies observed by the researchers was involving pupils in their work again. The recommended interaction is therefore short, very direct and to the point! The pupil is named, the misbehaviour is identified, and the teacher indicates what should be done instead. However, most pupils know they are misbehaving and a short reminder of the set task may be sufficient.

An alternative intervention is to remind pupils of rules and expectations already laid down. If the teacher has already established clear rules and thoroughly discussed the reasons for them, brief reminders can be used to correct inappropriate behaviour.

When reprimands do need to be used the effective teacher is aware of the factors that lead to the most successful use of this form of intervention. Kyriacou (1991) believes that reprimands should be used sparingly (because they undermine a positive classroom climate and pupils begin to feel the teacher is 'nagging'), and that effective reprimands have the following qualities:

- correct targeting;
- appropriate manner;
- appropriate content;
- consistency;
- avoid confrontations.

Correct targeting – it is vital that the pupil being reprimanded is the one who misbehaved and not a pupil who reacted to provocation by another. Also, reprimands involving the whole class should be avoided. However, there are times when a certain type of misbehaviour does involve a large number of the class. A useful strategy in this case is to either discuss with the class why the misbehaviour has been widespread, and thus be able to identify the problems causing it and reinforce good behaviour, or make reference to '... a large number of the class are not ...', thus avoiding blaming everyone for the poor behaviour. Similarly, making an example of one pupil who misbehaves and indicating that you will not tolerate anyone else behaving in such a way can be a useful ploy. But, the latter strategy needs careful implementation to avoid confrontations, as one HOD pointed out: 'Treat everyone the same. No favourites. Pupils soon pick on someone being treated differently to others'.

As far as manner is concerned, effective reprimands are delivered firmly and directly rather than tentatively, and they have their impact enhanced by such techniques as eye contact and pause. 'Reprimand – stare – pause for effect', is an effective reprimand cycle. Research suggests that children respond to rules that are enforced or 'followed through', but ignore those lacking conviction and enforcement (Kounin and Gump, 1958).

Calmness is also considered to be particularly important when delivering reprimands (Marland, 1992). There is a difference between displaying a firm note of disapproval in your manner and expressing intense rage, losing your temper and shouting at pupils. In Kounin's (1970) research, he found that 'rough' desists did not improve behaviour, they just upset the pupils. However, Marland (1992) believes that although fierceness is unnecessary: '... some children will put up with it and even become quite fond of it if the teacher reveals glimpses of a warmth behind the facade. One boy said, "He gets real wild with us sometimes, but you can tell he still likes us".' (p. 16)

As one HOD recommended: 'Stay calm, unless the situation warrants an outburst of anger'.

Most authors would agree that shouting is counter-productive in that it tends to raise the general noise level because the teacher is usually shouting over the pupils. In the teaching of PE it is often assumed that you need to raise your voice to make yourself heard in the sports hall, gym or on the field. To some extent this is true, but there are situations in the teaching of PE where 'quiet' teachers have been seen to be the most effective managers. Although such teachers rarely raise their voice in reprimand situations, as Marland (1992) notes: '... they usually have interesting voices – that is light and shade, variety of pace, relevant stressing of words, and above all, variety of tone'. (p. 16)

As far as the content of reprimands is concerned, effective reprimands should concentrate on the misbehaviour itself rather than the pupil. Remarks about pupils that are uncomplimentary, such as, 'What an idiot Jones!', 'Do you have to constantly show how thick you are Sarah!', and the use of sarcasm or ridicule can often lead to resentment, pupils being alienated, the teacher being seen as unfair and do not help the development of a positive classroom climate. Similarly, reprimands that make comparisons with other pupils, particularly if they are a relation of the misbehaving pupil, can also be seen as unfair, and resented.

Rhetorical or meaningless questions should also be avoided as they can often be interpreted as being direct attacks on the pupil. An example would be the, 'What's the matter with you?', type of question.

More effective reprimands are therefore task-centred and inform pupils of what they should be doing. 'Watch what I'm doing Sarah, so you know what to do', is better than, 'You're not paying attention Sarah!'.

What does not work particularly well is the use of empty threats. If you do state a consequence of the repeated misbehaviour, then it should be carried out.

Being consistent when giving reprimands is essential, and this point was reinforced by the majority of HODs in the TEPE Project. If expectations are made clear and the severity of reprimands are consistent with the offences, then pupils know 'where they stand', so to speak. Resentment can build up if the teacher suddenly 'over-reacts' and gives out over-severe reprimands, or is out of tune with his usual behaviour.

Above all, reprimands should not be done in such a way that they are likely to result in a 'slanging match' between pupil and teacher. If the teacher thinks that this might occur, because the pupil appears tense or agitated, it may be worthwhile using an investigative technique instead. Also, private reprimands are often more effective than public ones, unless the teacher wants the whole class to hear the reprimand in order to prevent others misbehaving. The private approach is often done quietly, with the pupil facing away from the rest of the class (otherwise they may wish to 'play to the gallery'), and is also less disruptive to the continuity of class work. If, however, a pupil being reprimanded does react emotionally, it may pay simply to ask to see the pupil after the lesson, rather than have a 'stand up row'.

Confrontations should be avoided if at all possible, but they do occur, so how should they be dealt with? Watkins and Wagner (1987) and Kyriacou (1991) suggest a number of principles for dealing with confrontations:

(1) Stay calm – be aware of the heat of the moment;
    – regain composure and allow the pupil to clam down;
    – think through rationally how best to proceed.
(2) Privacy – avoid a public area where the pupil can face his classmates and 'play to the gallery'.
(3) Defuse the situation – 'Is this so important that we need to get upset – just calm down and we'll talk about it at the end of the lesson'.
(4) Avoid making threats – especially any that could be thought of as being physical.
(5) 'Think through' an alternative or 'face saver', rather than tend to feel that your authority is at stake. A carefully thought out strategy may allow both parties to 'win' in a dignified manner.
(6) Use your social skills – particularly with a pupil who may be quite embarrassed about what she has done. This may entail going over

your own view of what happened and asking the pupil to explain their perception of the situation.

(7) Don't be afraid to ask for help.

The last point is an important one and the majority of PE teachers in the TEPE Project did recommend that student teachers should not be afraid to ask for help. However, it is also worth pointing out that at least two HODs felt that class control was very much a matter of individual style:

Work hard to establish your own style – don't necessarily follow other members of staff – it may work for them. Use their experience, but you need to do it your way.

I give hints on discipline techniques but emphasize that each teacher has his/her own way of class control whether it be extravert or a more quiet approach. Certain things are constant though, for example, don't let things go thinking they will settle down for themselves.

Investigations and counselling are important skills in the teacher's armoury. Misbehaviour situations will arise when the teacher is unclear about the nature and the cause of inappropriate behaviour, and it is then necessary either to gain more information by questioning or base a decision to reprimand on ones reading of the situation. There is no easy way of deciding which course of action is appropriate, it will depend on the individual pupil involved, the nature of the work being done and the teacher's anticipation of likely outcomes. However, if in doubt – find out!

The investigation may begin with a 'What's the difficulty?', posed in a quiet and sympathetic tone rather than a sharp, aggressive 'bark'. The questioning is primarily to establish the facts of the situation and should not be rhetorical, or to attack pupils. Questions like, 'Why can't you remember to use your head when being asked to do things?', would be totally inappropriate because there may not be an answer to such a question.

Investigations are better done in private with only the pupils directly involved, each having the opportunity to put their point of view. This may be done at the end of the lesson or at break time to avoid disruption of work. If the problem is not related to the work being done then the teacher has to decide whether counselling would be better.

Counselling needs to be done in a caring and thoughtful manner, and the pupil offered the opportunity to examine her behaviour and be aware of the consequences if the behaviour or attitude does not improve. The hope is that the counselling would be concluded with the pupil agreeing to behave well in the future.

If this approach is not successful then the teacher needs to discuss the matter with colleagues who are responsible for the pastoral care of the pupil. Such consultation with colleagues may result in a particular problem concerning the pupil being identified (e.g. problem at home, special needs, etc.), and the pupil offered the help they need. If this procedure fails then 'big guns' may have to be introduced, and this may entail the use of punishments. Schools also have other approaches to dealing with discipline and conflict situations. These include:

- putting pupils 'on report' and monitoring their behaviour;
- getting help from parents;
- contingency 'contracts' or rewards for good behaviour;
- special units for disruptive pupils.

## Punishments

Although the law requires teachers to act in the capacity of a reasonable parent, it also provides teachers with certain powers of control and the discharge of their responsibilities. This is particularly important in physical education where the issue of safety is paramount. Punishments are generally used as a last resort, as a deterrent, as retribution, to help the pupil understand that the behaviour was wrong and that they need to behave better in the future.

The punishments to be used in the school need to be supported by the governors and are governed by law, which, according to Wragg (1993): '... decrees that punishments must be ''reasonable'', defined by one judge as – moderate, not dictated by bad motives, such as is usual in the school, and such as the parent of the child might expect it to receive if it had done wrong'. (p. 35)

A survey conducted for the Elton Report (DES, 1989b) that examined the effectiveness of strategies used to deal with difficult pupils or classes concluded that although any strategy used skilfully and appropriately may be effective, reasoning strategies based on interview and counselling were seen as being the most effective. Many student teachers feel that the quick use of a 'big gun' like a punishment is the real answer to solving discipline problems. However, although the appropriate and skilful use of punishment is a useful way of dealing with certain discipline problems, an over-use of punishments may be at the cost of the development of a positive classroom climate, and can lead to resentment, anxiety, frustration and emotional reactions. As Good and Brophy (1991) point out in their review of the literature: '... punishment can control misbehaviour, but by itself it will not teach desirable behaviour or even reduce the desire to misbehave. Thus, punishment is never a solution by itself; it can only be part of a solution'. (p. 239)

How, therefore, might the teacher skilfully and effectively use punishments?

The starting point for the student or newly qualified teacher is to find out initially what established system of punishments the school and PE department use and how it relates to the school's rules and procedures. As one HOD recommended: 'Seek advice on normal discipline measures and don't be afraid to use them'. Also, it is worthwhile discussing with colleagues how they use the punishment system and how they deal with particular 'problem' pupils. Above all, if you are unsure or having a problem don't be afraid to discuss it with other staff, as several HODs in the TEPE Project recommended: '... ask for help when you need it. Don't be afraid of saying you have a problem – don't think that other staff have the answer with difficult pupils and it is just you. Nobody has the answer, we all try our best'.

There are a number of different types of punishment used in schools, each having advantages and disadvantages, and these are shown in Box 11.

Physical education departments are not always very good at giving student teachers information about discipline procedures, as 26% of the student teachers taking part in the TEPE Project discovered. It may therefore be up to you to ask for the information yourself. Exercise 4 is intended to help you to gather information on school and department policy concerning sanctions and punishments prior to teaching in a new school.

*Exercise 4   School and department sanctions and punishments*

- What is the policy concerning sanctions and punishments?
  (i)  At the SCHOOL level
  (ii) At the PE DEPARTMENT level
- What sanctions and punishments are used and for what types of misbehaviour?
  (i)  At the SCHOOL level
  (ii) At the PE DEPARTMENT level
- What is considered to be mild misbehaviour, and how is it dealt with in the PE Department?
- What is considered to be serious misbehaviour, and how is it dealt with in the PE Department?
- When observing other teachers make a note of any sanctions or punishments they use.

The skilful and effective use of punishments is very similar to the use of reprimands mentioned earlier, but in addition it is worth noting that punishments should:

- only be used when other strategies have failed and be part of a planned response to repeated misbehaviour;

**Box 11**
**Examples of Punishments used in schools**

| | Advantages | Disadvantages |
|---|---|---|
| Detention in break, lunch time or after school | Pupils generally dislike it | Inconvenience to teacher and decision of what to do with them. May require 24hrs notice. Problem of transport in rural areas. |
| Exclusion from class | Removes pupil from lesson to 'reflect' on misbehaviour | Not always seen by pupils as unpleasant and may wander off. Work to be set. |
| Writing lines or assignments | Done in pupil's own time | Older pupils may find it demeaning |
| Loss of privileges | If it involves loss of a school trip or break time pupils may find it upsetting | May be seen as vindictive or unfair |
| Isolation within class | Can be effective if it doesn't last for long | Disruption of work |
| Severe verbal reprimand | Unpleasant and quick | May lead to a confrontation, so needs to be private |
| Parental involvement | Sometimes very effective | Pupils may enjoy having status of being disruptive |
| Bad conduct marks | Mild formal punishment | Can be difficult to administer and communicate |
| Exclusion from school | May be the 'shock' the pupil needs or lead to special care | The last resort leading to school transfer |

*Corporal punishment is illegal in maintained schools.*

- be part of the school policy;
- fit the crime;
- be seen by the pupil as being fair, that they appreciate why the punishment has been given and have been duly warned in advance;
- be seen by the pupil as being in his own interests;

- be appropriately unpleasant to the pupil and reflect the seriousness with which you view the misbehaviour and the urgency of the need for future acceptable behaviour;
- be given as soon as possible after the misbehaviour and reflect your disapproval of the behaviour rather than your loss of temper.

It is also vitally important that there is some consistency in class management and use of sanctions and punishments, both within a department and throughout the school as a whole. This point is reinforced by the Elton Report (DES, 1989b):

We recommend that headteachers and their senior management teams should take the lead in developing school plans for promoting good behaviour. Such plans should ensure that the school's code of conduct and the values represented in its formal and informal curriculum reinforce one another; promote the highest possible degree of consensus about standards of behaviour among staff, pupils and parents; provide clear guidance to all three groups about these standards and their practical application; and encourage staff to recognise and praise good behaviour as well as dealing with bad behaviour. (p. 13)

The latter point made by the Elton Report is an important one, and the ability to recognise and praise good behaviour may be seen as an essential long-term class management and discipline strategy.

## Long-term class management and discipline strategies

One long-term strategy is that put forward by Wheldall and Merrett (1989) and known as 'Positive Teaching'. This approach is concerned with identifying and increasing appropriate behaviour and is based on the following five principles:

(1) Teaching is concerned with the observable – rather than attempt to offer labels or explanations for pupil behaviour, teachers should concern themselves with what the pupil actually does.
(2) Behaviour is the result of learning – more appropriate behaviour can be learned in place of bad behaviour.
(3) Learning involves a change in behaviour – this can be observed (e.g. the pupil does exactly as told), recorded and compared with previous behaviour.
(4) Behaviour changes as a result of consequences – learning occurs as a result of repeated behaviour which is followed by desirable and rewarding consequences. Behaviours are not repeated if the consequences are seen to be aversive. The authors therefore emphasize that rewarding appropriate behaviour is more effective than punishing inappropriate behaviour, and they quote their own

research in support of this view (Wheldall and Merrett, 1989; Houghton *et al.*, 1989).

(5) Classroom contexts may influence behaviour – pupils may experience a wide variety of different classroom contexts in a day, and each context may have its own specific appropriate behaviour. Pupils have to learn therefore to behave appropriately according to the context, and each teacher, whether art, science, PE or technology, is likely to have established her own rules and routines for work within that context.

The 'positive teacher' is therefore involved in constantly identifying and praising desirable behaviour and also reminding pupils of classroom rules, routines and acceptable behaviour. The Positive Teaching technique of RPI (Rules, Praise and Ignoring) is central to the Wheldall and Merrett approach. For example, using the simple rule of 'We should put up our hand when we want to answer a question'; this would be reinforced and pupils and the class as a whole praised regularly when they adhered to the rule, but infractions may be ignored. As mentioned previously the whole question of ignoring certain inappropriate behaviour is a delicate one, and not always advisable as far as the beginning teacher is concerned. Wheldall and Merrett (1989) elaborate on this point:

… ignoring is often more difficult for teachers and is frequently misunderstood. It refers only to the behaviours governed by the rules and does not mean that teachers should not intervene if a fight breaks out or if pupils are about to do something dangerous. The idea is to avoid responding to rule-related misbehaviours since to do so may be counterproductive if the pupils involved find any form of teacher attention rewarding. It also detracts from the overal positive approach. (p. 75)

Wheldall and Merrett (1987, 1988) have produced two training packages called BATPACK and BATSAC for school based in-service training in the Positive Teaching approach. These are designed to develop teaching skills related to effective rule setting, 'catching them good' or finding appropriate times for praise, observing the most common class behaviour problems and concentrating on positive rather than negative strategies to bring about changes in behaviour.

In the teaching of physical education, Hellison (Hellison, 1985; Hellison and Templin, 1991) has designed a system to help pupils develop, understand and practise self-control and self-responsibility. The Hellison system is therefore an intrinsic motivation system, based on the premise that pupils do want to get on well with others and take responsibility for their own behaviour, rather than always relying upon the teacher to praise good behaviour.

The Hellison system is also based on the view that pupils go through developmental phases that may correspond to discipline and motivational problems. The framework put forward by Hellison, and shown in Box 12, is designed to help teachers to appreciate not only why certain management strategies work for certain pupils and not others, but also to be able to plan accordingly. The framework takes the form of a set of hierachically arranged levels of self-responsibility. However, as all pupils are individuals, not all will go through each level of development at the same pace, and therefore individual pupil progression cannot always be clear cut.

---

**Box 12**
**The levels of self-responsibility within Hellison's Humanistic approach to Physical Education**

**Level 0 – Irresponsibility** describes students who are unmotivated and undisciplined. Their behaviour includes discrediting or making fun of other students' involvement or interrupting, intimidating, manipulating, and verbally or physically abusing other students or the teacher.

**Level 1 – Self-Control** describes students who may not participate or show much mastery or improvement, but they are able to control their behaviour enough so that they don't interfere with other students' right to learn or the teachers' right to teach.

**Level 2 – Involvement** describes students who not only show self-control, but are involved in the subject matter, and willingly accept challenges and practise motor skills.

**Level 3 – Self-responsibility** describes students who not only show self-control and involvement but are also able to work without direct supervision, eventually taking responsibility for their intentions and actions. They can identify their own needs and begin to plan and execute their own physical education programmes.

**Level 4 – Caring** describes students who are motivated to extend their sense of responsibility by co-operating, giving support, showing concern, and helping.

*Source: Hellison (1985) pp. 6–7.*

---

Hellison's 'Humanistic approach' is based on his work with 'delinquency-prone' young people in which he used physical education as a medium for the personal and social development of his charges through enhancement of their self-esteem, self-understanding, and self-responsibility, as well as the development of interpersonal skills. Except for Hellison's own work with disaffected young people, there is little research evidence of the scheme's value in the teaching of PE in schools. However, Smith (1990) has attempted to use this approach in the development of self-responsibility with a class of 20 pupils aged between 11 and 13 years, using a three-week unit of PE consisting of fifteen 40 minute lessons. As with all discipline strategies, the model had to be clearly explained to the pupils. They were also given typed copies of the levels of responsibility, and had the different types of behaviour explained to them with the aim of encouraging the pupils to 'strive' to work at the 'caring' level (Level 4) in their physical education lesson. Next, the pupils were given a personal contract adapted from Hellison's (1978) version, which involved the pupils in planning a personal activity programme. During the teaching of the unit Smith used the following strategies recommended by Hellison (1985) to promote higher levels of self-responsibility in his pupils:

(1) referring to the levels of self-responsibility during a 'teachable moment';
(2) modelling the levels through one's own attitudes and behaviours;
(3) reinforcing appropriate behaviours;
(4) giving pupils time to reflect on their own attitudes and behaviours;
(5) encouraging pupils to share their thoughts and opinions on some aspect of the programme. (p. 30)

The author concluded that the pupils that began the work at a lower level (0, 1, 2), did achieve higher levels (3 and 4), that pupils did improve on their levels of self-esteem and self-understanding because they had to hold themselves accountable for their own success and failure, and that, resources permitting, this Humanistic approach was workable in the 'normal' school setting.

The work of Underwood (Underwood and Williams, 1991), also supports the use of collaborative, peer tutoring and reciprocal teaching strategies for pupil personal and social development, and, in particular, the notion of giving pupils the responsibility for helping each other acquire physical skills. Such approaches may help pupils to develop an appropriate social attitude towards their school work by establishing a cooperative, supportive and positive learning ethos and environment.

As discussed earlier in this chapter, the creation of a positive learning environment in which pupils respect and support other pupils, pupils respect and cooperate with teachers, and teachers respect and understand the feelings of pupils, is seen by many teachers as being part of a long-term class management and discipline strategy. The effective teacher may use a variety of strategies to achieve this.

### The effective class manager

The effective classroom manager is capable of maintaining an effective learning environment by developing the teaching skills discussed in this chapter and Chapter 6. Good and Brophy (1991) and Silverman (1991) in their reviews of the literature agree that effective teachers:

- take account of pupil developmental characteristics when designing learning experiences, and match pupil ability levels to the task to ensure appropriate levels of success for pupils;
- plan for preventative management by establishing structured management routines that pupils learn and become accustomed to;
- create a positive, supportive and business-like classroom climate through the planning of interesting lessons, allowing pupils to share in decision making, and providing pupils with greater opportunities to learn and achieve within a warm and enjoyable learning environment;
- make task expectations and management routines clear to pupils through effective communication;
- present material and task requirements in such a way that pupils understand the concepts to be learned and what is required of them;
- organise and manage classes to ensure maximum opportunities for learning;
- monitor pupil activity and progress to ensure pupil's are 'on task', and also hold pupils accountable for their own learning and completion of tasks;
- use positive rather than coercive management styles.

In conclusion, it is interesting to compare the aforementioned skills of effective class managers with Wragg's (1993) summary of the literature on pupil's views of their preferred teacher. In general, pupils seem to prefer teachers who:

- are slightly strict, but not over-severe or permissive;
- are fair in their use of rewards and punishments;
- treat them as individuals;
- are interesting and provide a variety of stimulating work;
- are friendly and good humoured, but not sarcastic;
- explain things clearly.

We have a lot to live up to – but it's nice to know what the customer expects of us!

# CHAPTER 8

# Teaching styles and teaching strategies

## Introduction: What is a teaching style and what is a teaching strategy?

In Chapter 4 it was suggested that one of the characteristics and skills of effective teachers of physical education included having a repertoire of teaching styles and knowing how and when to use them to facilitate pupil learning and understanding.

HMI (DES 1985) have supported this belief in that they consider that 'good' teachers need: '... a variety of approaches and patterns of working and the flexibility to call on several different strategies within the space of one lesson'. (p. 4) ... and be capable of: '... a skilful matching of teaching style to pupil's needs and ability'. (p. 6)

Also, the DFE (1992) see the competencies required of newly qualified teachers including the ability to: 'employ a range of teaching strategies appropriate to the age, ability, and attainment level of pupils'. (para. 2.3.4)

These quotations illustrate the importance attached to the need for teachers to develop a repertoire of teaching styles. They also show that terms such as 'teaching style', 'teaching strategy' and 'teaching approach' may be used interchangeably in the literature, thus leading to a degree of confusion on the part of teachers concerning their real meaning.

What then, is a teaching style?

In his classic text, *Teaching Physical Education*, Mosston (Mosston and Ashworth, 1986) refers to 'landmark' teaching styles that may be used in the teaching of physical education. The basis, or 'anatomy' of each style is the result of three sets of decisions made by the teacher: decisions made before the lesson related to the planning of curricular and managerial issues; decisions made during the lesson concerning the actual delivery or implementation of the lesson; and decisions made during and after performance of the task concerned with evaluation of performance. Therefore, according to Mosston, teaching style refers to the teacher's decision making, delivery and evaluation of an episode of teaching.

Mosston believes that personal idiosyncracies are not part of a teaching 'style', but Siedentop (1991) disagrees and provides the following definition of a teaching style:

Teaching style refers to the instructional and managerial climate for teaching; it is often most easily seen through the teacher's interactions. The climate for teaching can range from clearly negative to clearly positive with a neutral climate in the middle. Teachers can be 'upbeat' or 'laid back'. They can be frequent interactors or infrequent interactors. They can be very challenging or very supportive, or even both at the same time. Students experience a teacher's 'style' through the interactions the teacher has with the class as a whole, with groups and with individuals. The blending of these many interactional features produces each teacher's distinctive style. Terms such as 'warm', 'caring', 'businesslike', 'demanding', 'aloof', and the like are used to describe teaching styles. (p. 228)

Siedentop appears to suggest that a confusion may exist between the term teaching 'style' put forward by Mosston, and 'instructional format', the latter being: '... the different ways teachers organise the delivery of instruction and, particularly, how the student role changes as a result of the changing format'. (p. 228)

Other research workers in the field of pedagogy have suggested other interpretations of the term teaching 'style'. Two of the major studies of teaching styles in the United Kingdom investigating science teaching (Eggleston, Galton and Jones, 1976) and primary school teaching (Galton, Simon and Croll, 1980) emphasized the notion of teaching 'strategy' within their concept of teaching 'style'. The idea of a teaching 'strategy' was first put forward by Taba and Elzey (1964) and developed further by Strasser (1967). According to Taba a 'strategy' involves a teacher's attempts to translate aims into practice, but Strasser actually identified the different strategic decisions that teachers might make before and during lessons to implement strategies. These strategic decisions may include curriculum decisions concerning what to teach, instructional decisions concerning how to teach, and organisational decisions related to the management of learning.

During the process of teaching these strategies are implemented through 'transactions' taking place between teacher and pupils, which Galton and his colleagues (Galton *et al.*, 1980) refer to as teaching 'tactics'. Teaching 'tactics' may have, for example, a class control, personal and social, or cognitive function. According to both studies (Eggleston *et al.*, 1976; Galton *et al.*, 1980), when a teacher begins to use a consistent set of teaching tactics, then this is considered to be their 'teaching style'.

In another study of primary teaching by Bennett (1978), the term teaching 'style' was largely based on descriptions of the organisational and curricular strategies used by the teacher, with little reference to teaching 'tactics'.

The following two chapters are concerned with the various teaching approaches that a physical education teacher may use to achieve his objectives for a particular teaching episode or lesson, and the teaching skills, transactions or tactics that may be needed to implement that teaching approach. This will include an examination of the teacher's curricular, instructional and organisational decisions, and the teacher-pupil, pupil-teacher, and pupil-pupil interactions that cement the overall teaching approach. According to Eggleston et al (1976), Galton et al (1980) and Mosston and Ashworth (1986) we are probably referring to teaching 'style', but Siedentop (1991) may prefer to use the term 'instructional format'. In this text the terms teaching 'strategy' and teaching 'approach' will be used because the former is the term used by the Department for Education (DFE, 1992) in their document Circular 9/92, in which they refer to the competencies expected of newly qualified teachers, and the latter is used in physical education National Curriculum documents (CCW, 1992).

Whatever term we are using to describe the way the teacher transforms aims into practice, the ability of the teacher to use a variety of teaching approaches and the 'skills' or 'tactics' to implement them effectively, appears to be necessary in order to achieve the objectives laid down in the National Curriculum end of key stage descriptions and cross-curricular guidelines (NCC, 1990; 1992) The language used in the Order makes it clear that pupils should be offered the opportunity to 'compare' and 'make judgements', 'analyse', 'review', 'describe', 'refine', 'adapt', 'interpret', 'plan', 'design and evaluate', in order to develop the knowledge, skills and understanding through planning, performing and evaluating their own and others work. As one National Curriculum document points out (CCW, 1992), pupils will need to become: '... more self-reliant and achieve greater independence in their mode of working'. (p. 50)

In addition to learning and performing physical skills pupils are now expected to think much more about their work, develop language, communication, problem solving, decision making and personal and social skills (NCC, 1990). Consequently, a variety of teaching approaches may be required to achieve these objectives, and the selection of an appropriate approach is very much a matching of teaching strategy with intended learning outcomes or lesson objectives. But, this is not the only issue to take into account when choosing a teaching approach.

## Factors influencing the selection of a teaching strategy

There are four main factors that should be considered when selecting a teaching strategy (Williams, 1993; Siedentop, 1991):

- *intended learning outcomes* and lesson objectives
- *the learner*
  - preferred learning style;
  - previous experience of different teaching approaches;
  - stage of learning the activity;
  - standard of behaviour.
- the *content* of the lesson
- the *context* of the teaching situation in terms of facilities and possible safety issues.

The key issue concerning selection of an appropriate teaching approach is that it should 'match' your objectives for the course, lesson or episode of teaching. This means that even within the same lesson one might intend to achieve different objectives by using different teaching approaches in sequence throughout the lesson, or organising pupils in a group work situation in which different teaching strategies may be experienced. In this way the teacher can mix or 'blend' different teaching strategies to suit particular learning outcomes, pupils' learning style or previous experience, as Joyce and Weil (1986) point out:

Very few models of teaching alone are sufficient to define an entire curriculum, although one can serve as the core. Most models can be strengthened by being combined with a variety of others, both to be more effective in achieving any given set of desired learning outcomes and to increase stimulation and variety. Effects can be increased by an artful pyramiding of the power of several models. (p. 404)

A major consideration when selecting a teaching approach is whether or not it will suit all pupils in terms of their preferred learning style, previous experience of different teaching approaches, their stage of learning the activity, or their standard of behaviour.

The literature concerning pupil learning styles is in its infancy but there are one or two interesting pieces of research information of value to teachers.

Conceptual systems theory developed by Hunt and his colleagues (Harvey, Hunt and Schroder, 1961; Schroder, Driver and Streufert, 1967), suggests that teachers should shape their teaching strategies to match the learner's personality and stage of information processing. When a teaching strategy is matched to a learner's conceptual level then learning is more likely to occur. However, additional factors such as the learner's motivational and value orientation (or beliefs), and their preferred sensory orientation (some may learn more effectively through certain sensory modalities), may need to be considered by the teacher. The research suggests that individuals may have a low, moderate or high complexity in terms of their information processing system, and that certain learning environments or teaching strategies may suit different levels of complexity. For example, individuals of a low conceptual complexity may be better suited to learning environments having a high 'structure', such as lecture, direct instruction and learning from teacher presentations. Those of high complexity, being capable of generating new concepts and different learning perspectives, might 'thrive' within teaching approaches of low structure, such as non-directive teaching strategies in which the teacher acts more as a facilitator, and the pupils have greater responsibility for their own learning (Joyce and Weil, 1986, p. 451).

In the research looking at how learners respond to unfamiliar teaching strategies, Joyce and Weil (1986) cite research which indicates that if pupils are matched to teaching strategies that do not suit their level of complexity, learners not only tend to show 'discomfort' with the learning environment, but also they may 'pull' their teachers towards their preferred learning style. In other words, if they preferred a more independent learning environment they were noticeably uncomfortable with a highly structured teaching strategy. Although the researchers recognised that those learners who felt most discomfort in mismatched learning environments should have their learning environment matched to their preferred style to avoid frustration and poor learning, they were largely of the opinion that teachers should attempt to mismatch learner and environment deliberately in order to challenge the learner's conceptual system, thus allowing them to move towards a more advanced form of information processing. The suggestion is, that if pupils are exposed to new forms of teaching and learning, they will be able to develop intellectually, as Joyce and Weil (1986) point out: 'To help students grow we need to generate what we currently term a "dynamic disequilibrium". Rather than matching teaching approaches to students in such a way as to minimise discomfort, our task is to expose the students to new teaching modalities that will, for some time, be uncomfortable to them.' (p. 440)

In the world of teaching physical skills as opposed to intellectual skills, there is evidence that individual differences in learning related to perceptual or cognitive style do exist (Witkin, Moore, Goodenough and Cox, 1977; Bakker et al., 1990), and therefore skill learning may be affected by the teaching strategy selected by the teacher. However, there is a dearth of research relating cognitive style to learning environment.

In the teaching of gymnastics in schools, Williams (1993) believes that particular teaching strategies may suit certain pupils and not others as:

... there are pupils who like to be given the answer and work towards it and who dislike unknown expectations. Others like to discover new ideas for themselves and dislike teacher oriented classrooms, repetition and drills. Some dislike individual work with no student interaction, while others dislike group projects. The fact that a single approach is thus unlikely to maximise learning opportunities for all pupils is a further reason for using a range of teaching styles rather than relying upon a single approach. (p. 31)

Williams also believes that a pupil's previous experience of different teaching strategies is an important factor when choosing a teaching approach, particularly when the teacher is trying to offer pupils opportunities to take responsibility for their own learning and make decisions for themselves:

> If I ask pupils to move equipment with a minimum of intervention from me, in a school where they are used to being closely supervised and directed in all aspects of school life, it is more than likely that they will be unable, in the first instance, to cope with the additional freedom and responsibility. If I have done this against my better judgement, then my reaction is likely to be that I knew all along that it wouldn't work and I have just proved it. What I have actually done of course is asked the pupils to do something for which they are not ready, not something of which they are not capable. In order to enable them to work more independently, I will need to introduce the approach more gradually than would be necessary in an environment where personal responsibility was a high priority throughout the school. (p. 31)

Siedentop (1991) considers that other learner characteristics need to be taken into account when selecting a teaching strategy, including the learner's previous experience in the activity. For example, a teacher might approach the teaching of an activity differently if the pupils were beginners compared with advanced performers, or if they were children with special educational needs such as those with a physical handicap or behavioural problems.

The content of the activity being taught may also influence the choice of teaching approach, as might the issue of safety. A more direct teaching approach may be seen to be necessary when introducing potentially dangerous activities such as certain gymnastic movements, rock climbing, or when teaching pupils to throw the javelin in athletics. However, a more indirect approach may be used when, for example, introducing basic ball handling skills. Also, introducing the basic skills of an invasion game such as rugby may be approached differently from the teaching of more advanced tactics and principles of play.

The teaching context may also influence the choice of teaching strategy, and this might include the availability of facilities and equipment, or safety issues. For example, a limited number of rings and backboards for teaching a particular shot in basketball may mean that a group practice strategy is more appropriate as opposed to a teaching approach in which pupils work in pairs coaching each other.

Siedentop (1991) would also add that the personal preference and skills of the teacher is an influence on the choice of teaching approach:

> Some teachers feel more comfortable with some formats rather than others. Personal preference is a legitimate factor in the teacher's choice of which format to adopt, especially when that preference derives from a professional belief in the validity of a format. Teachers no doubt tend to perform better

when they work from a format that they believe to be effective, one with which they are comfortable. (pp. 226–7)

However, while taking this latter point into account, one might argue that the teacher has a moral and professional obligation to offer pupils what are considered to be the best possible circumstances for learning, and to attempt to develop their cognitive, physical, problem solving, communication and personal and social skills. This may require the teacher to use teaching approaches that they are not comfortable with, but are necessary for the effective delivery of the National Curriculum for Physical Education.

## Building a repertoire of teaching strategies and teaching skills

In addition to the range of teaching 'models' available to all teachers (Joyce and Weil, 1986), there are a variety of teaching strategies that have been used by physical education teachers over the years, each approach being designed with particular objectives in mind. Also, for each teaching strategy to be effective and achieve its objectives, a 'bonding' of curricular, instructional and organisational decisions with appropriate teaching skills and 'tactics' may be necessary. For example, a teaching strategy based on questioning may only be effective if the teacher is capable of asking the appropriate questions at the appropriate time. A teaching approach requiring clear presentation of new material to pupils means that the teacher must be capable of an accurate presentation, possibly in the form of a demonstration.

Sometimes teachers have decided to try out a new teaching strategy without being aware of the need to acquire new teacher-pupil interaction skills that form the basis of the new teaching approach. Too often those advocating new and innovative teaching strategies have purely provided the teacher with the philosophy underpinning the new approach, and have not offered sufficient guidance to the teacher concerning the teaching skills and tactics needed to implement the new strategy successfully. The point being made here is that different teaching strategies may have their own specific teaching skills or tactics linked to them, or a modified version of a skill primarily used in another teaching approach.

Teaching strategies may fall into two broad categories:

(1) Direct teaching strategies, including:
- Command
- Practice
(2) Teaching strategies for greater pupil involvement in the learning process and the development of cross-curricular skills, including:
- Pupil self-appraisal strategies;

- Peer support and collaborative strategies;
- Teaching strategies for the development of higher order cognitive processes.

The following two chapters will examine each of these teaching strategies in turn, and their associated teaching skills and tactics. These teaching approaches are not necessarily exclusive, and an effective teacher is likely to display the ability to switch and mix styles to suit her objectives. As objectives for learning vary within a lesson or episode of teaching, the effective teacher will move between different teaching strategies and the use of the appropriate teaching skills and tactics related to each approach. One should not, therefore, view these different teaching approaches as necessarily a way of teaching a particular lesson or unit of work. The teacher must, therefore, begin by deciding what she wishes to achieve and then choose the best approach to realise those objectives.

# CHAPTER 9

# Direct teaching strategies and teaching skills

## What is direct teaching?

As the term implies, 'direct teaching' involves the teacher in telling or showing pupils what to do, directly supervising their progress and then evaluating their achievements. The teacher selects the content, designs the progression and communicates the task. To physical educators such as Rink (1985), this approach is termed 'interactive teaching', to Siedentop (1991), 'active teaching', and it is known to many PE teachers as 'traditional teaching'.

Direct teaching has been one of the most popular models of teaching used in all aspects of education for many years, and as 'direct instruction' (Rosenshine, 1979), or 'explicit instuction' (Rosenshine and Stevens, 1986), it has considerable empirical support as a model of effective teaching (Housner, 1990).

But, what is direct instruction? According to Housner (1990) the basic components of direct instruction are:

- set clear goals and make sure pupils understand them;
- present a sequence of well organised tasks;
- give pupils clear, concise explanations of the subject matter including liberal use of demonstrations and illustrations;
- ask frequent questions in order to check pupils' understanding of the presentation and then re-teach if necessary;
- give pupils frequent opportunities to succeed in tasks and make feedback available.

In addition, Housner's (1990) review of direct instruction models suggests that the following teaching skills and tactics are also at the heart of a direct instruction strategy:

- designing learning experiences that are progressive, motivating and promote success;
- making the purpose of the lesson clear to pupils and how it relates to previous lessons or activities;
- provide guided and independent practice with diagnosis of errors

through observation and questioning and appropriate feedback to enable pupils to progress;
- provide a supportive climate with high, realistic expectations and pupils made accountable for their work;
- provide end of lesson reviews.

Direct teaching is also about teachers making most of the decisions about the learning environment with little opportunity for decision making on the part of the learner. The teacher selects the content, designs the progression, communicates the task and evaluates progress.

However, there are different forms of direct teaching. Mosston (Mosston and Ashworth, 1986) has identified a continuum, or 'spectrum' of teaching approaches (referred to as 'styles') ranging from the more direct to the less direct. A teaching approach is placed more to the indirect end of the continuum if it offers greater decision-making opportunities for pupils concerning lesson content, topic, structure of learning environment, equipment, and evaluation of learning. At the direct end of the continuum are what Mosston terms the 'command' and 'practice' styles of teaching which provide very little opportunity for decision making on the part of the learner.

## Teaching by command

Mosston's 'command' style entails the teacher making all of the decisions concerning the content of the lesson and the learner or group imitating exactly what the teacher presents to them, and possibly responding as a group. You may wish to use this approach if your objectives for a teaching episode are concerned with:

- safety, discipline, conformity, uniformity and immediate response or replication of the teacher's model precisely and accurately;
- a synchronised response;
- efficient use of time for acquiring skills.

Teaching by command may not be considered to be appropriate for lesson objectives that are related to pupils' cognitive development, or for the development of pupils' ability to plan, evaluate or communicate. Also, the command style offers little opportunity for differentiation in mixed ability teaching situations. However, this approach may be suitable for working towards National Curriculum objectives concerned with being taught formally 'how to prepare for and recover from specific activity', and 'to perform set dances'. This approach may also be appropriate in the early stages of 'being taught the techniques and skills of outdoor and adventurous activities', certain athletic throwing events such as javelin and discus, and the teaching of other high-risk physical activities where safety is paramount. Such activities as aerobics, formal (e.g. ballet) and folk dances, and certain martial arts and self-defence activities are commonly taught using a command teaching strategy.

### 'Practice' teaching strategies

Many feel that Mosston's practice style is the most commonly used strategy for teaching physical education. When using a practice teaching strategy the teacher still makes most of the decisions concerning lesson objectives and content (including repetitions and time allocated to practice), roles of the teacher and learner, task presentation, choice of general work area, pupil assessment and evaluation; but the pupils may be allowed to make decisions concerning the choice of specific practice area. Mosston believes that there is a shift in nine decision-making aspects of the learning situation from teacher to pupil when a teacher uses the practice approach compared with teaching by command. These nine areas include: posture, location, order of tasks, starting time of tasks, pace and rhythm, stopping time of task, interval, attire and appearance, and initiating questions for clarification. This shift in decision making from teacher to pupil is what Mosston refers to as the first stage in the individualisation process leading towards total pupil independence and responsibility for the learning process. However, one must realise that each of Mosston's styles of teaching are 'landmark' styles, meaning that there can be variations or modifications to each of the styles. Therefore, a teacher may or may not allow pupils to make all of the decisions that the landmark style suggests. For example, the teacher may wish to allocate specific work areas, to make decisions concerning when to start and when to finish an activity, and to increase the pace of the activity. The teacher may also wish to make decisions concerning safe and appropriate attire!

A teacher may choose this teaching strategy if the objectives for a teaching episode include:

- to practise an assigned task as demonstrated or explained by the teacher;
- to help learners become aware of the relationship between time practising a task and proficiency or quality of outcome or performance;
- to help learners become aware of the importance of feedback from the teacher being associated with improved performance;
- to make learners accountable for appropriate use of their practice time according to the objectives of the episode and the expectations of the teacher.

According to Mosston, one can increase the efficiency of the practice strategy by using a task sheet. A task sheet may keep pupils on-task for a longer period of time. The purpose of a task sheet is to:

(i) help the learner to remember the task in terms of what to do and how to do it, thus 'freeing' the teacher from repeated explanations;

(ii) help the learner to follow written instructions;

(iii) facilitate the recording of pupil progress.

To be effective, task sheets need to contain specific information about what to do and how to do it (such as clear and concise explanations and specific teaching points for successful performance), and should, ideally, include an illustration of the sequences of the movement leading up to the completion of the task. Mosston believes that the task sheet should also contain details of:

- the number of repetitions or length of time for practising the task;
- a means of recording progress (e.g. number of successful attempts out of a total number of attempts);
- teacher and pupil feedback comments concerning the performance.

Box 13 provides an example of a task sheet recommended by Mosston for use in the teaching of basketball shooting and dribbling.

Task sheets may be used in a modification of the practice style known as 'task' or 'station' teaching. This is really an organisational framework that allows continuous practice for groups of pupils working on different tasks at the same time. It is a particularly useful strategy to use when facilities or equipment limit the teaching of a particular task, as in the case of a teacher only having a small gym available with only two backboards for basketball shooting practice. The arrangements for station teaching as shown in Figure 8 might then be used.

Station teaching is also appropriate for the teaching of health and fitness work such as weight training and exercise circuits, and for skills circuits related to particular games activities. In teaching these activities using a station teaching approach the teacher may present (explain and demonstrate) the different tasks at the beginning of the teaching episode so that everyone knows what to do and how to do it, and then provide posters or task cards to aid practice. Generally, only skills that have already been taught and practised are appropriate for station teaching, but a modification of this approach is to use one station to teach a new skill. In this case the role of the teacher is to present the new material and guide the practice at this station, while at the same time keeping an 'eye' on what is happening at other stations, and providing appropriate feedback from afar.

**Box 13**
**Task sheet for the teaching of Basketball shooting and dribbling**

Perform each task as described in the programme below and place a check next to the completed task

| Tasks | Dates | | | | | | Teacher's Feedback |
|---|---|---|---|---|---|---|---|
| **A. Shooting** | | | | | | | |
| 1. Set shots—foul line    25 shots | | | | | | | |
| 2. Set shots—45° angle left of basket    25 shots | | | | | | | |
| 3. Set shots—45° angle right of basket    25 shots | | | | | | | |
| 4. One-hand shot—foul line    25 shots | | | | | | | |
| 5. One-hand shot—right side of basket    15 shots | | | | | | | |
| 6. One-hand shot—left side of basket    15 shots | | | | | | | |
| 7. Jump shot—from centre, left and right. Do 15 shots from each side—foul line distance | | | | | | | |
| 8. Repeat No. 7 from greater distance | | | | | | | |
| **B. Dribbling** | | | | | | | |
| 1. Right hand—width of gym    6 times | | | | | | | |
| 2. Left hand—width of gym    6 times | | | | | | | |
| 3. Around obstacle course    10 times | | | | | | | |
| 4. Dribbling sideways— width of gym    6 times | | | | | | | |
| 5. Dribbling backward— width of gym    6 times | | | | | | | |
| 6. Zig-zag dribbling around the obstacles in area 4    10 times | | | | | | | |

*Source: Mosston and Ashworth (1986) p. 42–3.*

The teacher is also responsible for deciding on the time allocation for all stations and in organising the movement of pupils between stations. It may be necessary to ask pupils if they understand what to do before signalling the start of practice at each new station. It is also important that the selected station tasks take about the same amount of time to complete and are self-motivating, otherwise management problems may occur.

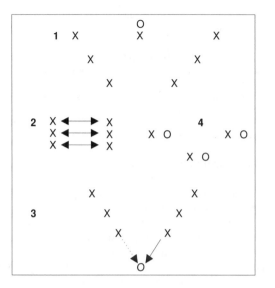

**Key: 1** Set shot pepper pot practice

**2** Chest pass practice in pairs

**3** File lay up shot practice

**4** Practice of protected dribble in pairs

*Figure 8    Station teaching for basketball using a small gym*

One disadvantage of station teaching occurs when the teacher is actually teaching a new skill at one station and is therefore unable to observe and offer frequent feedback to individual pupils or groups working at other stations. However, if this teaching approach is combined with Mosston's self-check style (in which pupils record their own progress and self-appraise their personal skill levels), or the reciprocal style (in which pupils provide each other with learning support and feedback), then this disadvantage may be partially overcome. In fact, for station teaching to work well there needs to be a clearly defined accountability system other than the overall supervision of the teacher, and preferably one that offers incentives, such as the accumulation of points for individuals and groups. All the same, even with this type of scoring system, the teacher has to ensure that pupils are disciplined and honest in their approach to the work, otherwise limited 'quality' practise will occur.

In addition to the difficulty of monitoring quality of pupil practice and performance, some activities are more suited to station teaching than others, as Rink (1985) points out:

Some kinds of content work better than others in station teaching. In most school situations limited provisions for task communications make new or complex skills difficult to work with in a station teaching format. Process-oriented tasks, such as those emphasising form, are difficult to communicate and to establish accountability systems for. Individual self-testing and product-oriented tasks without a great need for development (extension or refinement) usually are the most successful. (p. 200)

The station format does have the advantage of allowing the teacher to set up a work area before the lesson, and it does offer the teacher the time to give personal attention to those pupils having difficulties while the rest of the class continue to work.

The practice teaching strategy may satisfy the National Curriculum requirements for 'practice and performing', 'being taught how to prepare for particular activities and recover afterwards', and pupils being taught 'to extend the skills learned in earlier years to develop techniques applicable to a variety of games'. This approach also allows for 'refining' a skill, and in some cases 'adaptation, understanding and evaluation', if pupils are allowed some element of choice.

It is thought that one of the main difficulties with the station teaching approach is the design of progression within stations. Therefore, free-standing tasks that are not part of a progression are generally recommended. However, with modification the practice teaching strategy may offer differentiated activity to suit different abilities. This may take the form of differentiated tasks for certain groups of pupils at different stations using appropriate task cards. Williams (1993) describes how this can be done in the teaching of handstands and forward rolls in gymnastics: 'Instead of practising handstands as a class activity pupils can be asked to practise their choice of a limited range of options which go from trying to take their weight on their hands for a second, maybe using a wall as support, to, at the other extreme, trying to take weight on hands from a two foot take off into an inverted balance.' (p. 30)

Williams suggests that forward rolls: '… can be differentiated by offering a choice of finishing positions which make different demands, for example ending in a long sitting position, or in a 'V' sit position or in box splits position'. (p. 30)

If the teacher wishes to extend the opportunities for pupils to work at their own level, and progress in small achievable stages towards a given skill or movement, then work stations with task cards might offer gradations of practices building up to the final skill or movement. According to Mosston (Mosston and Ashworth, 1986), when a teacher uses this differentiated modification of the practice style then they are actually using the 'inclusion' style of teaching. This is particularly the case if the pupil is able to make a decision concerning the stage at which they enter the learning situation. In Mosston's inclusion style of teaching the pupil chooses the degree of task difficulty, while the teacher makes all the decisions concerning content, presentation and evaluation. However, in adapting aspects of Mosston's inclusion style to a more differentiated form of the practice style, the teacher does not in fact always allow the learner to choose at which stage to enter the learning process. Research has shown (Goldberger, Gerney and Chamberlain, 1982; Goldberger and Gerney, 1986), that it is easy for pupils to make inappropriate decisions concerning the level of difficulty at which they should be entering the skill learning situation. Therefore, a more differentiated form of the practice style would require the teacher to guide the learner into the most appropriate practice level of difficulty, or, at least, be 'on hand' to see that the pupil appreciates what might be an appropriate level.

A differentiated form of the practice style may include the use of the station teaching format with task cards or posters illustrating clearly the different levels of progression.

The addition of a more differentiated aspect to the practice style means that the following objectives may be achieved when using this format, which we might term 'differentiated practice':

- individual differences in ability levels are accommodated;
- pupils involvement and success at an appropriate level of difficulty is maximised;
- pupils have the opportunity to establish realistic aspirations in terms of their personal progress;
- progress is individualised.

What Williams (1993) refers to as 'teaching through limitation' is similar to 'differentiated practice'. It involves the learner in making decisions about the level at which to enter the learning situation, and it helps the learner to understand which task is more difficult and why. Examples of tasks suggested by Williams for the teaching of gymnastics in this way include the following: 'Choose a shoulder balance, a headstand or a handstand and practise it'. 'Practise headstands either with your legs tucked, or going from a tuck to straight legs, or lifting up with your legs straight throughout'. 'Now roll either forwards or backwards finishing either in a straddle position or on two knees'.

The practice teaching strategy may also cater for social objectives, although many would argue that more direct teaching approaches offer little opportunity for such outcomes. Even when pupils are practising a gymnastic movement together they have to cooperate in the sharing of a mat, and groups of pupils may need to work together when practising either a group skill (e.g. scrummaging in rugby), or an individual skill at a practice station. The National Curriculum (SCAA, 1994b) requires that: 'To develop positive attitudes, pupils should be taught: (a)· to observe the conventions of fair play, honest competition and good sporting behaviour as individual participants, team members and spectators'. (p. 2) 'be taught the rules, laws and scoring systems specific to different games'. (p. 6)

In terms of these National Curriculum objectives, Goldberger and Howarth (1993) would argue that the practice strategy would be appropriate for teaching the learner to understand and apply certain rules, and then practise them in a game, followed by appropriate feedback from the teacher.

As with all teaching strategies, effective direct teaching involves more than just content, curricular and organisational decisions by the teacher. Certain teaching 'skills' or 'tactics' are necessary for the effective delivery of the various approaches or forms of direct teaching.

There are three categories of teaching skills for the effective use of direct teaching approaches, and which are equally applicable to other teaching strategies, albeit often in modified form:

- presentation skills – creating interest and gaining pupil attention;
  – clarity of communication;
- observation skills;
- guidance and feedback skills.

## Teaching skills for effective direct teaching: Presentation skills

Effective teachers present new material by explaining new concepts and tasks clearly to pupils using certain communication skills. The teaching skills and tactics needed to present material effectively include:

(i)  Creating interest and gaining pupil attention;
(ii) Clarity of communication.

### (i) Creating interest and gaining pupil attention

Whatever the teaching approach being used for pupils to attend to the teacher's presentation, they need to be interested in the material being offered. This may depend upon how the teacher makes the material interesting and the relevance of the material to anything previously learned. Making the material interesting involves the teacher showing interest in it ... in other words, being enthusiastic about it, as Good and Brophy (1991) point out: 'When teachers are enthusiastic about the subject matter students are likely to pay attention and develop enthusiasm of their own'. (p. 472)

Although not strictly a 'teaching skill' (more an attribute or aspect of personality), enthusiasm was mentioned by most of the teachers, lecturers and advisers in the TEPE Project as an essential teaching skill for an effective teacher of PE. As one HOD mentioned: 'Enthusiasm ties in with presence. Perhaps *the* most important part of the job is enthusing young people about PE!'

The research literature also provides some evidence to support the view that teacher enthusiasm may be positively associated with teacher effectiveness and pupil achievement both in classrooms (Rosenshine, 1970; Berliner and Tickunoff, 1976; Rosenshine and Furst, 1973), and, although the evidence is inconclusive, in physical education settings (Carlisle and Phillips, 1984). There have been some negative findings and criticism of the physical education research since 1970 (Behets, 1991), and this has been largely concerned with problems of definition, measurement and the difficulties of manipulated rather than genuine enthusiasm. On the whole, most workers in the field of teacher effectiveness and practising teachers, would tend to agree that enthusiasm is an important part of a teacher's general 'presence', particularly when presenting new material.

'Set induction', or the ability to focus the learner's attention on what is to be learned by gaining their interest, is more likely to occur if the teacher is enthusiastic and interested in the subject matter. Pupils may then be inclined to model or imitate the teacher's interest in the activity.

Being enthusiastic is in fact a part of what has been termed 'varying the stimulus', an essential teaching skill for presenting new material. According to Perrott (1982), varying the stimulus: '... is based in learning theory which indicates that uniformity of the perceived environment tends to lead people into mental inactivity, while changes in the perceived environment attract the attention and stimulate mental activity'. (p. 28)

So, what really is enthusiasm? As it appears that PE teachers can be trained to be more enthusiastic (Carlisle and Phillips, 1984; Locke and Woods, 1982; Rolider *et al.*, 1984), then it may be possible to identify the components of this general teacher characteristic.

According to Good and Brophy (1991), there are two main aspects of enthusiasm:

- the ability to convey sincere interest in the subject (e.g. demonstration or modelling of the skill/movement to be learned);
- vigour and dynamics.

However, Good and Brophy are quick to point out that those teachers who don't have a dynamic voice and manner can compensate for this by using other techniques.

Two of the major attempts to identify the components of teacher enthusiasm in physical education were made by Rolider *et al.* (1984), and Behets (1991). Rolider asked 13 experts in teacher education, 100 teachers, and 245 pupils to write down what they thought were the visual and behavioural aspects of teacher enthusiasm. From their comments and descriptions Rolider and his colleagues identified the nine classes of enthusiastic behaviour shown in Box 14.

---

**Box 14**
**Definitions of Enthusiastic Behaviour in the teaching of Physical Education**

- Use of voice inflection – a large change in teacher's voice, volume or rate of speech.
- Use of gestures – movement of hands or arms linked with a verbal comment, also clapping hands, thumbs-up sign, etc.
- Smiling and laughing.
- Teacher modelling – demonstration.
- Use of physical contact – patting pupil on back, hand on shoulder, shaking hands.
- Hustling – verbal statements and gestures to initiate or increase the pace of pupil activity.
- Providing general positive feedback – e.g. 'Good try!'
- Providing specific positive feedback – positive statements mentioning some specific aspect of pupil motor or social performance, e.g. 'Good follow through Dave!'
- Use of positive prompts – general positive feedback followed by a prompt to correct some aspect of performance, e.g. 'Good effort, but try to hit through the middle of the ball next time'.

*Source: Rolider et al. (1984) pp. 48–9.*

---

In his study, Behets (1991) used an enthusiasm observation instrument to measure the enthusiasm of 17 physical education teachers. Behets rated teachers as displaying high, low or medium enthusiasm, and the descriptors for the seven items and three rating levels are shown in Box 15.

So, what exactly is enthusiasm? Good and Brophy (1991) sum up what has been included in the various descriptors of enthusiasm already discussed: '... qualities such as alertness, vigour, interest, and voice inflection are important. Enthusiastic teachers are alive in the room; they show surprise, suspense, joy and other feelings in their voices; they make material interesting to students by relating it to their

## Box 15
### Descriptors for the seven variables of Behet's Enthusiasm Observation Instrument

| ITEM | LOW | MEDIUM | HIGH |
|---|---|---|---|
| 1. Vocal intonation | Monotonous voice, minimum vocal inflection, little variation in speech, drones on & on & on | Pleasant variations of pitch, volume & speed | Great & sudden changes from rapid excited speech to a whisper. Varied lilting, uplifting intonation. Many changes in tone, pitch. |
| 2. Articulation | Poor articulation | Good articulation | Very good articulation |
| 3. Word selection | Mostly nouns, few descriptors/ adjectives | Some descriptors/adjectives or repetition of the same ones | Highly descriptive, many adjectives, great variety |
| 4. Encouragement | Little indication of encouragement, may ignore students | Some praises, but frequently repeats same ones | Quick and ready to praise and encourage with many variations |
| 5. Gestures | Seldom moves arms out or outstretched toward person or object. Never uses sweeping movements, kept arms at side or folded across body, appears rigid. | Often points with hand, using total arm. Occasionally makes sweeping motion using body, head, arms, face. Steady pace of gesturing is maintained. | Quick & demonstrative movements of body, head, arms, hands, face, sweeping motions, clapping hands, head nodding rapidly |
| 6. Body movements | Seldom moves from one spot or movement mainly from a sitting position to a standing position | Moves freely, slowly & steadily | Large body movements, swung around, walks rapidly, changes pace, unpredictable, energetic |
| 7. Overall energy level | Lethargic, appears inactive dull or sluggish | Some variations from high to low in appearing energetic demonstrative but mostly an even level is maintained | Exuberant. Maintains high degree of energy & vitality, highly demonstrative, great & sudden changes in voice, tone, pitch, eye, head, arm & body movements. |

*Source: Behets (1991) p. 52.*

experiences and showing that they themselves are interested in it'. (p. 473)

However, we all do things differently. We have our own way of showing interest in what we are teaching. No one would want to see all physical education teachers giving the impression that they are trying to sell ice-cream to eskimos, and as a result display a false and manufactured form of enthusiasm. Also, teachers have been known to be a bit 'over the top' when it comes to being enthusiastic or energetic, and this may have a negative effect on pupil attention and learning. Studies by McKinney *et al.* (1983) suggest that a medium level of enthusiasm is quite sufficient, and that high levels of enthusiasm may overstimulate young children at the primary level.

We do have our own individual way of displaying sincere enthusiasm and interest in what we are teaching, and when appraising teachers this needs to be taken into account. We have all known those teachers who have that something 'special' – who can 'light fires' in children's minds concerning the subject they are teaching. Such teachers may appear 'shy' and don't have what might be considered to be an 'outgoing' personality, yet they may constantly have pupils 'eating out of their hands' and always attentive. There is therefore an 'unknown' element within a teacher's overall 'presence', 'manner' and ability to create interest – enthusiasm may be part of this ability, and individual teachers will have their own way of doing this. You can't completely put your finger on it. It is just there! Maybe this really is where the 'art' and 'science' of teaching meet, and an individual 'flair' for creating interest is part of that artistry.

How effective are you at creating interest when presenting new material? Ask a colleague to observe you teach and give their opinion on the various aspects of creating interest listed in Exercises 5a and 5b below, by placing a tick in the appropriate column. Alternatively, videotape yourself and analyse the tape afterwards using these exercises.

*Exercise 5a   Creating interest when giving presentations*

|  | You are good at this | You need to work on this | You have your own way of doing this |
|---|---|---|---|
| Vocal intonation |  |  |  |
| Articulation |  |  |  |
| Word selection |  |  |  |
| Gestures |  |  |  |
| Facial expression and use of eyes |  |  |  |

*continued*

*Exercise 5a continued*

|  | You are good at this | You need to work on this | You have your own way of doing this |
| --- | --- | --- | --- |
| Body movements |  |  |  |
| Overall energy level |  |  |  |
| Modelling and demonstrations |  |  |  |
| Use of pupils' previous experience to create interest in the material |  |  |  |
| Use of anecdotes to create interest |  |  |  |

You have your own personal way of creating interest in the presentation – it includes

You created interest in the material by

*Exercise 5b   Creating interest during your teaching*

|  | You are good at this | You need to work on this | You have your own way of doing this |
| --- | --- | --- | --- |
| Vocal intonation |  |  |  |
| Articulation |  |  |  |
| Word selection |  |  |  |
| Gestures |  |  |  |
| Facial expressions and use of eyes |  |  |  |
| Encouragement |  |  |  |
| Body movements |  |  |  |

*continued*

*Exercise 5b continued*

|  | You are good at this | You need to work on this | You have your own way of doing this |
|---|---|---|---|
| Overall energy level |  |  |  |
| Smiling, humour, laughing |  |  |  |
| Hustling |  |  |  |
| Positive prompts |  |  |  |
| Positive feedback |  |  |  |
| Demonstrations |  |  |  |
| Use of anecdotes to create interest |  |  |  |

## (ii) Clarity of communication

There is a considerable amount of research evidence to support the view that teacher clarity is a major factor in teacher effectiveness, pupil learning and achievement (Cruickshank and Kennedy, 1986). But, what is teacher clarity? In reviewing the research on teacher effectiveness in relation to the presentation of material in classroom teaching, Good and Brophy (1991) report that the characteristics of effective teachers include the following:

- Effective teachers communicate lesson objectives, lesson presentation and instructions clearly, enthusiastically and concisely;
- Effective teachers explain work clearly and go over practical examples with pupils before releasing them to work independently.

In his review of research on teacher effectiveness in physical education, Silverman (1991) considers that effective teachers of PE: '... provide accurate and focused explanations and demonstrations'. (p. 358)

Therefore, there appears to be four main aspects of teacher clarity in the teaching of physical education:

- planning for clear presentations;
- explaining for clear understanding;
- demonstrating and communication of movement features;
- checking for understanding.

## Planning for clear presentations

As mentioned in Chapter 5, in the early stages of teaching it is important to 'think through' presentations thoroughly. This may involve writing out the task description in the lesson plan, and possibly even transcribing the same words that will be used with the pupils. This might include details of the task, organisational and management details of the activities chosen and possibly even details of how pupils might evaluate their performance of the task.

When planning a presentation it is also important to:

- match the task and learning experiences to the objectives of the teaching episode/lesson;
- match the material to the learner's present knowledge and past experience, and attempt to 'bridge' past experience to the new task/activity;
- structure the material so that the purpose and objectives of the teaching episode/lesson are made clear to the pupils;
- sequence the material in an order that the pupils will understand, working from the simple to the complex.

Drawing on the past experience of pupils and relating the new material to what has been learned previously helps pupils to use the new information more effectively. The appropriateness of any new task to pupils' previous experience is highlighted by Rink and Werner (1987). Tasks were considered inappropriate if:

(1) they were not related to previous tasks;
(2) they were not logical in progression;
(3) they were too complex for pupils considering their previous experience;
(4) their complexity was increased before any refinement of the previous task.

Rink (1985), in fact, believes that 'personalising' presentations by referring directly to particular pupil experiences may facilitate clarity, a point also made by one HOD in the TEPE Project: 'always try to link material with existing knowledge, understanding and experiences'.

An example of this might include the use of pupils' familiarity with throwing a ball in a 'sideways on', bent arm throwing action.

Reminding pupils of this might be a useful introduction or 'lead in' practice for teaching the javelin in athletics, serving in tennis, or the overhead clear in badminton.

The importance of appropriate sequencing of material in a logical order, possibly working from the simple to the complex, was mentioned by a number of HODs: '... build up material bit by bit', '... teach basics and take one step at a time', '... break down and structure material in a meaningful way'.

Physical education teachers have certain preferred ways of structuring and sequencing the teaching of aspects of the physical education curriculum. Progressive practices may be used in the teaching of certain gymnastic or athletic movements, and complex skills, such as the lay-up shot in basketball, may be broken down into a set of more simple, yet linked movements. Others would rather introduce the whole skill first and then correct any problems that may occur, possibly taking a component out of the whole skill for practice prior to putting the 'whole' back together again. The most important point to make here is that it is essential to 'think through' the structuring and sequencing of the movement prior to planning the presentation.

Helping pupils to understand why they will be practising a particular movement is part of what has been termed 'cognitive set' or 'set induction'. Set induction is not just about creating interest in what has to be learned, it's also about helping pupils to understand the context of what is to be learned.

Making sure that pupils understand the purpose of the lesson, how previous experience is associated with lesson objectives, how what is to be taught in the lesson relates to an ultimate goal or skill, is often referred to as 'scaffolding'. Noticeably, one of the OFSTED (1993a) criteria for assessing the quality of teaching is 'pupil awareness of lesson objectives'.

## Explaining for clear understanding

Clarity of explanation of a task is about communicating a clear understanding of what to do and how to do it. But, explaining a task well involves more than just focussing on the details of the skill or movement, it also involves a full description of the context in which the task will be practised, and possibly how pupils might evaluate their performance.

Pupils need to know:

- who they will work with, the size of groups and how the groups will be formed;
- what equipment they will need;

- when to start and when to stop;
- the conditions for the activity/practice/game (e.g. changing roles in a practice, number of attempts, rules, etc.).

Organisation of groups, equipment and work areas should ideally be dealt with prior to further explanation of the task, thus allowing pupils the opportunity to practise immediately after the explanation/ demonstration.

After an explanation by the teacher, pupils should have a clear idea of what to do and why they are doing it, how to do it and what the teachers' expectations are. Work by Ausubel (1960, 1968) and Gage and Berliner (1975) suggest that if teachers tell pupils exactly what they will be doing before the teaching episode begins, it will help orientate the learner to the objectives of the lesson. This use of what Ausubel refers to as 'advance organisers', help structure explanations and presentations, and assist pupils in relating parts of a lesson to the objectives of the lesson as whole. For example, in the teaching of tackling skills in rugby, one teacher introduced a lesson as follows:

Today we are going to look at tackling and how you can do this safely and effectively in a game. We are going to practise the different stages of learning to tackle so that you only need to concentrate on one aspect at a time, and gradually we will build up your experience so that you are then able to tackle safely in a small game.

HODs in the TEPE Project offered the following advice to beginning PE teachers concerning clarity in the presentation of new material:

Explain exactly what you intend them to do.

Explain why – and ask for questions.

Be clear, decisive, and above all – organised!

Take your time with explanations of new material, especially if it involves a 'new way' of organising the pupils (something they are new to).

Keep instructions concise and brief.

Remember that your language may not be that of the pupils.

These suggestions are well supported by the literature on teacher effectiveness. Both Perrott (1982) and Brown and Armstrong (1984) have identified similar basic teaching skills related to effective explanations.

- Organisation of material – Perrott (1982) refers to the importance of 'continuity', or the need to keep a strong connecting thread running through the lesson. Brown and Armstrong (1984) emphasise the need for a logical and clear sequence within the explanation, and the use of 'link' words and phrases.

- Clarity, fluency and explicitness – both Perrott, and Brown and Armstrong refer to the need to define new terms through the appropriate use of explicit language and avoid vagueness.
- Simplicity – in support of many of the comments made by HODs in the TEPE Project, Perrott emphasises the importance of 'simple, intelligible and grammatical sentences', and avoidance of the inclusion of too much information in any one sentence. The language used should be within the pupils' own vocabulary, and teachers should avoid using subject specific language unless pupils are previously introduced to the terms used. Teachers often think that pupils understand more than they do, and PE teachers in particular can be guilty of using sports coaching 'jargon' without making it clear to pupils what the terminology means.
- Use of examples – Brown and Armstrong (1984) refer to the use of clear, appropriate, and concrete negative and positive examples to support explanations, and Perrott (1982) emphasises the need to use visual means for communicating complex explanations. In the teaching of PE, the use of examples in the form of demonstrations has commonly been used in direct teaching to communicate to pupils the skill or movement to be learned.
- Emphasis and interest – Brown and Hatton (1982) see the need for good explanations to have voice variation, use of pauses to highlight points, repetition of main issues and verbal cueing of key ideas.
- Pace and conciseness – good explanations also involve appropriate pacing; talk slowly and don't rush explanations, and be concise in order to minimise pupil inactivity in PE lessons.
- Checking for understanding – before work commences, pupils need to have the opportunity to voice their level of understanding. The teacher may therefore either ask if there are any questions, or ask certain pupils particular questions in order to check if the main points have been understood. The teacher needs to be particularly clear that his expectations in terms of pupil work is clearly appreciated.

Use the exercise below to appraise your explanations in terms of the points discussed. Ask a colleague to observe you, or alternatively audio or videotape a lesson and analyse the lesson afterwards.

*Exercise 6   Analysing and appraising explanations for clear understanding*

| | Always | Usually | Never | Comments |
|---|---|---|---|---|
| Were pupils clear about the lesson objectives? | | | | |
| Were pupils clear about the lesson context?<br>– work area to be used<br>– boundaries of work area<br>– who they will work with<br>– equipment to be used<br>– when to start/stop<br>– changing roles<br>– number of attempts<br>– rules | | | | |
| Was material organised in a logical sequence? | | | | |
| Were appropriate links made with:<br>– previous material?<br>– future material? | | | | |
| Was it demonstrated clearly? | | | | |
| Were precise and intelligible sentences used? | | | | |
| Was vagueness avoided? | | | | |
| Were simple and appropriate words used? | | | | |
| Was the amount of information offered appropriate? | | | | |

*continued*

*Exercise 6 continued*

|  | Always | Usually | Never | Comments |
|---|---|---|---|---|
| Did the teacher make good use of:<br>– voice variation?<br>– pause for high-lighting?<br>–repetition of main points?<br>– verbal cueing of key ideas?<br>– appropriate pace of speech? |  |  |  |  |
| Did the teacher offer pupils the opportunity to ask questions? |  |  |  |  |
| Did the teacher check understanding by posing certain questions? |  |  |  |  |
| Was the teacher's expectations for the work made clear? |  |  |  |  |

## Demonstrations and the communication of movement features

They say that 'a picture is worth a thousand words', and in the case of learning movements and physical skills, although the research is not conclusive it is generally believed that an image of the movement in the form of a demonstration or film may help the learner to remember and reproduce the movement (McCullagh, 1993). Often referred to as 'observational learning' or 'modelling' (Bandura, 1977) it is suggested that the imitation, copying or reproduction of any action initially executed by another person, results in the learner developing a cognitive perceptual representation of the movement in memory. Such a process may be important in the early stage of motor skill learning which is believed to be highly cognitive (Pollock and Lee, 1992). Observation of an appropriate model is particularly important at this early stage of learning because learners need a clear idea of what they are aiming to achieve. Having a clear idea of what to do and how to do it is referred to as a 'reference of correctness' by Adams (1971), and this cognitive process is later refined after receiving feedback from attempts to reproduce the skill or movement.

Although it is agreed that additional research needs to be done on the use of demonstrations as an effective strategy in the teaching of physical skills (McCullagh, 1993; Newell, Morris and Scully, 1985), the literature is still generally supportive of the use of demonstrations. However, experts in the field do suggest certain guidelines for the effective use of demonstrations or modelling as a teaching skill. Bandura (1969), for example, emphasises the importance of four processes for observational learning to occur:

- Attention – the imitator must be fully attending to the most important, significant or relevant aspects of the demonstration. Burwitz (1975) found that learners could not always attend to the most important aspects of the image provided by the demonstration and needed help in doing this.
- Retention – the imitator needs to be able to retain the information from the demonstration in short-term memory until ready to practise the movement physically.
- Motor reproduction processes – the learner has to have the ability to reproduce the movement physically.
- Incentive conditions – the imitator has to be motivated to want to reproduce the movement.

Several points arise from these suggestions and from the research literature in sports psychology/pedagogy that are important for the effective use of demonstrations in the teaching of PE:

- the nature of the demonstration itself;
- the verbal cueing to support the demonstration;
- the context of the movement or practice;
- the organisation of the demonstration.

## The nature of the demonstration

Issues that relate to who offers the model (whether expert, teacher or pupil), the accuracy of the model, and what is actually picked up by the imitator are of particular importance to the teacher.

Most of the research investigating the nature of the model has focussed on certain characteristics of the person doing the demonstration, and in particular the competence, status and similarity of the model to the observer (Gould and Weiss, 1981; Gould and Roberts, 1981; McCullagh, 1986, 1987). There is one suggestion that if the person demonstrating has a high level of skill, competence and social status (e.g. teacher), then the observer is more likely to attend to the model and be motivated to perform than with a less skilled, less competent, or low-status model (Landers and Landers, 1973). However, Lirgg and Feltz (1991) suggest that the skill of the demonstrator is the most important factor, and therefore good peer or pupil performers might be quite appropriate for providing a demonstration if the teacher's level of competence was in question, or if the teacher wanted a more able pupil to make a contribution to the lesson.

There is also the suggestion from the work of Pollock and Lee (1992), that watching a demonstration by someone who was not performing in an expert way (e.g. a fellow learner), and who is actually going through the process of learning and receiving feedback themselves, may facilitate both observational learning and learning generally as a problem solving process: 'Watching someone improve performance on a task engages the observer in many of the problem-solving activities undertaken by the learning model. When the observer then has the opportunity to perform the task, the cognitive representation developed through observation has obviated some of the initial problem solving a novice must learn through physical practice'. (p. 78)

As far as the accuracy of the model or image of the action is concerned, it appears that while slow motion demonstrations may be useful in the early stages of learning (to emphasize aspects of the movement such as order and direction of limbs), normal speed demonstrations are more important at the later stages of learning to help the learner to acquire the correct speed and flow characteristics of the movement (Williams, 1986; Scully, 1988). Also, performing the whole action at the appropriate speed and in the correct context is important for many skills, even when parts of the skill are being emphasized (e.g. arm action in swimming the crawl stroke).

Accuracy of the demonstration also relates to the angle at which the learner is viewing it. For example, it is important for pupils viewing a demonstration of the set shot in basketball to see the action and position of the shooting arm from the side and front/back in order to have the total 'picture'.

In addition to 'live' demonstrations, physical education teachers use videotape films and posters to illustrate a particular movement. Pictures and posters do have the disadvantage of not showing the real life timing and fluency of a movement, but may be useful to illustrate a particular mechanical aspect of a movement that is difficult to 'freeze frame' in a real life demonstration. Examples might include the position of the arms and body at the top of the jump shot in basketball, or the 'hang' position in long jumping. Pictures and posters may also be useful to illustrate theoretical points and concepts in health-related exercise lessons (e.g. target zone for heart rate according to age).

Videotape is a useful device for showing expert models for a wide range of skills. In addition, there are certain video-recorders that have the facility to emphasize and enhance various key coaching points and kinematic features of movements, which Williams (1986) believes is a useful aid to learning. However, it is possible for commercially manufactured instructional tapes to contain too much information for the learner, and therefore need to be used selectively.

## Verbal cueing to support the demonstration

As already pointed out, observational learning is very dependent on the learner attending to and accurately perceiving the significant or key features of the model offered by the demonstrator. In his research, Burwitz (1975) noted that learners cannot always attend to the main points contained in a demonstration, and need help in attending to the most important aspects of the model by verbal cueing (Roach and Burwitz, 1986). Effective teachers therefore need to select and organise the learning cues required carefully to support the demonstration. What is a learning cue? According to Rink (1985) a learning cue is: '… a word or phrase that identifies and communicates to a performer the critical features of a movement, skill or task'. (p. 217)

Rink goes on to identify the following four characteristics of good learning cues that will help the learner to establish an accurate image of the movement being learned:

* accuracy;
* critical to the task being presented;
* appropriate to the learner's age and stage of learning;
* conciseness.

It is naturally expected that the teacher is knowledgeable about the task or activity being taught and is therefore able to select the appropriate learning cues or teaching points. Also, these teaching points would have been identified as a result of task analysis and included in the lesson plan. In one study by Werner, Rink and Hinricks (1984), it was noted that the accuracy of the learning cues offered by the PE teacher was critical for pupil learning and performance.

In the early stages of learning a new task the learner has to attend to a large number of cues and therefore it is important that the teacher identifies the most relevant learning cues for successful performance. The information processing literature refers to helping the learner to 'selectively attend' to the most appropriate and critical cues for successful performance (Marteniuk, 1976; Abernathy, 1993), and that in the early stages of learning it is essential that the learner's information processing system is not 'overloaded' by the provision of too much information. As at least two HODs emphasized this point in their advice to beginning PE teachers on the presentation of new material: 'Keep it simple', 'Don't give too much information'.

In their study of task presentation in physical education, Rink and Werner (1987) considered that three or fewer new learning cues was sufficient. Rink (1985) also recommends that a thorough task analysis at the planning stage might involve breaking down movements into preparation, execution, and 'follow through' phases, in order to identify the most important learning cues.

One way of helping pupils to appreciate the nature of a movement is to use 'action words' or 'verbal labels' when planning teaching points or learning cues. Graham (1992) calls these 'reminder words or phrases' that offer pupils a 'mind picture'. It is particularly useful if such words or phrases really do 'mediate' or sound like the actual action. For example, 'snap' the wrists when following through in the basketball chest pass, 'punch' the racket in the tennis volley.

Learning cues may vary according to the type of activity being taught. If the skill or movement does not require any perceptual decision making or choice of response, then the learning cues need to relate simply to the key verbal and visual cues for sound execution of the movement shown in the demonstration. However, if the skill to be performed is set in a more complex, perceptual or 'open' skill situation, and decisions have to be made concerning choice of response (e.g. involving opposition in a game situation), then learning cues might be concerned with the selection of the appropriate response.

The selection of learning cues should also take into account learner characteristics, particularly the age and stage of learning. Young children at primary school not only have a limited movement experience to bring to a new skill learning situation, but they also have a limited information processing capability, including less developed selective attention and memory strategies that are important for observational learning (Gallagher, 1982, 1984; Gallagher and Thomas, 1984; Gallagher and Hoffman, 1987). Because of these developmental considerations Weiss and Klint (1987) and Thomas (1980) suggest that a combination of modelling and the development of verbal rehearsal and verbal self-instructional techniques should be used when presenting new material to younger children. According to Weiss and Klint these verbal rehearsal strategies are useful in helping young children to attend selectively to the most appropriate cues and relevant task components, and to remember the specific order in which components of a skill are executed.

The use of appropriate language for young children with limited movement experience is also an important consideration. This may entail using phrases that are less abstract and analytical than might normally be used in sports coaching. For example, when teaching young children about the use of the legs and hips when landing from a jump, referring to 'squashy' landings may help them to verbalise and visualise the movement.

For younger children the 'key' learning cues or components of a movement may need to be emphasized by 'freeze framing' the movement during the demonstration but, as has already been pointed out, a whole movement real life, real speed demonstration should also accompany this form of model otherwise the timing and flow characteristics of the movement may be lost.

In addition to the dangers of offering pupils too much information when presenting new material, there is also the problem of spending too much time on presentations resulting in pupil inactivity. Therefore, it is important to be concise and precise when providing explanations, learning cues and organisational details, so that pupils can quickly practise. Don't be sidetracked – it is easy when you are enthusiastic about an activity to spend too much time referring to relevant anecdotes. While these do help to create interest in the activity being taught, they can be overdone at the expense of pupil activity and may inhibit pupil memory of the main points of the demonstration. However, the teacher must spend time in making sure that pupils are clear about safety issues and appreciate the practice context.

## Context of the movement

In the teaching of many physical education activities management problems may occur following a demonstration if the context in which the movement is to be practised is not made clear. Offering pupils purely a demonstration of the movement to be practised without also informing them of the organisational details of the practice/game, such as the changing roles of members of the practice group, or the number of practise attempts before roles change, can lead to chaos following the demonstration. The teacher may then have to spend valuable teaching time going over these organisational details with individual groups. Therefore, it is important that the practice context of the movement is incorporated into the demonstration. This can be done by first of all setting up one practice group in the work area while the rest of the class are watching. If the teacher is demonstrating the skill, he may then take the place of one of the group members. The movement is then demonstrated a few times followed by a demonstration of the practice organisation. However, the teacher may wish to step out of the group after the demonstration of the movement, and the pupils in the demonstrating group go through an example of the practice organisation.

To make sure that pupils know what to do, the teacher might then check for understanding.

## The organisation of the demonstration

According to the literature on motor skill learning, the image of the movement provided by the teacher's demonstration is first of all transferred into the learner's short-term memory (Posner, 1969; Marteniuk, 1976). The retention of movement-related information in short-term memory is supposedly limited by time, and it may therefore be important for pupils to have the opportunity to rehearse or practise what they have seen as soon as possible after seeing the demonstration in order for the information to be remembered. Only by rehearsal or practise is such information transformed into long-term storage for retention and later recall. The possible implications of this for the planning and organisation of demonstrations are threefold:

- Pupils need to be able to see clearly the demonstration and hear/understand the learning cues;
- Pupils need to have the opportunity for immediate rehearsal or practise following the demonstration;
- Teachers need to monitor that pupils do practise the task as demonstrated immediately following the demonstration.

For pupils to be able to see the demonstration and hear the key learning cues offered by the teacher, they need to be totally attentive and not distracted. This means that the teacher needs to organise the class so that they can all see the demonstration and hear the teacher. Try to avoid having pupils looking into the sun, near a busy road, facing another activity in progress or looking out of a window and this will help to maintain attention. Some teachers prefer to have pupils sitting or squatting down and not standing one behind the other (the pupils in the second tier are usually those who are likely to interfere with those in front of them!), in certain formations so that the teacher can see everyone throughout the demonstration, and be able to project his voice in their direction. Teachers have been observed using formations similar to the following:

```
      X  X  X                XXXXXXX      XXXXXXX
   X           X             X       X
 X               X           X       X
 X               X           X       X
 X             X             X       X
      T                          T              T
```

To enable pupils to practise the movement immediately after the demonstration, and to avoid any confusing organisation and management details being given at the same time as the demonstration, some teachers deal with organisation of groups, equipment and even allocation of work areas before the demonstration. When given the signal to do so, pupils can then go off to practise immediately following the demonstration, or when the teacher has checked for understanding. This approach avoids organisational details 'interfering' with pupils' short-term memory of the image of the skill to be learned.

However, even if the teacher has planned to allow pupils to practise immediately following the demonstration, there is no certainty that pupils will do exactly what they have been told. It is therefore essential that when pupils have been sent to their work areas to practise, the teacher should then 'scan' the group for immediate compliance and provide appropriate reminders when necessary. A degree of preventative management is also recommended. For example, during the demonstration the teacher might not only check for understanding, but also briefly outline what is expected of pupils when they are sent to their work area to practise. Also, the way pupils are dispersed for practice should be linked to this reminder of expectations. The key instructions should be: 'When I say "go" I want you to ... .' One should certainly not have pupils wandering off before an explanation of the task has been completed and expectations made clear. An orderly dispersal is more likely to lead to a business-like and disciplined approach to the task in hand!

There are several aspects of demonstrations that one may wish to evaluate using a colleague observer or self-analysis of videotape, and these are included in Exercise 7 below.

## *Exercise 7   Appraisal of Demonstrations*

(1)  Pre-demonstration phase
- Was the demonstration well planned beforehand?
- Were pupils organised into their working groups prior to the demonstration?
- Was the purpose of the activity made clear?
- Were all members of the class able to see the demonstration and hear the teaching points made?
- Were there any distractions that caused pupils to lose concentration on the demonstration?

(2)  The demonstration itself
- Was the demonstration a good model of the movement?
- Were the essential, specific, teaching points given?
- Were too many teaching points given?
- Was the organisation of the activity also shown in the demonstration?
- Was the skill demonstrated in it's appropriate context?
- Were practice/work expectations made clear to pupils?

(3)  Post-demonstration phase
- Did pupils have the opportunity to seek clarification?
- Was dispersal to work areas speedy and efficient?

## Teaching skills for effective direct teaching: Observation skills

When the teacher has completed the presentation of the new skill, and pupils have been sent to practise in their work areas, the guidance and feedback role of the teacher is then put into operation. As this role is important for learning it is not surprising that physical education teachers do give a lot of feedback (Pieron and Delmelle, 1982). However, research evidence suggests that the quality of this feedback in terms of the specificity of learning cues offered is variable (Armstrong, 1986). This suggests that some PE teachers may lack the knowledge and skills to give effective feedback and guidance (Lee *et al.*, 1993). Being able to give guidance and feedback effectively initially involves being a good 'observer' of movement.

According to Barrett (1983), 'observing' is defined as: '... the ability to perceive accurately both the movement response of the learner and the environment in which the response takes place'. (p. 22)

Barrett sees the teaching skill of observation as both a managerial skill and an essential skill for the teacher to be able to give effective feedback.

As a managerial skill, whole class observation or 'scanning' is important immediately after sending a class away to work to ensure that they adhere to the teacher's expectations. Such 'scanning' is an essential feature of good class monitoring as discussed in Chapter 7. In this section we are mainly concerned with observation as a diagnostic teaching skill that enables the teacher to make accurate decisions about a learner's performance and possible learning difficulties, in order to provide appropriate guidance and feedback.

Barrett (1983) believes that observing as a teaching skill may have the three basic components shown in Figure 9.

To be an effective observer of movement the teacher needs to decide what to observe. This requires the ability to analyse movement and identify 'critical features' that are essential for successful performance. In this way observing is linked closely with movement analysis. But, what does the ability to analyse movement actually entail?

It is believed that experienced observers develop strategies to enable them to 'search' efficiently for the important aspects of a skill, or 'critical feature', to concentrate on and to ignore, the less important. Critical features are components of a movement and it's environmental context that are 'critical' for successful performance at a particular point in time.

The teacher of physical education can become better at movement analysis by planning how to observe. Barrett (1983) sees such planning involving three stages:

- selecting the specific critical features that will be the focus of the observation;

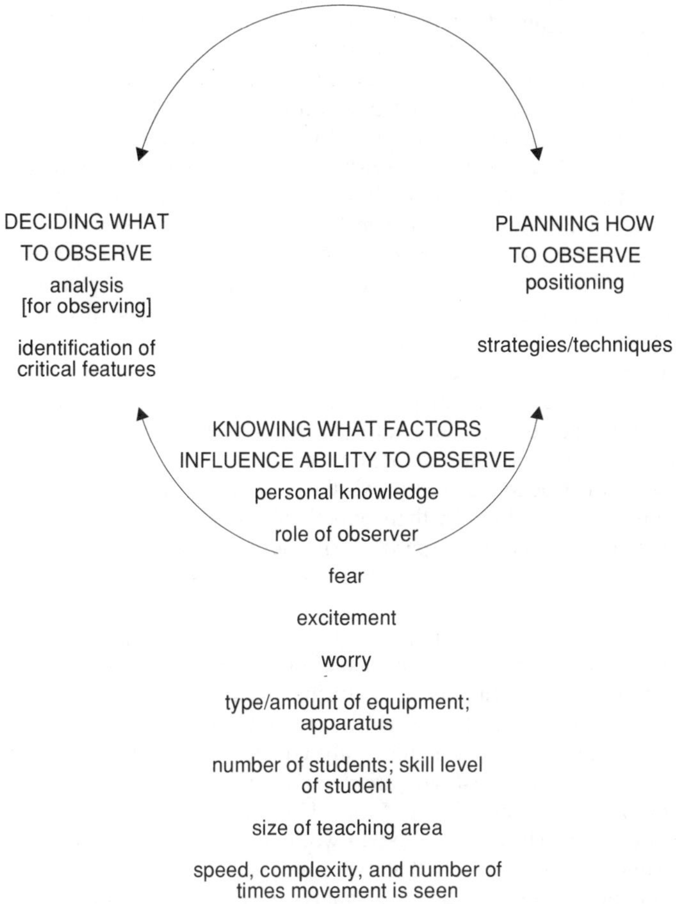

DECIDING WHAT
TO OBSERVE
analysis
[for observing]

identification of
critical features

PLANNING HOW
TO OBSERVE
positioning

strategies/techniques

KNOWING WHAT FACTORS
INFLUENCE ABILITY TO OBSERVE
personal knowledge

role of observer

fear

excitement

worry

type/amount of equipment;
apparatus

number of students; skill level
of student

size of teaching area

speed, complexity, and number of
times movement is seen

*Figure 9   A model for conceptualisng observing as a teaching skill*
*Source: Barrett (1993) p. 23.*

- identifying the best positions from which to observe these features;
- deciding how to actually look at these features in terms of what to look at, when, and for how long. (p. 25)

When observing a movement it is important to watch the learner's skill attempts from different angles of vision. This will involve the teacher in moving around rather than staying in a fixed position so that the performer can be seen from different viewpoints. Moving around the periphery of the class and avoiding being caught in the middle of the group is also important for efficient class monitoring.

Rink (1985) suggests that with large groups, it might be advisable to start by 'scanning' the whole group for one particular aspect of the movement, then select a few individuals of varied skill to observe for a period of time. This, she suggests, avoids the problem of 'looking but not really seeing', when 'confronted with a sea of performers' (p. 252).

So, what should the teacher look for when observing?

The general advice from research workers is that the learning cues the teacher has planned to emphasize in the presentation should serve as the selected observation cues to focus on during movement analysis. These then become the 'critical features' that direct and 'focus' the teacher's observation. These learning cues need to be pre-planned and as a direct result of the developmental skill analysis discussed in Chapter 5.

In the same way that PE teachers use demonstrations to help learners to acquire an 'image' of the movement to be learned, so it seems that the teacher may improve her observation and movement analysis by developing a mental image of the movement to be analysed. PE teachers can improve their ability to observe and analyse movement by building up their experience of watching and analysing movements and activities (particularly those they may be less familiar with), and structuring their observation to look for examples of movement errors.

Teachers don't necessarily have to be experts in a particular skill to be proficient at movement analysis. However, the more experience and practice the teacher can get at analysing specific movements the better they can become. But, the ability to analyse movements may be specific to the movement being analysed. Just being a PE teacher does not necessarily mean that you are good at analysing all skills. Research evidence (Armstrong, 1977, 1986; Hoffman and Sembiante, 1975; Armstrong and Hoffman, 1979; Imwold and Hoffman, 1983; Pinhiero and Simon, 1992) suggests that expert or 'good' teachers or coaches of a particular activity are better at analysing performance errors in that activity than non-experts. Although experience of teaching an activity may improve one's ability to analyse movement, many feel that courses of specialised systematic training including conceptual or pedagogical kinesiology and movement analysis training, may help to develop a teacher's expertise in movement analysis (Beveridge and Gangstead, 1988; Nielson and Beauchamp, 1991; Pinhiero and Simon, 1992).

Having a strategy for how one might observe a movement seems to be important, and Barrett (1983) interviewed a number of experienced coaches to ascertain how they observed performers and what they looked for.

An athletics coach spoke of 'locking in, holding the movement pattern in his mind's eye long enough before the movement is passed on into another pattern'. Generally, expert coaches of athletics and golf indicated that they observed relationships, 'relationships among and between parts of the body, not just a single action of one part' (Barrett, 1983, p. 26). These expert coaches considered that this ability is not easily acquired and would naturally be easier for the athletics or gymnastics coach who is only observing one performer at a time. In physical education lessons with upward of thirty pupils, PE teachers have to cope with a number of distractions that can affect the quality of their observation. In Barrett's (1979) study of student teachers, it was noted that factors such as knowledge of the movement, excitement, worry, type/amount of equipment/apparatus, size of work area, skill level of pupils and the speed, complexity, and number of times a movement had to be seen, all contributed to distractions that influenced effective observation. The suggestion is that PE teachers may be poor observers because their attention is frequently being diverted and they are unable to control this. Barrett believes that one answer may be to provide student teachers and NQTs with the opportunity to observe pupils working in a range of different teaching environments. However, if the teacher is aware of the possible distractions prior to teaching a particular activity, then a strategy may be put into operation to overcome these problems. This may entail not only planning to look for and focus on certain 'critical features' or learning cues that have been provided in the presentation of the movement, but also to focus on these cues during observation of pupil skill attempts.

Having planned and carried out a movement analysis of the pupil's skill attempt, how does the teacher use this information? Hoffman (1983) believes that such information is used for 'clinical diagnosis', or the: '... decisions made by skill instructors regarding the nature of the learner's performance problems and the factors that give rise to them' (p. 36).

In other words, the teacher's job is to watch the learner and judge the extent of the discrepancy between the learner's skill attempts and the behaviour required to achieve the skill goal. This diagnostic-prescriptive model of skills teaching put forward by Hoffman is shown in Figure 10. The model suggests that an accurate diagnosis is essential for the teacher to be able to provide the appropriate guidance and feedback for the correction of movement errors. Hoffman suggests that teachers of physical skills have three main clinical diagnostic decisions to make:

**1. Has the learner performed the skill correctly?**
In skills where there is a simple yes/no answer (e.g. catching a ball, shooting in Netball), then this is easy, but in some skills there are gradations of success (e.g. passing a hockey ball to a teammate, triple jump, gymnastics), and the teacher needs to have considerable knowledge of the skill and of standards of performance to make an accurate decision.

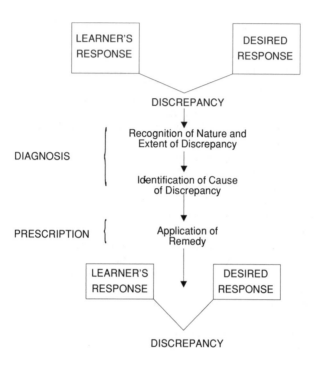

*Figure 10   A diagnostic-prescriptive model for skills teaching*
Source: Hoffman (1983) p. 37.

**2. If the learner has not performed the skill correctly, what aspects of the performance are incorrect?**
The problem here is to decide how much the performance differs from the ideal model of the skill, and the teacher will use her experience of identifying and interpreting the most relevant and important movement cues to make an accurate diagnostic decision about the success or otherwise of the movement (Pinhiero and Simon, 1992). Hoffman believes that skill errors are either primary or secondary errors. For example, poor contact between racket and ball in a tennis ground stroke may be due to incorrect grip, poor racket preparation, poor preliminary footwork or incorrect point of contact. In the tennis service

poor contact or direction may be due to incorrect grip, body position or inappropriate toss. Therefore the teacher or coach should always be looking for the primary error or 'root cause' of the problem.

### 3. Having identified the real cause of the movement error what prescription should the teacher offer?

The effective teacher should be able to draw upon a 'bank' of experience and a range of teaching/learning cues and remedial practices to help the learner with the primary error causing the movement problem.

Although criticised by Pinhiero and Simon (1992) for lacking empirical support, Hoffman (1983) has put forward the diagnostic problem-solving model shown in Figure 11, that teachers might use when giving skill instruction.

The initial question to ask when using this model is 'Was the Goal attained?', and answers may vary according to the age and experience of the learner, and the level of performance the learner is working towards. If the goal was not achieved then it is suggested that the teacher may work through the process to find out why. This may entail using the information from the secondary errors to identify the primary errors causing the problem. According to Hoffman (1983), such hypothetic-deductive reasoning: '... is a process of collecting data or cues and generating alternative hypotheses about the nature of the problem under investigation'. (p. 39)

Consequently, as the teacher works through the model some hypotheses will be discounted and new ones presented. There are three hypotheses about the learner's performance that may be considered by the teacher:

- lack of basic abilities to perform the skill;
- skill deficiencies;
- psychological factors.

If the teacher feels that the learner does not have the basic physical abilities to perform the skill successfully, then he may have to consider an alternative skill goal within the capabilities of the learner. For example, some pupils have difficulty with the underarm stroke used to start a rally in badminton because they lack the coordination to be able to make contact with the shuttle. In such cases an alternative form of starting a rally or game may be used which, while not legally correct, does allow pupils to begin a rally or game.

A second hypothesis may be that the learner has a skill deficiency. These may be of three types: technique errors, perceptual errors and decision-making errors.

Technique errors will normally have a primary error causing the secondary problem and movement analysis should enable the experienced teacher to identify the source of the problem.

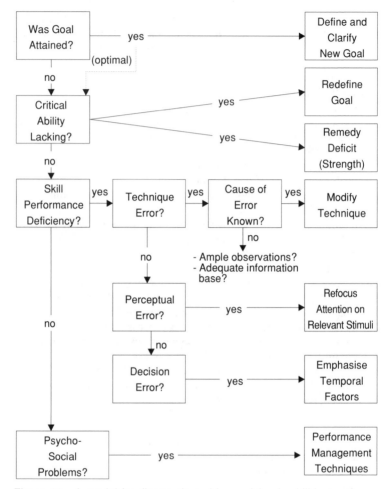

*Figure 11    A model for diagnostic problem-solving in skill instruction*
Source: Hoffman (1983) p. 39.

If the technique is satisfactory but the learner is still not achieving the desired goal, the problem may be a perceptual or decision-making error. Perceptual errors are caused by an incorrect interpretation of the sensory input. In the case of decision-making errors the correct interpretation may have been made but an inappropriate decision taken concerning what to do and how to do it. For example, in cricket, the learner may have displayed a technically perfect on-drive, but was caught out trying to hit a good length ball. As Hoffman (1983) points out: 'Decision errors are eliminated only when the performer learns to pay closer attention to the temporal relationship between their movements and relevant signals in the environment'. (p. 40)

If the learner seems to have the necessary abilities, technique and perceptual/decision-making skills, poor performance may be due to psycho-social factors. Anxiety, lack of motivation, fear, etc., can all affect pupil learning and performance.

How long should a teacher observe a pupil? This may depend on what the teacher is looking for. It's possible to analyse some movements very quickly, others may require more careful observation and from different positions. With a large class the teacher has to be efficient in her use of time, and a rapid 'scanning' of a representative sample of the class can give the teacher an idea of the general areas of success and failure. If a large number of the class are having problems, then a further class demonstration or modification of the task may be required.

When the teacher has made a 'clinical diagnosis' of pupil skill attempts, the next stage in the guidance 'cycle' is to provide the learner with positive encouragement for her efforts, and then offer information on the success or failure of the performance and how the next attempt may be improved. This is the feedback and refinement stage.

## Teaching skills for effective direct teaching: Feedback and refinement skills

How important is teacher feedback for learning? What does research evidence tell us about teacher feedback as an effective teaching skill?

In Gagne's (1974) eight phases of a complete learning sequence, the last phase is the feedback phase in which the learner finds out the extent to which he has achieved the learning objective. Therefore, feedback, in simple information theory terms is the information that the learner receives as a consequence of a response, and which may guide and motivate the learner for future skill attempts. As part of an information-processing model of learning, Fitts and Posner (1967) believed that feedback could in fact serve three functions: 'It can provide knowledge, motivation and reinforcement. It can also serve as a reward, providing extremely strong motivation to continue a task, since it relates to the distance between a present state and a goal. Since feedback operates as a strong source of motivation it may be an important or even necessary condition of learning.' (p. 28)

Informative feedback may be considered to be intrinsic or augmented. Intrinsic or internal feedback is the information the learner receives from the sensory systems. Augmented feedback is that information provided by an external source such as the teacher, coach, videotape or computer, and may take the form of knowledge of results (information about the outcome of response), knowledge of performance (information about the actual characteristics of the movement response) and augmented sensory feedback, in which an external device may be used to offer additional sensory feedback. The motor skill learning literature has been generally supportive of the importance of feedback for learning, although such factors as the nature of the skill to be learned appears to be a major issue concerning the value of augmented feedback. The learning of certain skills may be dependant on augmented feedback, yet others may not require it, or may even find it detrimental to learning (see Magill, 1993 for a detailed review).

The teacher effectiveness research literature has been fairly positive about the important part played by augmented feedback in learning. In their review of process-product research in classrooms, Good and Brophy (1991) identified 'monitoring of pupil progress and providing feedback and remedial instruction as needed' (p. 443), as one of the characteristics of more effective classroom teachers in terms of pupil achievement gains. Although a few recent studies in the physical education teacher effectiveness literature (Masser, 1987; Boyce, 1991; Silverman *et al.*, 1992) do offer some support for the benefits of augmented feedback and task refinement for learning, in general, experts are cautious about the value of earlier research findings, and feel that more research is required (Lee *et al.*, 1993). Whereas laboratory studies in psychology have been able to control for the effects of intrinsic feedback (thus ensuring that subjects receiving feedback always appeared to be superior in learning to non-feedback groups), field studies in the physical education setting have had difficulty controlling for such variables as intrinsic feedback, the amount of practice, learner factors (such as skill level and ability to use the feedback) and issues related to the teacher's knowledge of the activity.

When learning skills in physical education pupils are always receiving some intrinsic feedback (e.g. they see where the ball lands in tennis), so it is difficult to eliminate all forms of feedback other than augmented feedback from the teacher.

Some studies of the teaching of physical education do suggest that more effective teachers tend to give a higher proportion of augmented and positive feedback (Pieron, 1982; Phillips and Carlisle, 1983; De Knop, 1986) but, the issue of equating the number of practice trials for all experimental groups does appear to devalue certain studies. The work by Silverman *et al.* (1992) is one example of a study that attempted to account for practice trials, and they noted that descriptive, prescriptive and corrective feedback were shown to be related to achievement.

The background of the learner is also an important issue. For example, Rikard (1991) noted that feedback was more effective for low-skilled learners, although it has to be pointed out that low-skilled learners did receive more corrective feedback (learner is told exactly what to do) than high-skilled learners. In fact, it has been reported that teachers tend to give more evaluative feedback (indicating how well or poorly the learner has done) to high-skill learners, whereas corrective feedback is given to the low-skilled (Lee *et al.*, 1993). The authors suggest that this may be due to teachers feeling that low-skilled learners need more corrective feedback to learn a particular skill.

Learners may also vary in terms of their ability to use augmented feedback. How two different pupils use the same feedback statement from the teacher may be very dependent on the motivation, skill level and perceived competency of the pupil in relation to the task. In fact, Lee *et al.* (1993) believe that until we know more about student mediation or understanding and use of the feedback they receive, we will not have a clear appreciation of the ideal conditions for effective feedback. For example, in one study by Keh and Lee (1994) a significant relationship was observed between learner use of teacher feedback and the number of correct practice trials in three badminton skills.

The effectiveness of the teacher's feedback may also be dependent on the teacher's knowledge of the skill or activity being learned. The inconsistency of teacher effectiveness research findings in physical education may in fact be due to the poor quality of the teacher feedback in certain studies, because incorrect feedback can inhibit learning. Evidence from at least two studies cited by Lee *et al.* (1993) suggest that more knowledgeable teachers may provide more specific skill-related feedback for the correction of errors. In their review of the feedback literature Lee and her colleagues are particularly critical of the research to date, and suggest that not only is there a need for more research on augmented teacher feedback, but that it must take into account the context in which feedback is given:

The appropriate amount and type of feedback will vary not only for different skills, but also for different students learning the same skill. What appears to be the right amount of feedback to promote learning for one student might inhibit learning for another. To make sense conceptually, the research on instructional effects of teacher feedback must include student perceptions as a variable (Lee *et al.*, 1993, p. 238).

As this short review of the research on teacher feedback has tended to highlight the shortcomings of teacher effectiveness research, and the possible reasons for the inconsistency of teacher feedback research findings, what implications might be forthcoming for physical education teachers who wish to improve their teaching skills and become more effective? Well, until more meaningful research is completed we have to accept that teacher feedback appears to be a very important component of effective teaching, particularly when combined with other aspects of effective teaching. In fact, certain workers in the field feel that effective teaching does require the combined use of a number of teaching behaviours (such as teacher clarity, demonstrations, accuracy of learning cues and feedback) and that no individual behaviour such as feedback should be expected to discriminate between more or less effective teachers (Graham *et al.*, 1983; Rink and Werner, 1987).

For the teacher of physical education it is therefore important to appreciate that not only might feedback be essential for learning, but that certain types of feedback may be more effective than others, and that the teacher's knowledge of the learner and the activity being taught could also be crucial factors in the equation. Therefore, the effective teacher of PE needs to be aware of the value of different types of feedback. These include:

- congruent and incongruent feedback;
- specific and general feedback;
- positive and negative feedback.

## Congruent and incongruent feedback

Congruent feedback focusses on the learning cues that were introduced to the learner during the teacher's presentation. While practising a skill pupils should be concentrating on a limited number of learning cues and therefore the teacher should make every effort to restrict her feedback to the specific cues provided in the presentation. The teacher may need to provide additional learning cues when modifying or differentiating activities but generally it may be better to focus on this limited number of specific and congruent cues, and avoid what Rink (1985) refers to as the 'shotgun approach'. The shotgun approach occurs when the teacher initially asks the learner to focus on certain specific congruent learning cues but then proceeds to offer a range of additional learning cues not provided in the demonstration.

Distractions can also lead to a loss of focus and concentration on congruent cues. An overemphasis on competition in the early stages of learning can lead to a lack of focus on the important learning cues. For example, moving quickly into competitive games when introducing short tennis may result in a loss of quality in ground strokes because pupils become more interested in hitting the ball hard to win a point, when a more cooperative type of game might help pupils focus on congruent learning cues.

Examples of congruent learning cues might include: 'Look up and pass the ball to feet' (Soccer). 'Try to reach up to place the ball on the backboard, aiming at the top right hand corner of the black square', (Basketball). 'Play the shuttle close to the top of the net' (Badminton drop shot).

Evidence from the work of Arena (1979), in which it was noted that 46% of PE teachers' initial feedback was not relevant to the learning cues provided in the presentation, does suggest that teachers may need to pay attention to this aspect of their teaching if they are to be more effective in terms of pupil learning. Not all feedback can be congruent, and the teacher should provide more 'extended' feedback or refinement (in which pupils are asked to improve a particular aspect of the movement) for those progressing well, and a lower level of refinement for those having difficulty. These might be termed 'differentiated cues'.

Exercise 8 may be used to analyse the congruency of learning cues offered when giving feedback. Ask an observer to watch one of your lessons and to write down in the left hand column the learning cues you provided in the presentation. The observer should then 'tally' the frequency of use of these congruent learning cues. The second part of the schedule is for the observer to record the frequency of use of any additional learning cues provided when giving pupils feedback, but not mentioned in the initial presentation. Some of these incongruent cues may be 'differentiated cues' and there is the facility within the schedule to distinguish both incongruent and 'differentiated cues' by recording a 'X' for the latter.

*Exercise 8    Congruency of Learning Cues in Teacher's Feedback*

| Learning cues provided in the presentation | Frequency of use of congruent learning cues in pupil feedback |
|---|---|
| | |
| | |
| | |
| Additional learning cues provided but not mentioned in the presentation | Frequency of use of incongruent learning cues* |
| | |
| | |
| | |

*Indicate with cross tally 'X' if a differentiated cue.

## Specific and general feedback

When learners are given clear, understandable, and congruent information that helps them to appreciate what they must do to improve their performance, then this is referred to as 'specific' or 'qualitative' feedback.

Although the stage of learning, degree of precision and amount of practice are important considerations, there is considerable motor learning research evidence to support the view that the more specific or qualitative the feedback or knowledge of results given to the learner, the more likely that learning will occur (Magill, 1993). Also, both Werner and Rink (1989) and Hardy (1990) provide some evidence to suggest that the provision of more specific instructional cues may result in more appropriate pupil responses than inaccurate information and general statements.

Examples of specific informative feedback might include: 'Try to stay sideways on when you hit the ball' (Tennis). 'Keep the hips up' (Swimming – backstroke).

More general feedback statements such as 'Fine', 'Good', 'OK', may be useful for developing a positive and motivating learning environment, keeping pupils 'on-task', and generally encouraging pupils prior to giving more specific feedback, but when teachers over-use general feedback in their teaching, pupils are unlikely to know what to focus on to improve their performance. Therefore, congruent specific feedback is likely to be more effective than general statements such as 'Try harder', 'Concentrate' or, 'You'll have to do better than that!'.

However, there is the question of feedback being too specific and precise, as this might 'overload' the learner and interfere with the learning process. For example, in the early stages of learning teachers might need to avoid using words that pupils do not understand. In one study by Magill and Wood (1986), it was important that learners understood what the instructor actually meant by such terms as 'too fast' or 'too slow' when learning a novel task. Only after a certain amount of practice and understanding of the terms used could the learner benefit from the specific feedback. This suggests that only those learners who have moved beyond the early stages of learning may be capable of benefiting from very precise and specific feedback.

## Positive and negative feedback

A lot of the earlier descriptive-analytic research on teaching in physical education seemed to suggest that PE teachers were more negative than positive in their responses to pupil skill attempts (Anderson, 1980). However, the research picture on this issue is somewhat inconclusive (Pieron and Cheffers, 1988). In some cases the negative feedback in these studies may well have been related to the tendency for PE teachers to be constantly involved in correcting errors. The effect of the publication of such data, albeit from a very limited number of studies, was that the PE profession considered negative feedback was 'bad', and that teachers needed to give much more positive feedback. It is now thought that there needs to be a more critical and yet balanced view of the whole issue of positive and negative feedback.

First of all, negative feedback in the form of 'extreme criticism' of pupil efforts and skill attempts is undoubtedly inappropriate and is unlikely to lead to learning or greater effort and, in fact, may lead to control problems (Dunkin and Biddle, 1974; Rosenshine, 1976). On the other hand, a teacher who spends the whole lesson going around the class saying 'Good', 'Great', the whole time, even when such praise is not deserved, is likely to decrease rather than increase motivation. Therefore, because the terms negative and positive feedback have these unfortunate connotations, it may be better to use the term 'supportive feedback' for feedback that might have a combination of positive, negative and corrective components. Feedback needs to be appropriate to the circumstances, and even what might be regarded as negative feedback, in which the teacher is informing the pupil of the nature of his errors, can be provided in such a way that it is encouraging, informative and supportive. Errors can be corrected in a positive and sympathetic way, and pupils do appreciate teachers displaying empathy when they are having learning difficulties (Branwhite, 1988). For example – 'You're working really hard Jane, but you're still having difficulty hitting through the middle of the ball because you're leaning back too much. Let me show you what to do. Try to step forward as you strike through the ball ... like this!'

In this way, supportive feedback is particularly useful for a pupil who has not been able to understand and apply the learning cues offered, even after frequent attempts to give feedback. It is also worth noting that effective teachers are more likely to refer to the actual performance of the learner, rather that to the learner as a person when providing feedback. So, instead of saying 'That's a poor strike John', it may be more considerate to say, 'Try to watch the ball onto the racket next time'. As mentioned in Chapter 4, effective teachers also 'individualise feedback and guidance for personal levels of mastery and understanding and do not make comparisons between pupils'. (p. 127)

It is argued that supportive feedback ought to have a strong 'reminder' component to it for pupils who do not really concentrate on the learning cues offered by the teacher, either because they think they 'know it all' or because they just don't listen. Firmer tones of voice might be used in such cases, with an emphasis on what was not satisfactory about the behaviour or skill attempt, and an indication of what is considered to be desirable. Naturally, there is an overlap between these forms of feedback interactions and those discussed in Chapter 7 related to 'Maintaining an effective learning environment'.

But, what about the quality of positive feedback or praise? Good and Brophy (1991) have produced a very useful set of guidelines for effective use of praise and these are shown in Box 16.

Exercise 9 is designed to help teachers to examine their use of a selection of different types of feedback by using either a colleague observer or when analysing a videotaped lesson. However, before

---

**Box 16**
**Guidelines for effective praise**

**Effective praise:**

- is delivered contingently rather than randomly and unsystematically;
- specifies the particular accomplishment rather than being a general positive reaction such as, 'Good';
- shows spontaneity, variety, paying attention to the pupil's accomplishment rather than being a bland conditioned response;
- rewards attainment of specified performance criteria rather than mere participation;
- provides information to pupils about their competence or accomplishments as opposed to no information at all or only information related to pupil status;
- orients pupils towards their own performance rather than comparing themselves with others;
- uses pupil's own prior accomplishments rather than the accomplishments of peers as a context for describing present accomplishments;
- is given in recognition for effort or success at personally difficult tasks;
- attributes success to effort and ability rather than to ability alone or to external factors such as luck;
- fosters a belief in pupils that their efforts to improve should be for intrinsic (they enjoy the task) rather than extrinsic reasons (to please the teacher);
- focuses pupils attention on what they are learning as opposed to purely compliance with the teachers authority;
- fosters interest and enthusiasm for the skill being learned.

*Adapted from: Good and Brophy (1991) p. 213.*

---

using the observational analysis schedule in Exercise 9 the descriptors for classifying the different types of feedback need to be learned.

## Exercise 9   *Use of different types of feedback*

*Descriptors for the different types of feedback*

- General positive feedback – is a positive statement that does not tell the learner what is good about the skill attempt but which may be used to encourage pupil effort.
  Examples: 'Well done', 'Good try', 'That's better'.

- Specific positive feedback – is a positive statement that gives a clear indication as to why the performance was good.
  Examples: 'Great extension of the legs Jane'.
  'That's much better length of drive Dave'.
- Negative feedback – is a general critical statement about the performance with possible reference to the pupil personally.
  Examples: 'That's rubbish'.
  'Come on Sarah, you're not really trying'.
- Supportive specific feedback – in which the teacher attempts initially to encourage the pupil concerning the skill attempt and then indicates what specific aspects of the performance are in error and what needs to be done to improve the movement.
  Example: 'You're trying hard but having problems with your footwork. Try putting your left foot in front of your right next time'.

## Observation schedule – use of different types of feedback

The observer simply puts a 'tally' ( / ) in the appropriate column whenever the particular type of feedback is used by the teacher.

| Type of Feedback (FB) | Frequency of Use (tally) |
| --- | --- |
| General Positive FB | |
| Specific Positive FB | |
| Negative FB | |
| Supportive specific FB | |

## Refinement

When pupils are having difficulty with the task the teacher may need to modify or refine the task by asking the pupil either to concentrate on more simple 'differentiated' learning cues, or perform an earlier movement in the skill learning progression. In this way the teacher is reducing what is expected of the pupil, and is 'individualising' or 'differentiating' learning based on his observation of pupil response to the task. Similarly, those performing well may need extending tasks to challenge them and 'extend' their opportunity to learn. In Masser's (1987) study of primary-age children learning a simple task, refinement had an immediate and long-term benefit on pupil achievement. High-skilled subjects in the Rikard (1992) study improved by 14% when receiving refining tasks, and low-skilled subjects responded well to refinement when it was followed by specific corrective feedback.

## Guidance cycles

When the different teaching skills of observation, feedback and refinement are used in combination with an individual or group to help 'shape' pupil behaviour towards the movement objective, then we might term this sequence of skills a 'guidance cycle'. The concept of a teaching or guidance 'cycle' implies that teaching skills or tactics may be more important in sequence than as isolated interactions (Bellack *et al.*, 1966; Dunkin and Biddle, 1974). Few studies have investigated sequencing or 'chaining' in the teaching of physical education and these have been mainly descriptive. Olson (1983), for example, analysed 24 physical education lessons and noted that teachers used general positive feedback chains (331 times) and corrective feedback chains (164 times) more than positive specific feedback chains (32 times). In Mawer's study of primary school teachers teaching physical education (Mawer and Brown, 1983) nearly three-quarters (72.7%) of all guidance interaction following presentations were general rather than specific, and only 43% of guidance interactions were terminated with positive feedback. Although there is a dearth of process product or experimental teacher effectiveness research to support the value of particular sequences or 'chains' of teacher behaviour in terms of pupil achievement in physical education, it may be reasonable to assume that appropriate combinations of some of the teaching skills discussed in this chapter may facilitate pupil learning. Naturally, other factors such as planning of appropriate learning experiences, sound presentation, etc., also need to be taken into account, and all aspects of teaching may be dependent on each other for a model of teacher effectiveness to be created (Rink and Werner, 1987). Assuming that the task set for the pupils is appropriate, has been presented effectively and pupils efficiently dispersed to their work areas to practise, what would a guidance cycle look like that had all the likely components of effective teaching? Figure 12 offers a suggestion for what might be termed a 'positive guidance cycle'.

A positive guidance cycle might begin with teacher observation and diagnosis of the pupil's skill attempts, with the teacher particularly focusing on the learning cues provided in the presentation of the skill.

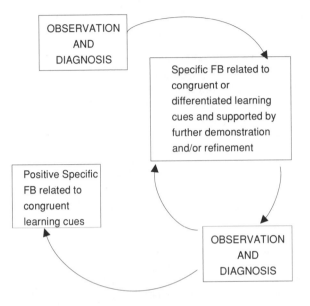

*Figure 12   A positive specific guidance cycle*

One of the most important aspects of the guidance cycle then follows. The teacher's initial contact with the pupil needs to be supportive and encouraging, particularly if the pupil has experienced a degree of failure. For example: 'Now John, you're trying very hard but I can see you are having a spot of difficulty'.

Within this second phase of the cycle the teacher may then offer a reinforcement of the learning cues covered in the presentation or differentiated cues. However, it is very likely that the pupil may not have remembered the image of the movement provided in the teacher's demonstration. Some children do appear to be poor 'imagers' (Fishburne and Hall, 1987), and really need a second opportunity to see the movement being performed. Therefore, a further demonstration to the pupil or group accompanied by an emphasis on the key learning cues may be appropriate, rather than just verbally telling pupils what they must do to improve. For example: 'John, let me show you again what to do. See how I am reaching up high with my right hand to nearly place the ball on the backboard in the top right hand corner of the black square. Now you have a go and I'll watch.'

Having offered a further presentation of the skill it is now essential that the teacher observes the pupil again and does not terminate the guidance cycle at this point. Further observation might show that the pupil has done exactly what the teacher has suggested and so specific positive feedback may be given. 'Well done John, that was a good reach and accurate placement in the right hand corner of the black square.'

An earlier study by the author (Mawer and Brown, 1983) suggested that teachers tended to terminate guidance cycles too early. After offering initial feedback concerning how to improve performance, the majority of teachers moved on without giving the pupil the opportunity to show their next skill attempt and hopefully receive positive feedback for implementing the teacher's advice.

Not all pupils will be successful after the teacher's guidance and feedback, and it may be necessary to repeat the cycle or offer a modification/refinement of the task from an earlier stage of the skill learning progression. Also, modified equipment or facilities (e.g. lower basketball backboards) may be available and appropriate for such differentiation.

When the teacher 'scans' the class in the initial stages of working she may note that a large number of pupils are having a similar problem and it may therefore be more efficient to offer a further presentation to the whole group, or even modify the task.

Also, when the teacher is moving around the class, or even offering feedback to a group or individual, he may spot an opportunity to offer positive and specific feedback from a distance. This opportunity should be taken because, in general, the sooner feedback is given after performance the more likely it is to be effective. This form of short, 'distance feedback' can also benefit the rest of the class by focusing their attention on the key learning cues. It may also serve as a valuable monitoring function to keep pupils 'on-task', particularly if specific praise is provided.

What teachers must avoid when giving feedback during guided practice is what Siedentop (1991) refers to as the 'correction complex', and what was identified by Mawer (Mawer and Brown, 1983) as a 'fault-finder' style of teaching. Having diagnosed the pupil's learning difficulties the teacher using this interaction sequence focuses the pupil's attention on the congruent learning cues, observes the pupil perform again, and then, instead of offering positive specific feedback when the pupil has succeeded in performing according to the teacher's advice, the teacher appears to look for additional problems with the pupils' performance. The teacher is thus preoccupied with correction of errors and gives the impression of always finding fault in the pupil's performance rather than looking for aspects of performance or effort to praise. Many of the 'fault finder' cycles identified in the Mawer study also tended to have negative feedback components, were largely verbal in nature and did not include additional use of demonstration.

## Other teaching skills used in direct teaching

Although most of the teaching skills and tactics used in direct teaching have been discussed, many skills used in other teaching styles and strategies are used by teachers in a mixed-tactics approach to direct teaching. For example, questioning may be used within guidance cycles that are largely direct in nature. For example: 'That's a good effort Fran, but what do you think you need to do to keep the ball down?'

In this way a question involves the learner in thinking about the skill and helps the teacher to find out whether the learner understands the key learning cues. Teaching strategies using a predominance of questioning as a teaching tactic will be discussed in Chapter 10.

# Teaching strategies for greater pupil involvement in the learning process and the development of cross-curricular skills

## Introduction

As discussed in Chapter 4, there is a need for the effective teacher to use a variety of teaching styles and strategies in order not only to achieve the objectives suggested by the end of key stage statements, but also to work towards the National Curriculum cross-curricular competencies. Pupils are now expected not only to 'analyse', 'adapt', 'improvise' and 'evaluate', but generally to think more about their work in physical education, and develop decision-making, problem-solving, and personal and social skills. This may involve pupils having greater responsibility for their own work and being more involved in their own learning.

A range of teaching approaches that offer pupils the opportunity to make decisions, to take the initiative, either to create or have to solve problems, may be appropriate, particularly if pupils are to become more independent and self-reliant in terms of their own learning. The more direct teaching strategies already discussed in Chapter 9 may not provide these possibilities, but there are a variety of recognised teaching approaches that teachers feel may offer pupils greater opportunities to become more involved in their own learning, and develop certain personal and social skills. These include peer support and collaborative teaching approaches, pupil self-appraisal strategies and teaching strategies that involve the teacher in posing questions to pupils and acting in a more facilitatory and mentoring role. Each of these strategies require the appropriate 'bonding' of curricular instructional and organisational decisions with effective teaching skills and tactics peculiar to the particular approach. Once again, Mosston (Mosston and Ashworth, 1986) provides an outline of the range of teaching styles or approaches that are available to the teacher and some of these will be discussed briefly in this chapter. The reader is referred to Mosston and Ashworth (1986) for a more detailed account of the 'spectrum' of teaching styles.

## Peer support and collaborative teaching/learning strategies

There appear to be considerable benefits in terms of both pupil learning gains and social development, of teaching strategies that reduce the size of the learning group or have a one-to-one tutoring role, or involve peer teaching or peer support (Bloom, 1984). Research does seem to support the view that children can effectively teach each other, provided the teaching programme is well structured and that pupils are trained for the role (Cooke, Heron and Heward, 1983).

Peer support teaching can be done in pairs or small groups depending on the activity being taught. What Mosston (Mosston and Ashworth, 1986) refers to as the 'reciprocal' teaching style, and Underwood (1991) as 'collaborative' learning, are peer support strategies which offer greater opportunities for social interaction, development of communication skills and empathy for each others learning attempts. In that pupils are helping each other learn and perform a task, such approaches involve pupils in appreciating the teaching points related to a movement, and in turn they may learn to understand the mechanics of performing the task. Also, pupils observe their colleagues' performance, compare it with a set of performance criteria provided by the teacher and then convey the feedback to their colleague. As Mosston and Ashworth (1986) point out, this approach develops a: '... social bond that goes beyond the task'. (p. 63)

In addition to the above points you might use this teaching strategy if your objectives for a particular episode of teaching were to work towards National Curriculum objectives such as: '... to develop, refine and evaluate a series of actions, with or without contact with others', 'to cooperate with others in regular practice in order to refine their techniques' (SCAA, 1994b, pp. 6 and 9) – and the development of interaction skills related to 'giving feedback on their own and others performances', and 'help and are helped by others' (NCC, 1992, p. D5).

These approaches are often used in combination with other teaching and learning strategies. In fact, it has been suggested that peer tutoring is most effective when the learning programme is well structured, is repetitive, has progression linked to learner mastery and with peer tutors well trained in their role (Cooke, Heron and Heward, 1983). However, there are peer tutoring approaches in PE in which a degree of choice is offered to each partner in terms of the selection of the activity to be learned (Williams, 1993).

The use of this approach does involve the teacher in considerable planning and the production of well-presented teaching materials in the

**Box 17**
**Criteria task card for the teaching of the basketball set shot**

# BASKETBALL
## ONE HAND SET SHOT

**THE TASK**

Each partner is to take 10 one hand set shots from a comfortable distance.
Switch roles after every 10 shots. Continue until called together.

**OBSERVERS ROLE**

1. Compare the doer's action with the "things to look for".
2. Tell the doer what he/she is doing well.
3. Correct if necessary; then comment on any improvement shown.

**THINGS TO LOOK FOR**

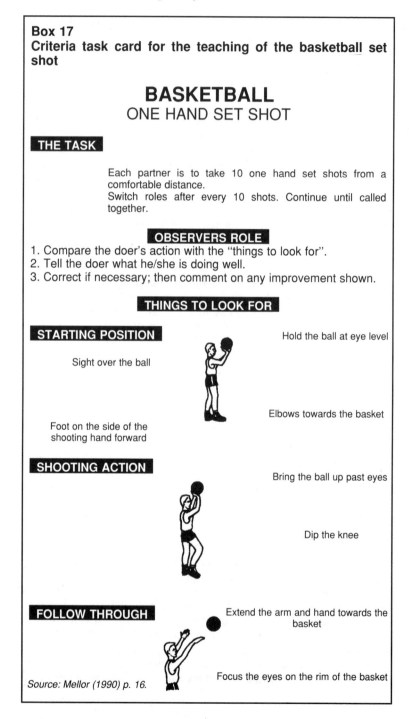

**STARTING POSITION**

Sight over the ball

Hold the ball at eye level

Elbows towards the basket

Foot on the side of the shooting hand forward

**SHOOTING ACTION**

Bring the ball up past eyes

Dip the knee

**FOLLOW THROUGH**

Extend the arm and hand towards the basket

Focus the eyes on the rim of the basket

*Source: Mellor (1990) p. 16.*

form of criteria task cards as an aid to the peer tutoring process. Also, peer tutors need to be trained to observe, analyse, give feedback, as well as develop the social skills that are essential for the success of this approach to teaching/learning. An example of a criteria task card is that suggested by Mellor (1990) and shown in Box 17. A selection of task cards for different activities are provided by Dudley Education Services (1991).

In using this teaching approach the teacher may be involved initially in demonstrating the task to be learned (or it may be presented via the task sheet), but the teacher must also emphasise to both the observer and the performer what their roles will be. The observer needs to know and understand what is on the criteria task card, and then observe their colleague performing. Having observed their colleague's skill attempt, the observer must then compare the performance with the information on the task card, and then offer feedback to the performer concerning the correctness of the performance and what needs to be done to improve. The observer may also need to inform the teacher about the feedback given. Pupils may then change roles.

Mosston (Mosston and Ashworth, 1986) emphasises the importance of the teacher's role when using the reciprocal teaching approach. It is, he suggests: '... to answer questions by the observers, to initiate communication only with the observers'. (p. 66)

In other words, the teacher should not take over or interfere with the observer's role otherwise the observer is not learning to observe, analyse, evaluate and develop the appropriate social skills. However, if the observer is making an incorrect observation, and consequently giving incorrect feedback to the performer, then it is the teacher's job to guide the observer's observations to the key aspects of the movement that need attention, and the most appropriate feedback to offer the performer. The teacher is therefore educating the observer to observe and understand the key features for successful performance of the movement. The skills required of the teacher in this role include:

- careful planning of the teaching and learning situation;
- 'training' of pupils to act as tutors;
- the ability to listen carefully to the feedback provided by the observer;
- giving positive and informative feedback to observers concerning the observation, communication and feedback offered to the performer, and if necessary, to direct the observer's attention to the important features of the movement and how they relate to the criteria on the task card;
- careful preparation of criteria task cards to ensure clarity of criteria and features of the movement to be observed. This may include presenting a series of pictures of the movement in sequence, and using appropriate language linked to these pictures.

It may also include reminders of the manner in which observers should execute their role. For example, task cards in the Dudley resource mentioned earlier state: 'Remember – we are all different, therefore be patient, give praise, co-operate, show honesty, look for detail, and show a responsible attitude'.

The effective teacher will therefore apply a modification of the guidance cycle described in Chapter 9, with feedback comments directed to the observer and related to their supporting role within this teaching approach. For example:

Well done Mary, you gave very clear instructions about the need to follow through.

Sam, I liked the way you emphasised the need to reach up high – well done.

In the case of observer errors, the teacher might pose a question, firstly to make the observer think, but also to ascertain exactly what she has been saying to the performer:

Which foot do you think she should take off on? What does the task card show?

What other part of the body other than the arms can help to get distance and height into the shot?

Sometimes the observer won't admit that they are having difficulties with their observation. Underwood (1991) offers an example of a sequence of teacher–pupil interaction and discourse that might occur when an observer has not been able to spot that her partner was taking off on the incorrect foot for a forward roll:

| | | |
|---|---|---|
| Teacher: | – | 'How is your partner getting on Fiona?' |
| Helper: | – | 'Fine, she's good'. |
| Teacher: | – | 'You say she's fine, but what does the picture tell you about the way she should take off for a forward roll?' |
| Helper: | – | 'She should take off on two feet'. |
| Teacher: | – | 'Can we watch your partner together to look at that point?' |
| Helper: | – | 'OK'. (Both watch) |
| Helper: | – | 'Oh, she's taking off on one foot, I hadn't seen that'. |
| Teacher: | – | 'Well done Fiona, you have spotted that well, now see if you can help her to correct it'. (p. 19) |

Although Mosston believes that the teacher should only communicate with the observer, for reasons of safety, maintenance of an appropriate social ethos, or when there are specific learning difficulties, he may need to intervene either on a pair or whole class basis. A potentially dangerous situation in gymnastics, for example, may need to be stopped immediately, and the whole class reminded of safe practice. A common problem of movement observation or feedback by a number of observers, may need to be relayed to the whole class rather than inefficiently mentioned to each observer in turn.

The creation of an appropriate 'social ethos' within this method of working may initially be the main problem for many teachers, particularly with classes that are familiar with a more command/practice teaching approach. It is difficult for some pupils to quietly 'slot into' a 'teacher' role. Underwood and Williams (1991) suggest a particular procedure which has been successfully used in collaborative learning in gymnastics to ensure that pupils learn the social skills required for working in this way.

(1) Ask the pupils to go with a partner.
(2) Give each pair a paper and pencil.
(3) Explain that they are going to work together and help each other.
(4) Ask them to discuss and then write down what they need to do to be able to work together happily.
(5) Ask them to decide which idea they consider more important.
(6) Ask each pair to state the most important idea, then list them on a blackboard or flip chart (e.g. ideas might include 'be patient', 'praise each other', 'be nice').
(7) Discuss with the class and clarify the meanings of the words in practice.
(8) Display the list of negotiated and agreed social qualities and expectations in the working environment in future lessons.
(9) Reinforce and remind pupils of these social expectations in future lessons.

Whether the teacher uses this procedure or not, the important point being made is that the effective teacher using this teaching approach will make their expectations for social behaviour very explicit from the start.

There may be other reasons for the teacher actually to interact with the performer. These might include occasions when the performer is having particular learning difficulties and needs specialist help, either at the request of the observer (because they were unable to help their partner), or because you as a teacher have observed a particular learning problem. In both cases it may be appropriate to ask the observer if you can both work together in helping the performer, thus allowing the observer to feel that they are still playing their 'helper' role.

One of the advantages of the 'reciprocal' or 'collaborative' teaching approach is that learners may receive more feedback as well as develop their social interaction skills, as Goldberger and Howarth

(1993) point out: 'Learners who have experienced this style offer more feedback, more positive feedback, and accept more feedback more readily than learners not having experienced the reciprocal style'. (p. 25)

However, research by Byra and Marks (1993) does suggest that observers are more likely to give frequent specific feedback to friends than non-acquaintances, and that performers feel more comfortable receiving feedback from friends.

However, some teachers may feel that because of the amount of talking between learner and observer, there is a lot of lesson time when pupils are inactive, and this may certainly be the case in the early stages of using this approach. When pupils have become accustomed to this new way of working they may benefit from being more aware of the requirements of the task, as Williams (1993) suggests:

… in the longer term, learning is enhanced. This is because each pupil receives more feedback than would be possible if it were given by the teacher. It is also because the act of playing the teacher role is an opportunity for the pupil to think through the task and how to approach it when the turn to be performer comes, with greater understanding which facilitates practical learning. (p. 30)

Research examining the use of the reciprocal style in the teaching of PE suggests that this approach does positively influence social interaction and the acquisition of motor skills (Goldberger *et al.*, 1982).

Other small scale studies of the use of reciprocal teaching in UK secondary schools have produced some interesting observations concerning what teachers feel are the advantages as well as the problems that may be experienced when using this approach (BAALPE, 1989b). The three schools taking part in the BAALPE project examining teaching and learning strategies in PE believed that the following benefits may be forthcoming when using the reciprocal teaching approach in gymnastics and basketball:

- teachers benefit because they are made more aware of the personal and social needs of pupils;
- improvement of skill in specific technique practice situations;
- high cognitive as well as physical involvement of pupils;
- greater pupil involvement in their own learning;
- improved pupil–pupil communication, better working relationships and positive influence on social development;
- improved pupil–teacher communication;
- possible improved self-esteem due to constant positive feedback from teacher and pupil observer;
- pupils who act as observer first appear to gain from the experience because they possibly learn the task more quickly;
- longer periods of active learning particularly with 'closed' skills;
- reciprocal teaching and use of task cards may be useful for evaluation of pupil progress and profiling.

However, all the groups in the BAALPE project experienced certain problems in implementing the reciprocal teaching strategy, even when this approach was only a part of the lessons taught. The problems experienced included:

- pupils found the transition from a more traditional teaching approach difficult because the new approach required more of them, which they found threatening, but also because they had difficulty with the lack of teacher feedback;
- teachers found the transition difficult because of the need to give feedback to observers on their observational and teaching skills, rather than directly to the performer;
- pupils tended to lose interest in the skill when they were having skill learning difficulties, suggesting that the use of this approach possibly needs to be restricted to short periods of time and selected tasks (e.g. closed skills/techniques);
- pupils sometimes had difficulties in reading and remembering specific coaching points from the task cards resulting in inaccurate and incorrect feedback. This in turn led to a lack of progress on the part of the learner, and teachers had to intervene to give feedback;
- because some pupils had difficulty in reading the task cards it was considered to be essential that task cards are clear and simple, written in a language that all pupils would understand (taking account of individual ability levels), and have clear diagrams which are well laid out and easy to understand;
- the whole teaching approach may take longer than more teacher-directed approaches.

The general impression that one gets from the limited experimental research and school-based action research literature is that the effective teacher of PE using this approach needs to:

(1) be sure that the activity to be taught is appropriate for the use of a reciprocal/collaborative teaching strategy, and facilities and equipment are available to support this approach;
(2) be sure that pupils are clear about the social expectations of their role within this teaching approach, and procedures put into operation to establish the appropriate social ethos (which may include appropriate pairing/grouping of pupils);
(3) be sure about her role in terms of looking to give feedback to the observer, but also be aware of the need to give performer and class feedback when required;
(4) design well-produced and carefully thought out task cards with clear diagrams and language at the appropriate level of pupil understanding;

(5) be aware of the need to give considerable help and training to observers in observation skills, teaching skills and social skills;

(6) have appropriately modified observation, listening and feedback skills to be able to improve not only the ability of the pupil observer to observe and give feedback, but also to be aware of the need to use questioning strategies to help the observer to become a more effective pupil teacher;

(7) be aware of the possibilities of using this approach for only part of a lesson.

## Pupil self-appraisal teaching strategies

In Mosston's (Mosston and Ashworth, 1986) self-check teaching approach the learner is given more responsibility for his own learning. In effect, the learner evaluates himself. However, it is expected that the learner has experienced both the practice teaching strategy and the reciprocal strategy prior to being allowed to 'self-check' their own learning. The learner does need to be reasonably proficient before being able to analyse and evaluate her own performance, as Mosston (Mosston and Ashworth, 1986) points out: '… for learners who have not attained basic proficiency in the task, this style may not be appropriate'. (p. 104)

It also helps if the learner has experienced using criteria task cards to give feedback to a colleague as with the reciprocal teaching approach, because similar criteria task cards are used in the self-check strategy. An example of a performance criteria task card to use when adopting this approach is shown in Box 18.

When using this approach the teacher should explain the purpose of this teaching approach, explain the role of the learner, and the role of the teacher, and then present the task to be practised. Pupils are then sent to their work areas to practise using the criteria task cards to evaluate their own performance. What does the teacher now do? The teacher's role is simply to assess how well the pupil is self-checking and either provide appropriate feedback or use questioning to help the learner to appreciate how to use the task card for self-checking.

The teaching skills used are modifications of the observation, guidance and feedback skills described in the previous chapter, and the use of convergent questioning discussed in the next section. Observation is directed towards not only the pupil's performance, but also how the pupil compares their performance with the criteria on the task card. Feedback relates to how well they have 'self-checked' their performance rather than just the performance itself. However, as Mellor (1990) points out:

If the learner after engaging in a self-check still has difficulties and cannot isolate the problem, then the teacher will furnish an additional explanation of the task, demonstrate the skill again, correct the error, or whatever the learner needs in order to move on with the performance of the task. The teacher for that moment shifts the behaviour to Style B (Practice Style). (p. 13)

Therefore, when required, the teacher will need to use many of the teaching skills discussed in the previous chapter.

---

**Box 18**
**Self-check performance criteria task card for basketball set shot**

| THE TASK | 1. Read the card |
| | 2. Take 5 shots and self-check |
| | 3. Use yes/no self check columns |
| | 4. Take 5 more shots and continue self check |
| | 5. Repeat until called in. |

THINGS TO LOOK FOR

| | Yes | No | |
|---|---|---|---|
| STARTING POSITION<br>1. Hold ball on the shelf hand at eye level<br>2. Sight over ball at rim of basket<br>3. Take staggered stance, placing foot on side of shooting hand forward | | | |
| SHOOTING ACTION<br>1. Dip the knee, and bring the ball up past the eyes<br>2. Extend the elbow towards basket<br>3. Release the ball with high arc | | | |
| FOLLOW THROUGH<br>1. Extend the arm and hand towards basket<br>2. Follow through with a limp wrist<br>3. Focus the eyes on the rim of the basket before and after the shot is released | | | |

*Source: Mellor (1990) p. 14.*

A teacher might use this teaching approach if her objectives for an episode of teaching were:

- to offer the learner a greater degree of independence within the learning process and thus develop greater self-responsibility for their own performance feedback;
- to offer the learner the opportunity to learn to self-appraise their own learning, and develop a degree of kinaesthetic awareness of their own performance on which to base personal self-assessment and self-improvement;
- to provide pupils with a learning situation in which they may learn to be honest and objective while engaging in self-checking, and to be able to recognise discrepancies and limitations in their performance;
- to individualise the learning process.

Certain skills in physical education are not suitable for this teaching approach. These include 'body orientation' tasks, such as gymnastics, diving and dance, because, as Mosston (Mosston and Ashworth, 1986) points out: 'The sense of movement may supply a general feeling about the performance, but it does not supply the accurate information needed for improvement'. (p. 106)

Tasks that are appropriate for use in this teaching approach include ball games (e.g. basketball, hockey, soccer) that have definite progressions, and some athletic events that do not involve a high degree of body orientation. There is the suggestion that the use of videotape replay and mirrors might help the learner to take greater advantage of this strategy, but more research is needed concerning the value of the self-check approach both for learning and the development of pupil self-concept (Goldberger and Howarth, 1993). Also, some pupils do enjoy working alone and being more independent, others do not, and this is an important issue that the teacher would need to consider prior to deciding to use this teaching approach.

## Teaching pupils to think in Physical Education: Teaching strategies for pupil cognitive development

Many believe that the movement medium in physical education is ideal for stimulating pupils' cognitive development. If we want pupils to explore, discover, create, analyse, apply, synthesise and evaluate in PE then more 'indirect' teaching approaches may be required. If we want to stimulate a more 'thoughtful' approach to learning and create independent pupils who, in National Curriculum terms, take initiative and acquire responsibility in 'planning and evaluating tasks', take more responsibility for their actions and response to tasks, to 'compare', 'monitor', 'interpret' and 'make judgements', 'compose', 'adapt', 'improvise', 'analyse and review' and develop problem-solving skills, then it will be necessary to plan an appropriate learning environment to achieve these outcomes.

More pupil-centred and 'humanistic' approaches to learning that are designed to create a situation in which pupils are more involved in, and take more responsibility for their own learning, may help to produce a young person who is better equipped to respond to the demands and pressures of a changing environment.

Most educators agree that it is a good idea to teach higher order thinking and problem-solving skills, but they tend to disagree on the best way to do it, and they are unsure of what can actually be achieved. There are those who believe that problem-solving skills cannot be taught directly, or have transfer benefits to everyday life. Yet there are others who are in favour of identifying teaching strategies for teaching higher order thinking skills and teaching them directly to pupils. Those in favour of teaching such skills to pupils either believe that more generic strategies should be taught that cross subject boundaries, or they consider that inquiry, creative thinking, decision-making and problem-solving skills should be taught in the context of applying specific subject matter knowledge, concepts and principles. Good and Brophy (1991) take the view that many of the teaching strategies used are based on the assumptions that: '... basic thinking and problem solving skills can be identified that are generic to all subjects and are needed in a broad range of life situations, and these skills can and should be taught in schools, ideally in separate courses or units of their own rather than just as part of subject matter teaching'. (p. 464) They quote the CoRT programme (De Bono, 1983; 1985) as an example of a specially designed programme to develop pupil thinking skills.

But, what of physical education? What teaching strategies are available to the PE teacher to help develop in pupils these higher order cognitive processes and problem-solving skills?

Mosston (Mosston and Ashworth, 1986) identifies a series of teaching approaches that offer pupils the opportunity to be involved in what he terms 'the discovery process'. This, he believes, involves such cognitive operations as – comparing, contrasting, categorising, hypothesising, synthesising, solving problems, extrapolating and inventing. According to Mosston, to engage the pupil in crossing what he terms the 'discovery threshold', a degree of 'cognitive dissonance', mental dissatisfaction, and motivation to inquire and find a solution, needs to occur. Mosston's 'guided discovery' and 'divergent problem solving' strategies are designed to initiate the crossing of the 'discovery threshold'. But, what is the teacher intending to achieve when using these strategies, and what teaching skills does the teacher need to develop to be an effective teacher of this approach to learning?

## The Guided Discovery teaching strategy

The guided discovery strategy involves the teacher in designing a series of questions that will eventually lead to one or more appropriate answers and ultimately the discovery of a particular concept, principle or 'movement solution' by the pupil. It is not a series of random questions, but a planned logical sequence of very carefully designed questions leading to a particular solution. Hence this approach to teaching is often termed 'convergent problem solving', because the teacher helps the pupil to 'converge' gradually on the solution to the problem. In fact, Goldberger and Howarth (1993) identify two guided discovery strategies. The first, described as 'guided discovery', is more teacher directed, gradually leading the pupil through a series of 'conceptual steps' to the answer to the problem the teacher has set. In the second, 'convergent discovery', the learner: '... must find the path to discovery by him or herself. In this style each learner experiments with different solution pathways until the desired answer is revealed'. (p. 25)

The guided discovery teaching approach might be used when the teacher's objectives are to:

- involve the learner in the convergent process of thinking about a particular conceptual or movement problem that usually has one or more correct solutions;
- sequentially lead the learner through a series of small steps (through the use of questions) to 'discover' the solution to a problem.

This teaching strategy has been commonly used in the teaching of a variety of aspects of the school physical education curriculum, but more particularly when the teacher wants pupils to think about the application of movement principles, concepts or tactics in games. In National Curriculum gymnastics, for example (SCAA, 1994b), it is recommended that 'pupils should be taught the factors that influence quality in gymnastic performances, including extension, body tension and clarity of body shape' (p. 6). National Curriculum recommendations for Key Stage 3 athletics state that 'pupils should be taught: to apply the relevant mechanical principles underpinning performance' (p. 7), and 'to apply and extend their techniques and skills to other events' (p. 7). In the teaching of health-related exercise it is suggested that pupils should 'be taught to plan, undertake and evaluate a safe health-promoting exercise programme', and 'to show understanding of the principles involved' (p. 9). National Curriculum guidelines for the teaching of dance include that 'pupils should be taught to describe, analyse and interpret dances, recognising differences' (p. 7), and in games, 'to extend the skills and principles learned in the earlier years to develop techniques, tactics and strategies applicable to a variety of games' (p. 6).

Each of these National Curriculum requirements may be approached using a guided discovery strategy in which questions are posed to the learner or group that lead them to discover an appropriate correct solution, whether it be a particular mechanical principle in athletics (e.g. preventing forward rotation and therefore loss of height in the long jump), gymnastics (e.g. position of centre of gravity in balances or landing from jumps), or principles of attack and defence in invasion games.

Recent developments in what has been termed 'Teaching for Understanding' (Thorpe, Bunker and Almond, 1986), have emphasised guided discovery approaches designed to help pupils to understand the 'principles' of playing games, and to encourage appropriate decision making within games. Suggestions from the teaching of both invasion games and net/court games can be found in the literature (Shearsmith and Laws, 1988; Spackman, 1983). Shearsmith, for example, offers a detailed, verbatim scheme of work for the teaching of invasion games using mainly a guided discovery/problem-solving teaching approach. In attempting to lead the pupils to an understanding of the principle of support in a ball handling invasion game, Shearsmith goes through the following example of problem setting within the context of small-sided games:

Teacher: – Play a game and discover what you have to do to help (support) your team mate who has possession?
Possible pupil response:
             – Find a space and move into it quickly.
Teacher: – Yes, remember the distance a receiver is from the passer varies game to game. In Netball it is closer than in Hockey or Football. This is because of size of pitch and distance the ball can be passed. In rugby you have to be behind the person in possession to support him. When the learner has found a space he needs to let the passer know. There has to be what between the passer and receiver? The word begins with 'c'.
Response: – Communication.
Teacher: – There are two ways that people can communicate. What are they?
Response: – Talking (verbal). Visual (signal).
Teacher: – What system do we mainly use in basketball and netball?

Paul Stoddart (BAALPE, 1989b), in the teaching of invasion games, posed the following problems for pupils in his lesson on 'How can we keep possession?'

Question: – What sort of passes are safest?
Answer: – Low, flat, fast passes over short distances.
Question: – What kinds of passes are least safe?
Answer: – High, slow lobs over long distances.
Question: – How do I choose the best receiver before I actually give a pass?
Answer: – 'Who is closest to goal, or who is in the best receiving position away from a defender.

Thorpe (Thorpe *et al.*, 1986), in introducing the game of short tennis poses the following questions related to the use of the volley in the game (p. 26):

| | | |
|---|---|---|
| Teacher: | – | Where do you want to hit the ball if you are going to volley? |
| Pupil: | – | If I don't think I can win or force a weak shot by hitting the side, I hit deep. |
| Teacher: | – | Why? |
| Pupil: | – | If she tries to hit past the side of me I have time to cover it if she is hitting from well back. |
| Teacher: | – | Try it. |
| Teacher: | – | What will you do then if you are at the back and the volleyer has the net covered? |
| Pupil: | – | Hit over the top. |

In gymnastics, Williams (1993) suggests that pupils may be guided towards making their own decisions about the best way to perform certain gymnastic movements: 'Balance on two hands and two feet, and then on one leg. Which is the easier? Why?'

When using the guided discovery or convergent problem-solving strategies there are a number of points that the teacher needs to consider if these approaches are to be used effectively:

- questions must be designed in a logical sequence, leading to the solutions concerned with the objectives and subject matter of the lesson;
- try to avoid giving the answer to the problem as this may lead to pupils being less willing to examine and think about solutions because the teacher 'always gives the answer'.
- rather than respond negatively to incorrect answers, it's better to ask, 'I don't quite understand, would you explain your answer to me'.
- short episodes of this approach (e.g. use of questioning) can be used to clarify a task when using other styles, and when providing individual and group feedback.

The benefits of these teaching strategies are that they not only involve the learner in thinking about solutions or 'answers' to questions or problems posed by the teacher, but, because of the continuous success of the pupil in each small stage of discovering the solution to the problem, they may experience positive effects in terms of their self-esteem and a sense of accomplishment. Also, if this strategy is used in a group format, there may be positive benefits related to group cooperation and a willingness to listen to each other's point of view. However, little research has been done related to this teaching approach in physical education. Both Lawton (1989) and Turner and Martinek (1993) attempted to compare a skill or technique-oriented approach and game-centred ('teaching for understanding' or tactical focus) approach to teaching badminton and hockey respectively and found no significant difference between groups in terms of skill, knowledge and understanding of tactics, decision making or games playing ability.

## Divergent problem solving

Whereas all previous teaching approaches that have been discussed have involved the learner in producing a response prepared by the teacher, in divergent problem solving the pupil is offered the opportunity to discover and produce alternative answers to the question or problem set by the teacher. In other words, there may be a number of appropriate solutions to a movement problem set in gymnastics, dance, or games, or in the preparation of a fitness programme in health-related exercise. Although the teacher may be involved in preparing the general subject matter of the lesson, or the topic or problem to be encountered by the pupil or group, the pupils provide the answers and evaluate their own responses. Consequently, the initial response may actually determine the next move in the discovery of the final solution to the problem.

A teacher might decide to use this strategy if his objectives for a lesson or episode of teaching were to encourage pupils to:

- use their cognitive capacities;
- develop insights into the structure of an activity;
- discover multiple solutions to problems set by the teacher;
- become more independent and confident in terms of thinking about problems and evaluating solutions to problems.

This approach to teaching may be suitable for working towards National Curriculum objectives in dance, gymnastics and games. In dance at Key Stage 4 pupils should be taught: 'to perform and create dances in a range of styles, showing understanding of form and content'. In gymnastics at Key Stage 3 pupils should be taught 'to refine a series of gymnastic actions into increasingly complex sequences, working alone and with others, that include variety, contrast and repetition, using both floor and apparatus'. In games teaching at Key Stage 3 pupils should be taught to 'appreciate strengths and limitations in performance and use this information ... to outwit the opposition in competition', and at Key Stage 4 'to use increasingly advanced strategies and tactics of competition play and adapt these to the strengths and limitations of other players' (SCAA, 1994b).

In gymnastics this approach requires a greater degree of creativity on the part of the pupil because it allows for different solutions to a problem. For example: 'Create a sequence using a variety of different methods of travelling'. 'See how many different balances you can find using only three points of the body in contact with the floor'.

In games, using this approach might involve pupils in, for example, finding different ways of beating a defender with different types of passes, or having a group discuss and practise the sort of team defence they might set up in basketball and explain the advantages of such a tactic to the rest of the group.

In her 'contextual approach' to games teaching, Read (1993) suggests that tasks should be designed so that pupils have to find potential solutions to the game problem, and test these solutions out prior to group discussion. For example, a simple 2 v 1 attacking situation in hockey can be varied according to the positions of defenders as shown in Figure 13 using four grids or a channel with a goal.

Simple 2 v 1 problem-solving situations in rugby can be developed into 2 v 2, 3 v 2, 4 v 2, and 4 v 3 game-related practices as shown in Figure 14. In this way players are offered greater opportunities to work out solutions to game problems in context.

The need to combine teaching approaches is particularly important when considering the use of the divergent problem-solving strategy. Pupils do vary in terms of their ability to cope with different teaching approaches, and this may have something to do with their preferred learning styles. Not all pupils respond to problem-solving approaches or being offered the opportunity to be involved in their own learning. Some prefer to be given the answer! Others enjoy and benefit from being involved in the process of discovery. Schroder *et al.* (1967) might refer to the latter type of learner as having a high cognitive complexity (the complexity of their information processing system), whereas those feeling 'uncomfortable' in a problem-solving learning environment might be of low cognitive complexity or 'marginal' learners. The reader is referred to Joyce and Weil (1986) for a detailed discussion of this issue.

Mosston (Mosston and Ashworth, 1986) recognises that this teaching approach may be stressful to some pupils because of 'the demand of divergent production', and having to 'face the unknown'. Anyone who has to expose their ability to think and solve problems has a 'fear of failure' and revealing one's limitations. Mosston, therefore, recommends that with novice performers simple problem-solving episodes may be a more appropriate entry point to experiencing this learning approach. Those pupils who are more comfortable with this approach may respond positively to what Mosston calls 'branching off', which involves the provision of problems that have 'multiple solutions', such as a less predictable positioning of opponents in the development of attacking possibilities against two defenders in invasion games.

**Problem 1**   Defender must start in back quarter of grid
opposite the ball and move to challenge in entry grid

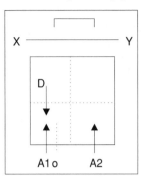

**Problem 2**   Defender starts diagonally opposite entry
square and must challenge in that square

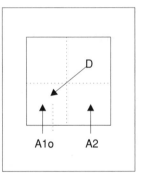

**Problem 3**   Defender starts in centre behind midline and takes
two steps over that line to respond to 'A's actions

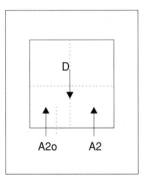

*Figure 13   Attacking problems in a hockey 2 v 1 situation*
*Source: Read (1993) p.13.*

AIM: TO PRACTISE HOLDING AND CREATING SPACE AGAINST
OPPOSITION

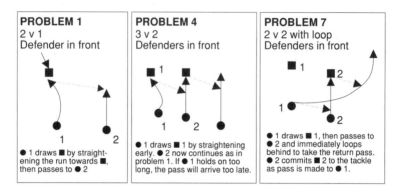

**PROBLEM 1**
2 v 1
Defender in front

● 1 draws ■ by straight-
ening the run towards ■,
then passes to ● 2

**PROBLEM 4**
3 v 2
Defenders in front

● 1 draws ■ 1 by straightening
early. ● 2 now continues as in
problem 1. If ● 1 holds on too
long, the pass will arrive too late.

**PROBLEM 7**
2 v 2 with loop
Defenders in front

● 1 draws ■ 1, then passes to
● 2 and immediately loops
behind to take the return pass.
● 2 commits ■ 2 to the tackle
as pass is made to ● 1.

N.B. In the early stages always condition the defenders so that
the attack can develop.

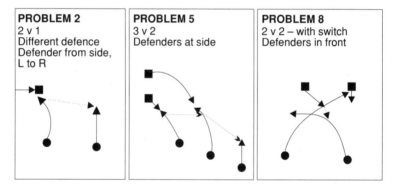

**PROBLEM 2**
2 v 1
Different defence
Defender from side,
L to R

**PROBLEM 5**
3 v 2
Defenders at side

**PROBLEM 8**
2 v 2 – with switch
Defenders in front

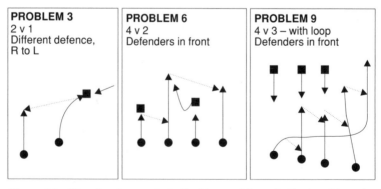

**PROBLEM 3**
2 v 1
Different defence,
R to L

**PROBLEM 6**
4 v 2
Defenders in front

**PROBLEM 9**
4 v 3 – with loop
Defenders in front

*Figure 14   The development of attacking problems in the teaching of
rugby*
*Source: Rugby Football Union (1992) p.14.*

Combining other teaching strategies with divergent problem solving is important for pupil learning. Mosston (Mosston and Ashworth, 1986), for example, points out that:

Performing the discovered movements must follow the discoveries. The learner needs to repeat some (or all) of the discovered movements to both verify the solutions and to reach the developmental purposes of the given activities. Episodes in style G (divergent problem solving) then, should be followed by a series of episodes in B (practice) or D (self-check). The episodes are designated as G/B or G/D combinations. (p. 219)

In her 'contextual approach' to teaching games, Read (1993) emphasizes the importance of returning to a 'practice' format for pupils who are unable to solve the game problems because of faulty or inappropriate technique. She suggests that this additional practice of skills and techniques may be done: '... individually, in small groups or with the class working as a whole using technique improvement cards to individualise learning through a reciprocal or self-check style'. (p. 13)

The teacher's role when using this teaching strategy is to act as more of a 'mentor' or 'facilitator', observing pupils working, giving neutral feedback and posing additional questions. In fact, the skill of questioning is at the heart of both the convergent and divergent problem-solving approaches.

### Questioning as a teaching skill

What is a question? Brown and Edmundson (1984) suggest that a question may be: 'Any statement intended to evoke a verbal response' (p. 99). But they do make the point that this definition does not include questions that are really commands, such as 'Would you mind being quiet!' However, questions are asked for a variety of reasons, as shown in Box 19, and not always to encourage pupil thinking.

In Brown and Wragg's (1993) report of the Leverhulme Primary Project 57% of questions were management oriented (e.g. Have you got a pencil?), 24% involved the recall of information (e.g. What do they call a female pig?), and only 8% were higher order questions which involved pupils in analysing, making generalisations or inferences about knowledge they had acquired. Evidence does suggest that teachers do tend to ask mostly factual questions, with fewer questions requiring pupils to think beyond the recall of information (Galton *et al.*, 1980; Stodolsky *et al.*, 1981). Such an emphasis on recitation has its place in education, in that teachers need to check pupils' knowledge and understanding and diagnose pupil learning difficulties. But, in order to develop children's cognitive skills and level of thinking, higher order questions are required. Questions, in fact, may range across a wide cognitive level, and researchers have

---

**Box 19**
**Reasons given by teachers for asking specific questions**

|  | N |
|---|---|
| Encouraging thought, understanding of ideas, procedures and values | 33 |
| Checking understanding, knowledge and skills | 30 |
| Gaining attention to the task to enable the teacher to move towards a teaching point | 28 |
| Review, revision, recall, reinforcement of a recently learned point | 23 |
| As a management tactic, to get the class to settle down and draw attention to the teacher | 20 |
| To teach the whole class through pupil answers | 10 |
| To give everyone a chance to answer | 10 |
| Asking bright pupils to encourage others | 4 |
| To draw in shyer pupils | 4 |
| To probe pupils knowledge after critical answers or redirect questions to the pupil who asked the question | 3 |
| To allow expressions of feelings, views and empathy | 3 |

*Source: Brown and Edmundson (1984) p. 101.*

---

identified the categories and hierarchies of questions based on their cognitive level.

Good and Brophy (1991) review the literature and suggest a hierarchy of questions based on the work of Bloom (Bloom *et al.*, 1956):

- Low in cognitive demand – knowledge questions;
- Intermediate cognitive demand – comprehension and application;
- High cognitive demand – analysis, synthesis and evaluation (p. 475).

Brown and Wragg (1993) categorise questions as:

(1) Conceptual – concerned with ideas, definitions and reasoning;

(2) Empirical   – requires answers based upon observation, recall of facts, or experimentation;

(3) Value   – are concerned with relative worth or value (e.g. moral or environmental issues).

Questions may also be considered to be narrow (convergent) or broad (divergent). The former leads to a specific answer and the latter provides the opportunity for alternative possible answers or solutions and are more open-ended.

Although some research does seem to support the view that higher order questions do produce higher order pupil responses and pupil achievement, the evidence is mainly inconclusive, indicating that higher order 'thinking' or divergent questions may not necessarily be more effective than factual, convergent or lower order questions (Good and Brophy, 1991).

The important issue appears to be the sequencing or combining of questions planned with particular objectives in mind, and as a part of a well-designed package of instruction. For example, if the teacher wanted to remind pupils of certain facts first of all, and then encourage them to apply their facts to a problem, she may start with a lower order question and conclude with higher level questions.

The effective teacher, therefore, needs to consider the purpose of the questions that are to be asked, the quality of the questions themselves, and how they relate to other questions and interactions in a teaching episode or period of discourse with pupils. To achieve this, teaching episodes need to be thoroughly planned. Poor questions may result from a lack of planning and good questioning does not always arise spontaneously, as Brown and Wragg (1993) point out: '... if we want to ask questions which get children to think, then we've got to think ourselves about the questions we are going to ask them'. (p. 14)

Consequently, they suggest an 'IDEA' approach to planning questions (p. 46):

I – Identify the key questions in relation to your objectives for the lesson;

D – Decide on the level and order (timing) of the questions;

E – Extend the questioning. Think of supplementary and subsidiary questions to ask;

A – Analyse the answers that you are likely to receive and the responses that you might give.

What about the quality of questions and the tactics and skills of good questioning?

A good question naturally depends on the context in which the question is being asked, but there are some suggestions from the literature concerning the characteristics of good questions (Groisser,

1964; Brown and Wragg, 1993). Good questions are well structured clear, brief, in natural and simple language, well sequenced and thought provoking. The key tactics of effective questioning involve structuring, directing and distributing, pausing and pacing, using prompts and probes, and listening and responding.

## Clarity of questions

Questions should make it clear to pupils what the teacher's intention is, and, in the case of a guided discovery or convergent teaching approach, be specific and highly focussed. In other words, they should guide pupils to respond in a particular way. Vague and unclear questions result in a waste of time and the teacher may be asked to clarify or rephrase them.

Questions are also unclear and confusing if they are part of a rapid sequence, because pupils may not really know which particular question the teacher is actually asking. Also, any answers to such a stream of questions may mean that some pupils don't hear the answers because they are distracted by the range of questions.

Questions should also be brief – pupils may have difficulty understanding long questions, and they should be 'pitched' at the pupil's level of understanding, and in simple language pupils are likely to understand. PE teachers often use a great deal of coaching 'jargon', and unless new terminology is clearly explained to pupils it can lead to confusion.

Well-planned and purposeful questions are also likely to be clearer to pupils than improvised questions that can often prove to be vague, confusing and irrelevant.

## The skills and tactics of effective questioning

Questions are often used successfully to focus the minds of pupils on the subject matter to be dealt with in the lesson. This is called 'structuring', and is similar to the 'advance organiser' concept described in Chapter 9 in which the teacher uses a question to direct pupils towards what is to be learned. For example, a PE teacher might pose a question related to a demonstration of soft landings in gymnastics: 'What am I doing to make sure that I land softly without falling over?'

– or shooting in soccer: 'What do I need to do to keep the ball low?'

Questions can too easily be posed to, and answered by the most bright and outgoing members of the class, or those within the teacher's line of vision. Therefore, the effective teacher distributes her questions to each pupil in turn, or randomly around the class, making sure that those at the back or side of the group have an opportunity to answer. It is also important to direct questions to individuals, otherwise chaos can occur when a whole barrage of answers are thrown at the teacher. This can be done by name, or nods of the head, facial expression or gesture. Carefully observing pupils and their facial expressions can give the teacher a clue as to who might not have understood the concept, or who is not paying attention.

Inexperienced teachers tend to ask too many quick questions, therefore not allowing pupils the time to think about the question and the possible answer. A pause after a question not only keeps pupils on their toes (because they don't know who the teacher will ask to answer the question), it may also encourage more pupils to answer questions, provide the opportunity to offer longer answers and for them to pose more questions themselves (Tobin, 1987). Pupils also need a short period of time (say 3–5 seconds) to think about and formulate their answer. When using a problem-solving approach in PE, teachers also need to be patient and allow pupils time to think about and work out their solutions to the problem. If they are working in groups they will need to discuss their solutions, and if the task involves creating a movement sequence, time will be needed to practise and 'polish' the final product. Too often inexperienced teachers of PE can become 'task setters', posing a rapid series of movement problems without allowing pupils the time or opportunity to think about and formulate their solutions (Mawer and Brown, 1982). Therefore, pausing and pacing questions is an important questioning skill.

If the pupil answer to a question is inappropriate or incorrect, the teacher might use 'prompt or probe' follow-up questions that direct the pupil to a more accurate or precise answer. In using the convergent problem-solving or guided discovery approach in PE a probing question might be used to help lead the pupil towards the correct answer, rather than simply say that she was wrong. 'Can you explain that to me ?' or, 'How does that work?', 'How would that be done?', might be examples of prompting or probing questions posed in an encouraging or thoughtful rather than a threatening way. However, one has to be careful not to spend a long time attempting to get a particular answer from one pupil as this can lead to other members of the class losing interest, which, in turn, can lead to class management problems.

Teachers do need to be careful about not responding at all to pupils' answers, or responding in a limited way, such as: 'Oh, oh'. In one study of primary school teachers teaching PE, 60% of questions asked of pupils were either simple isolated questions without further focusing on the answer, without positive feedback or were followed by a rejection of the answer (Mawer and Brown, 1982).

Responding to pupils' answers to both verbal and movement problems involves listening and observing. It's easy not to really listen properly to pupil answers to questions, to do what Brown and Wragg

(1993) term 'skim listening'. It's important to listen to pupils in such a way that you are trying to identify any misunderstandings pupils may have, and to attempt to appreciate the underlying meanings of what the pupil is trying to tell you. Whatever, it's important to show that you really are interested and are positive about the pupil's attempts to answer the question. This is not always easy because you often have to learn to distinguish between pupils who are really not trying to answer the question and are fooling about, and the pupil who is honestly trying but has not really solved the problem.

Many inexperienced teachers have difficulty in responding appropriately to pupil answers to questions, yet these teaching 'moves' are the crucial component of effective discourse using questions. This is particularly the case with convergent problem-solving strategies, in which the response of the teacher is vital to keeping the discourse on line towards the eventual 'correct' answer(s) to the problem. Whether responding to convergent or divergent problem-solving answers, it is important to both reinforce and provide feedback to pupils, and in a manner that continues to encourage them to sustain interest in the problem. Being enthusiastic and positive is therefore very important, particularly in divergent problem-solving situations in PE when pupils need to feel 'comfortable' in trying out new ideas and not be afraid of failing. Provided the pupil has really been trying to solve the movement problem, even the most limited solution may need to be reinforced in order to encourage the pupil, or group, to keep working at the problem. A negative response may result in pupils not wanting to be involved in the problem-solving learning process.

However, the teacher has to be careful when offering positive responses to all pupil answers to questions or skill attempts, regardless of the quality of the response. When using a convergent problem-solving strategy the teacher must balance the need to keep the discourse on line, yet not put off a pupil who provides an incorrect answer. In divergent problem-solving, when a variety of answers are possible and within the capabilities of the learner, it is easier to be positive and reinforcing about a range of possible answers to the problem. Knowing your pupils and what they are capable of is therefore very important when responding to their answers to problems. In divergent problem-solving situations a very supportive atmosphere needs to be created, and therefore most of the feedback statements from the teacher may be neutral. Also, it often helps if the teacher highlights certain pupil responses so that the rest of the class appreciate the diversity of responses that are possible.

## Questions to avoid

The literature is full of advice on questions to avoid. Groisser (1964) suggests that there are four types of questions that teachers should particularly refrain from using. Overuse of 'Yes/No' type questions, for example, because they tend to be 'lead in' questions for more thoughtful discussion, tend to waste time and confuse pupils, and teachers might as well pose the intended question first of all. Also, while pupils can easily guess answers to 'Yes/No' questions, the teacher does not find out what the pupil really knows. Similarly, guessing-type questions need to be used sparingly and with particular objectives in mind. They can be used to interest pupils as a lead in to a discussion, but if overused pupils are encouraged to guess rather than think. They may, however, be used as part of a carefully thought out teaching strategy designed to encourage pupils to think carefully about a solution to a particular problem. For example, 'What do you think may have caused Colin Jackson to perform badly in the Olympic hurdles final?', might be a suitable introduction to a discussion about the various psychological factors that may affect an athlete prior to major competition and lead to a poor performance.

Bullying or nagging pupils who don't appear to know the answer to a question with, 'OK, come on then, what else...', is often self-defeating and it may be better either to help the pupil answer the question correctly by giving clues, rephrasing the question, or even giving the answer.

Rhetorical or leading questions such as, 'Don't you think it would be a good idea...?', should also be avoided unless the teacher really does want an answer. Otherwise they can lead to over-dependence on the teacher.

The 36 teachers in Brown and Edmundson's (1984) study felt that the most common questioning errors by student teachers were related to the structuring, presentation and delivery of questions, and the handling of pupil answers. Student teachers tended to 'not look at pupils', 'spoke too fast in an inappropriate volume of speech', and lacked 'clarity of speech'. Also their questions were often too complex, ambiguous and lengthy, and contained vocabulary beyond the understanding of pupils. In handling pupil responses a major fault was concerned with 'accepting those answers which the teacher wanted or expected', and alternative answers were not really considered. Students appeared to ask questions because 'it seemed a good idea at the time', and failed 'to provide background information' to pupils to help them to answer questions. Also questions tended to 'lack a logical sequence', and were 'disjointed – jumping quickly without linking ideas, making a point or discussion too difficult to follow' (p. 117). Students also made mistakes in targeting questions, either concentrating too many questions to too few pupils, or asking too many questions to the whole class. The teachers in the study recommended that student teachers should:

- plan questions beforehand by actually writing them down in the lesson plan with a number of 'correct' answers alongside:

- think carefully about their approach to handling questions before the lesson, particularly allowing time for pupils to think about answers, and being prepared to hear alternative answers;
- ensure that all pupils can hear both the question and the answer;
- develop rules and routines to avoid calling out;
- observe experienced teachers and discuss feedback of one's personal performance and how a questioning technique might be improved.

In the teaching of physical education there are a number of common errors in questioning when used with the divergent and convergent problem-solving strategies. Asking such questions as, 'How many ways can you ...?' may result in the learner providing one particular answer to the movement problem, and leaving it at that! Some learners have difficulty with this type of question, are afraid to offer a solution, and tend to 'freeze'. It is therefore better to ask, 'Show me four different ways of ...', which can then be followed by, 'Show me three more ways ...'.

The effective teacher, therefore, makes every effort to develop their professional expertise in posing questions, and avoids errors in the use of questioning.

How good at questioning are you? Exercise 10 describes a range of common mistakes made by teachers when using questioning as a technique. Ask a colleague to observe you teach (or alternatively audio or video record a lesson), and put a tally in the first column whenever a mistake is made. An observer may make additional comments in the right-hand column. It is not necessary for an observer to attempt to focus on all of the aspects of questioning in Exercise 10.

*Exercise 10   Focusing on mistakes in Questioning*

| **Delivery of Questions** | Number of occurrencies | Observer comments |
|---|---|---|
| Unclear questions | | |
| Speech too fast | | |
| Volume of speech | | |
| Asking too many questions | | |
| Asking questions in a threatening way | | |

*continued*

*Exercise 10 continued*

| Delivery of Questions | Number of occurrencies | Observer comments |
|---|---|---|
| Not looking at pupils when asking questions | | |
| **Type of Questions** | | |
| Inappropriate language | | |
| Too difficult/complex | | |
| Too easy or too factual | | |
| Too many 'Yes/No' questions | | |
| Bullying/nagging questions | | |
| Too many guessing questions | | |
| Irrelevant questions | | |
| Insufficient probing questions | | |
| Too many rhetorical questions | | |
| **Target of Questions** | | |
| Not spread around the class | | |
| Too many whole class questions | | |
| To only brightest/able | | |
| **Context of Questions** | | |
| Not in context of lesson | | |
| **Responding to answers** | | |
| Answering questions yourself | | |
| Not providing 'wait time' to think | | |
| Ignoring answers | | |

*continued*

*Exercise 10 continued*

| **Responding to answers** | Number of occurrencies | Observer comments |
|---|---|---|
| Not correcting incorrect answers | | |
| Expecting only correct answers | | |
| Not having routines for pupil answers | | |
| Not correcting calling out | | |
| Failing to 'build on' answers | | |

## Sequencing of questions

What is probably more important than the type or cognitive level of questions is how questions are put together in sequences, particularly when using guided discovery and problem-solving teaching strategies. But, it is not just the questions in the sequence that are important, it is the way the teacher responds to pupil answers that is the crucial feature of interactions within a guided discovery teaching episode.

In the Leverhulme Primary Project (Brown and Wragg, 1993), 47% of teacher's questions were part of a sequence of two or more questions, the remainder were individual questions by the teacher. In one study of the teaching of primary school gymnastics, 60% of all questions were isolated questions, not preceded or followed by teacher guidance, feedback or additional questions (Mawer and Brown, 1982).

Brown and Edmundson (1984) identified a number of different types of sequences of questions and these are shown in Box 20.

Effective use of the guided discovery and divergent problem-solving teaching approaches is likely to include the 'extending and lifting' and 'step-by-step' types of questioning sequences in which pupils are gradually led from simple recall towards more complex levels of thinking. Allowing pupils to work initially at lower levels of thinking might give them the confidence to engage then in higher levels, or be able to put forward their own ideas and solutions to problems.

A major difficulty for inexperienced teachers is keeping the pattern of discourse 'on course'. It is very easy to wander away from the main point of the teaching episode and be sidetracked. Staying on course requires thorough planning of sequences of questions and answers with emphasis being placed on 'key questions'. From these 'key questions' are built a number of possible shorter and more specific questions.

**Box 20**
**Sequences of questions**

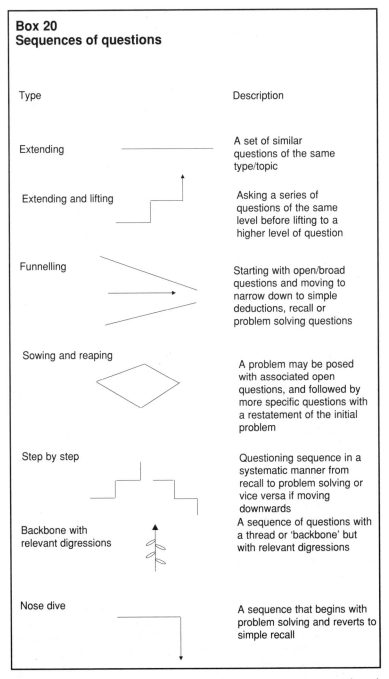

| Type | Description |
|---|---|
| Extending | A set of similar questions of the same type/topic |
| Extending and lifting | Asking a series of questions of the same level before lifting to a higher level of question |
| Funnelling | Starting with open/broad questions and moving to narrow down to simple deductions, recall or problem solving questions |
| Sowing and reaping | A problem may be posed with associated open questions, and followed by more specific questions with a restatement of the initial problem |
| Step by step | Questioning sequence in a systematic manner from recall to problem solving or vice versa if moving downwards |
| Backbone with relevant digressions | A sequence of questions with a thread or 'backbone' but with relevant digressions |
| Nose dive | A sequence that begins with problem solving and reverts to simple recall |

*continued*

**Box 20 continued**

| Type | | Description |
|------|---|-------------|
| Random walk | 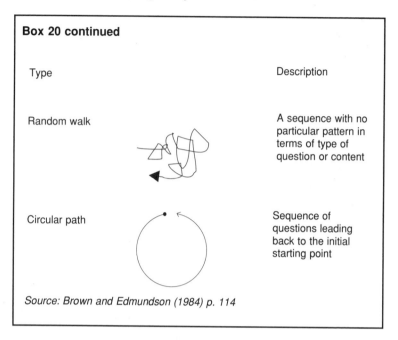 | A sequence with no particular pattern in terms of type of question or content |
| Circular path | | Sequence of questions leading back to the initial starting point |

*Source: Brown and Edmundson (1984) p. 114*

At present we know very little about sequencing or teachers' tactics when using questioning in PE as part of discovery learning and problem-solving teaching strategies, but the classroom research related to conducting discourse and discussion does offer a few pointers, particularly for the use of more divergent problem-solving approaches. Good and Brophy (1991) believe that the teacher's role is particularly important in discussions using an inquiry teaching approach: 'Instead of acting as the primary source of information and the authority figure who determines whether answers are correct or incorrect, the teacher is a discussion leader who structures the discussion by establishing a focus, setting boundaries and facilitating interaction'. (p. 486)

The teacher therefore acts as more of a facilitator or mentor and may use question and answer initially, but the discussion may develop into more of an 'exchange of views', with pupils responding to each other and actually posing questions themselves. The teacher may then act as a summariser, clarifying, elaborating and inviting pupils to contribute.

The role of the teacher as a consultant is practically completed within what Mosston refers to as the 'Individual programme – learner's design', and 'Learner-initiated' teaching approaches, both strategies that offer pupils much greater independence in the learning process (Mosston and Ashworth, 1986).

## Teaching strategies for greater pupil independence in the learning process

The 'Individual programme – learner's design' strategy involves the teacher in selecting the basic subject matter and topic, but the learner then designs his own programme, seeking the teacher's help when required. The teacher monitors the pupil's progress, affirms the pupil's decisions, and engages in supportive dialogue with the pupil.

It is advisable for pupils to have experienced other teaching approaches in Mosston's spectrum, and be reasonably proficient and knowledgeable performers prior to being involved in this approach to learning. It is intended to be a highly disciplined learning strategy and not a 'do as you like' situation. For example, a group of pupils might put together what they have learned in terms of technique, etc., to create a dance, but with the music selected by the teacher. In health-related exercise, pupils who had been taught about the various components of everyday fitness and how to design a personal fitness programme, may be asked to design a programme for a relation with a particular occupation. The pupil, therefore, has the freedom to choose her own subject for the task. Such an approach may be suitable for working towards the Natoinal Curriculum Key Stage 4 programme of study introductory statement that pupils 'should be taught to plan, undertake and evaluate a safe health-promoting exercise programme', and 'to show understanding of the principles involved' (SCAA, 1994b, p. 9).

The pupil has complete independence in the 'Learner' Initiated' teaching approach – they make their own decisions concerning subject matter, learning experiences and evaluate their own progress. They experiment, examine and discover their own answers to the problem they have set themselves. It is a very individualised strategy and not all pupils will be ready for working in this way. The teacher's role within this teaching approach is similar to that, '... of a consultant in the business world' (Goldberger and Howarth, 1993, p. 25); to observe, to listen, to ask questions and to possibly at times make the pupil aware of aspects of their work they may not have considered. However, the teacher is a supporter or facilitator and should not try to 'hawk' or impose their own ideas. This approach might be appropriate for working towards the National Curriculum Key Stage 4 activity specific objectives related to:

- Dance – 'to compose and perform, accurately and expressively, increasingly complex and technically demanding dances that successfully communicate the artistic intention'.
- Outdoor and adventurous activities – 'to prepare to undertake a journey safely, e.g. fell walking, in an unfamiliar environment'.
- Athletic activities – 'to plan, carry out and evaluate an effective personal training schedule for a selected event'.

- Games – 'to cooperate with others in regular practice in order to refine their techniques ...', in, for example, planning practices to improve a particular technique as skill' (SCAA, 1994b, pp. 9–10).

These teaching strategies do enable the teacher to increase the opportunities for pupils to progress towards greater independence, to plan, perform and evaluate their own activity programmes, to take more responsibility for their own actions, and, as the NCC (1992) point out, this experience should: '... help them to continue with physical activities after leaving school'. (p. D4)

## Mixing and blending of teaching strategies

The teaching approaches described in this and the previous chapter are not necessarily exclusive, and the effective teacher will have the ability to switch, mix and blend teaching strategies to suit his objectives and pupil responses. As objectives for learning vary within a lesson or episode of teaching, the effective teacher will move between different teaching strategies and use the appropriate teaching skills and tactics for each strategy. One should not, therefore, view a single strategy as just one way of teaching a particular lesson or unit of work. The teacher should begin by deciding what she wants to achieve, and then choose the most suitable approach for achieving that objective for that episode of teaching.

Therefore, developing a repertoire of teaching approaches, and the teaching skills to support them, is only a part of being an effective teacher of PE. The really effective teacher is aware of when to use which strategy, and with which pupils – and, knows when to change a strategy if it doesn't appear to be working! Thoughtful planning and flexibility are the names of the game!

# Assessment of pupil progress

## Introduction

The National Curriculum, as part of the 1988 Education Reform Act, has the aim of ensuring that schools not only teach a balanced range of subjects and set clear objectives, but also monitor pupil progress. Assessment is: '... an integral part of the National Curriculum' (DES, 1989a, para. 6.1.), – and, considered to be 'at the heart of the process of promoting children's learning' (DES, 1988b).

Schools are required to keep records of their pupils' progress, and the record should be updated at least once a year. There is also a statutory requirement to report a pupil's progress in all National Curriculum subjects, including physical education, against the end of key stage descriptions. However, assessment in Physical Education does not include the use of standard assessment tasks (SATs). Instead, it was considered that teacher assessment would be sufficient for providing the appropriate information for both curriculum planning and for reporting to parents.

Although many PE teachers are familiar with the detailed assessment of pupils as part of their teaching of GCSE, the National Curriculum has greatly increased the role of the PE teacher within a whole school policy of assessment, particularly at Key Stage 3. Effective assessment of pupil progress requires the development of a number of teaching skills, but also an awareness of the basic principles underpinning a sound assessment policy.

## The principles of effective assessment

It is important that assessment is seen as an integral part of the whole teaching process, as SEAC (1991) has suggested:

Teacher assessment is part of everyday teaching and learning in the classroom. Teachers discuss with pupils, guide their work, ask and answer questions, help, encourage and challenge. In addition, they mark and review written and other kinds of work. Through these activities they are continually finding out about their pupil's capabilities and achievements. This knowledge then informs plans for future work. It is this continuous process that makes up teacher assessment. It should not be seen as a separate activity necessarily requiring the use of extra tasks or tests. (p. 1)

Assessment is not, therefore, a 'bolt on' to the teaching/learning process, but should evolve naturally out of it and provide, as the DES (1988b) suggest, opportunities for both feedback and feedforward. It should offer pupils the opportunity to show what they can do, know, and understand, and should support their optimum progress. Planning for assessment is therefore a part of the overall planning of a scheme of work or lesson, and should be built into all tasks that are set. In this way assessment is seen as a continuous process, making use of a wide range of assessment techniques and providing a complete picture of the extent to which objectives are being achieved. Consequently, methods of recording pupil experiences should be built into schemes and units of work. However, such careful planning should not mean that unexpected pupil achievements are not recorded.

A planned programme of assessment is therefore an integral part of course planning and the teaching/learning process, but what other reasons are there for assessing pupil progress? Why do we assess pupils? Why have an assessment policy?

According to Kyriacou (1991) and Robinson (1992), assessment serves a number of purposes:

- It provides the teacher with feedback concerning pupil progress in that it establishes what a pupil knows, understands and can do. This information can then help the teacher to –
  (1) inform curriculum review and evaluation;
  (2) determine to what extent curricular aims are being met;
  (3) aid future curriculum planning and the identification of progressive learning objectives;
  (4) determine the level at which a pupil can apply skills, knowledge and concepts and therefore identify individual pupil needs and readiness for learning, with a view to providing clear and realistic targets for individual pupils;
- It provides pupils with informative feedback so that they can –
  (1) relate their performance to the standards and expectations set by the teacher;
  (2) use the feedback to develop and improve their performance.
- It helps to motivate pupils through a balance of intrinsic and extrinsic motivation in which their knowledge of levels of success may stimulate them to achieve more in the activity.
- It helps to provide a record of progress which can help the teacher to –
  (1) plan appropriate future learning for pupils and the teaching of similar groups;

> (2) communicate and provide information for other teachers, parents, and governors;
> (3) provide information to facilitate interphase and interschool continuity.

- It provides a statement of attainment at a particular point in time which can be used to communicate a formal statement to parents, employers, etc., or for qualifications and certification.
- It can also help the teacher with –
  (1) self-appraisal of teaching skills;
  (2) evaluation of teaching strategies;
  (3) a focus for teacher observation.

As one of the main purposes of assessment is to help the teacher plan the next stage of learning, it is not surprising that the OFSTED (1993a) criteria for the guidance of inspectors involved in assessing the quality of teaching includes an examination of 'the effectiveness of use of assessment to inform subsequent work', and how assessment is 'used by teachers in their planning to respond to the needs of groups of pupils'.

In order to achieve this particular purpose, ongoing, continuous, formative assessment is essential, as well as the end of course, end of key stage summative assessment.

### Formative and summative assessment

Teachers are 'formatively' assessing all the time as they are teaching, and this formative assessment in the form of informative feedback is not only helping the pupil to learn at that point in time, but also helping the teacher to plan the next stage of the pupil's learning. For example, in a lesson a teacher may set a task and find, after observation, diagnostic assessment and giving feedback to a number of pupils, that the task is too difficult for some, and too easy for others. Consequently, the teacher may then modify the task for different groups so that they are able to achieve a degree of success in the task. In this way formative, diagnostic assessment is being used not only to identify errors or learning difficulties, and provide feedback, but also to modify the task to facilitate pupil learning in a progressive and appropriately differentiated fashion. After the lesson the teacher may make notes related to the formative assessment which will be used as part of a summative record, and will then report at the end of the scheme or unit of work possibly in the form of a 'Record of Achievement'. Summative assessment is therefore the systematic recording of the pupil's overall progress and achievement, and is made up of a series of formative assessments. However, if the pupil assessment is only designed for 'end of course' summative purposes, then it would not be possible to extract formative information about the pupil's achievements and learning difficulties during the course.

## Approaches to assessment

Although there has been a shift towards greater use of criterion referenced assessment (the pupil is assessed against set criteria) within GCSE and the National Curriculum, Carroll (1993) believes that PE teachers use a mixture of criterion, norm-referenced (relating to others), and ipsative (relating to self and one's previous performance) forms of assessment. Whereas norm-referenced assessment focusses on how the individual pupil's performance compares with the average or norm for the age group, criterion-referenced assessment looks at the pupil's achievements against specific criteria or objectives. With criterion-referencing teacher assessment depends on what the pupil *can do*, and helps to establish what has been successfully learned in readiness for planning the next stage of individual and class learning. According to Robinson (1992), criterion-referencing in PE also: '... allows for skills, knowledge and concepts to be assessed in the context within which they are used'. (p. 40)

A comparison of the three different approaches to assessment, with examples from PE are provided by Carroll (1993) and shown in Box 21.

With the advent of pupil profiling and records of achievement (DES, 1988c; 1989c), more aspects of pupil achievement are being used for assessment purposes. Also, with National Curriculum guidelines leading to a more accurate specification of learning objectives and a greater involvement of the individual pupil in assessment, a more individualised pacing of learning should occur. However, assessing pupils in physical education is often seen as being a little different from assessing other subjects in the school curriculum. Rather than always having a written permanent record that occurs in many other subjects, a lot of assessment in PE (other than in PE and Sports Studies theoretical examinations) is of movement and bodily actions that only occur for a brief second. It is therefore not an easy task for the PE teacher because his judgement and interpretations have to be instantaneous and occur during the teaching of a lesson. Videotape can be used to record movement but it is not always practicable. However, regardless of the problems, PE teachers have succeeded in making these difficult assessment judgements, but they have to be well organised and have clear objectives. The need to have clear and well thought out plans for assessment of pupil practical work in GCSE PE has provided PE teachers with the necessary background skills to develop effective programmes of assessment of pupil physical performance for the requirements of the National Curriculum. All the same, the need to assess pupil progress in terms of their ability to plan

# Box 21
## A comparison of three approaches to assessment

| | Ipsative Reference | Norm Reference | Criterion Reference |
|---|---|---|---|
| Example | Pupil's educational gymnastics sequence of own creation. | Pupil's fitness test score. | Pupil's attempts at scoring a number of baskets from a set position. |
| Ideology | Child centred. | Group centred. | Activity centred. |
| Purpose | Comparison with pupil's own previous sequence. To assess progress. | Comparison with group fitness scores. To assess how fit pupil is in relation to other pupils of same age. | Comparison with a standard (scoring baskets). To assess how much pupil has mastered skill of scoring baskets from a set position. |
| Diagnostic | Whether pupil needs to work on the sequence and what part of the sequence. | Which pupils need remedial fitness work. | What needs remedial work. Whether scoring at baskets does. |
| Interpretation of Assessment/ Scores | How well or badly pupil has done in relation to previous sequences. Improving or not. | To see the relative position of pupil in the group in terms of fitness. | Indicates level of mastery of scoring baskets from set position. |
| Variations in Assessment/ Score | Other pupil's assessment not important. Pupil's own assessment important (i.e. self-assessment). Variation in own assessments indicate improvement or otherwise in sequence. | Needs a range of scores amongst pupils on standardised set of scores. | Range of scores not important unless wishing to differentiate as in GCSE. Depends on uses. Variation indicates different level of mastery of scoring. |
| Items in Assessment | Task difficulty related to what pupil can do. | Items related to the group to obtain norm or distribution. Number of items usually required. | Task difficulty not important. Related to specific criteria, e.g. scoring baskets from set position. |
| Role/Uses in Education | Value for own sake. What aspects of the sequence or go on to next sequence. Readiness. Motivation – self performance and progress. Accountability – self. | How fit a person is. Selection for sport/action. Fitness gradings. What aspects of fitness to work on. Motivation – other performance norms. Accountability – do better for group. | Selection based on mastery of skill, e.g. basketball team. Decide whether to go on to next skill or further practice required. Motivation – mastery of skills. |
| Logical inference | Pupil shows a performance in a sequence which is better or worse than previous performances. | Pupil shows an amount of fitness which is greater or less than the mean of those tested for fitness. | Pupil shows an amount of mastery of scoring baskets which is greater or equal to criterion score. |

*Source: Carroll (1993) p .12.*

and evaluate their own and others work are relatively new requirements that the National Curriculum has created.

Being aware of these developments and what they mean in terms of the PE teacher's role is part of being an effective teacher of PE. So, what then are the skills of effective assessment of pupil progress?

Whereas PE teachers were happy to plan for the vigorous assessment procedures of GCSE PE, they visualised a massive time constraint and over-bureaucracy attached to Key Stage 3 assessment for all pupils. Consequently, one of the main skills of the effective teacher of PE is the management of time for assessment within the 'hurly-burly' of a teaching day. Beyond this, essential assessment skills are concerned with the accomplishment of three tasks.

The first task for the teacher is to work out exactly WHAT it is she wants to assess. This will involve identifying learning objectives and establishing criteria for assessment, and then planning, presenting and teaching towards these objectives and criteria so that pupils are able to 'show' what they can do (performance), know and understand. As pointed out in Chapter 5, planning of units of work, lessons, and assessment tasks, should not only be progressive, but indicate within units and lesson plans when there might be opportunities for assessment to occur.

The second task for the teacher is to establish HOW he wishes to assess. This will entail:

- collecting evidence of progress;
- recording the evidence;
- involving pupils in providing evidence.

The final task is the reporting of pupil progress to other teachers, parents and future employers.

The first two of these tasks have implications for choice of teaching strategy.

## Deciding what to assess

Although the National Curriculum Council (NCC, 1992) suggest that PE teachers should develop criteria that may be used in assessing pupil's work in PE, they do not actually prescribe ways of doing this. However, they do suggest that the criteria that might characterise good performance in PE may include descriptions such as accuracy, efficiency, adaptability, ability to do more than one thing at a time, good line or design, sustaining participation and imaginative performance. They also recommend that teachers might use the National Curriculum end of key stage descriptions as a basis for developing learning objectives and criteria, taking into account the need to be flexible in their selection of such descriptions in the case of pupils with disabilities or learning difficulties. Of course, this may mean that the teacher will have to establish which of his criteria are actually assessable, and whether by objective or subjective means.

Therefore, one very important teaching skill regarding assessment is the ability to devise and set criteria related to learning objectives, against which to assess pupil progress. However, this cannot be done effectively unless the teacher has already analysed what is to be learned and identified levels of progression. Progression can be interpreted in a variety of ways, and is likely to be different according to the activity area being taught. Also, McConachie-Smith (1991a) suggests that different elements of progression (such as difficulty, variety, quality, complexity) may progress at different rates, and therefore all may not improve at the same time. Consequently, the task for the PE teacher is to agree on descriptions that distinguish between different levels of achievement and progression.

The National Curriculum Council (NCC, 1992) suggest that there are at least two elements of progression within each of the three strands of the physical education 'process' of planning, performing and evaluating – 'difficulty' and 'quality'. In addition they put forward two further elements of progression related to pupils' personal and social development – 'independence' and 'interaction'. By independence they mean that a pupil may take more initiative and responsibility for planning and evaluating tasks and make increasing use of 'partnerships' between school and community. The development of interaction skills may occur when pupils gradually learn, for example, to share space and resources, work cooperatively in groups or competitively against others and eventually organise their own groupings.

It would be useful at this stage to offer an example of how a progression may be worked out for a particular activity in the PE curriculum.

McConachie-Smith (1991b) provides some suggestions concerning progression in the teaching of gymnastics. She puts forward the view that one needs to examine progression in terms of planning, performing, and evaluating in the following way:

- Planning – may include a progression,

from linking two movements together, of like or different kinds; to short phrases of 3/4 movements, or short series of movements to traverse a particular pathway over apparatus; to short sequences of movement within a short time span to longer compositions of over one minute. The constructions of the sequences and compositions will also progress by starting with simple elements of composition such as using different pathways, or different directions of movement moving at different levels on the apparatus. (p. 34)

McConachie-Smith suggests that a progression of demand needs to be worked out that allows the teacher to observe the pupil's ability to cope at different levels of demand. She also points out that the demands involved when planning for group and for individuals may be progressive because they: '... add the elements of negotiation and compromise as social skills involved in the process'. (p. 34)

- Performing – here the teacher needs to work out clear criteria concerning the expectations of pupils at the different stages of development of gymnastic skill. McConachie-Smith suggests that teachers need to set progressively more difficult tasks in order to establish each child's level of capability in that 'children may all satisfy the criteria set by the end of key stage statement but at different levels'. (p. 32) Therefore, a progressive level of difficulty needs to be worked out in relation to content (skills), process (level of control), and context (individual to partner to group). She offers the example of:

Children within KS1 initially have difficulty putting two movements together without a clear stop and restart. The qualitative sign that they have progressed and 'moved up a gear' will be their ability to execute two movements with continuity, and the next sign of increased fluency will be the logical move from one movement to the next using the natural directional flow. This may be further refined to incorporate the natural temporal qualities of the movement such that the movements merge into each other as a continuous whole. (p. 33)

- Appreciating and evaluating – according to McConachie-Smith a progression in ability to appreciate and evaluate movement in gymnastics might include: '... ability to comment on single actions, then short phrases of movement, building up to full compositions'. (p. 34) Also, in terms of the processes of skill development the pupil may be required initially to observe and identify aspects of body shape, extension, direction of travel, constraints of time (fast and slow), and this may progress to making comparisons between: 'performances which require the memory of both and identification of similarities and differences. Analysing a phrase or sequence into its component parts and identifying the elements contained within it'. (p. 34)

Such judgements naturally become more difficult as criteria become more abstract, such as 'use of space or exploitation of time'.

McConachie-Smith feels that teachers have not paid sufficient attention to the setting of progressively complex criteria concerning pupil observation, yet the ability to observe is so important to the process of evaluation.

Therefore, when starting the process of writing criteria for assessment, it is important to identify and plan for progression within the processes, content and context of learning. As previously mentioned, these criteria may develop from National Curriculum end of key stage descriptions, and also from key stage PoS activity specific and introductory statements. Taking an example from the area of health-related exercise, the key stage introductory statement for Key Stage 3 includes: 'pupils should be given opportunities to engage in health-promoting physical activity, where possible within the local community', and 'be taught the short-term and long-term effects of exercise on the various body systems'.

Therefore, the assessment criteria related to this key stage description as suggested by Harris and Elbourne (1992) might include:

Understanding of what happens to the body systems over a short period of time (e.g. 6 weeks) and over a longer period of time (e.g. 6 months to a year); demonstration of involvement in decision-making processes concerning healthy and enjoyable exercise. This includes knowing what's on in the local community (including the school), what activities they enjoy/dislike, what exercise is possible in and around the home, what activities improve their health. (p. 5)

Dickenson and Almond (1993) suggest that teachers should first of all reduce the end of key stage description to learning objectives for each activity area stated in simple terms, and then identify the assessment criteria. They give an example from Year 7 games related to the end of key stage description, 'Devise strategies and tactics for appropriate activities':

Learning objective – understand game strategies and devise simple tactics.

Criteria – Knows when to attack or defend, individually or in a group/team. Can work out simple ways to attack or defend'. (p. 24)

With these examples in mind now try Exercise 11 below.

### Exercise 11   Devising learning objectives and assessment criteria

Devise learning objectives and assessment criteria for an activity of your choice based on either of the following Key Stage 3 end of key stage descriptions:

'Adapt and refine existing skills and apply these to new situations.'

'Demonstrate how to prepare for particular activities and how to recover after vigorous physical activity.'

When setting criteria for pupil assessment it is important to acknowledge that maturation may play a part in pupil's performances in physical activities, and therefore teachers need to take this into account when drawing up assessment criteria in much the same way that criteria are modified and flexibility used in the interpretation of end of key stage statements for pupils with learning difficulties and special educational needs.

## Setting assessment tasks

Having planned the progression and established the criteria for assessment, tasks then need to be set that allow the pupils the opportunity to show what they can do, know and understand. The tasks need to assess what they are supposed to assess, and be relevant to the pupils' standard of ability and stage of progression within the task. In the case of invasion games, a task might be a particular skills practice, a full game situation, an attack versus defence game-related practice, or a small sided game. Consequently, a very important teaching skill in relation to assessment is the ability to organise and implement assessment with large groups of pupils within the normal teaching situation.

Taking another example from the area of health-related exercise, Harris and Elbourne (1992) suggest an example assessment task focusing specifically on the pupil's ability 'to prepare for and recover from particular activities', and this is shown in Box 22 below.

---

**Box 22**
**Example of an Assessment task: Warming up for a specific activity**

Select one of the following games: Hockey, Soccer, Netball, or Rugby. Either on your own or with a partner, design and perform a warm up that you could perform before playing a game.

1. MOBILISE THE JOINTS that you will be using in the game. Make the movements controlled and smooth. Try to mime some of the actions used in the game.

2. RAISE THE PULSE by moving on and off the spot. Build up the pulse gradually and do not raise it so high that the activity becomes exhausting. Try to include some equipment from your selected game in this part of the warm up.

3. STRETCH the main muscles that you are going to use in the game and hold each stretch still for 6–10 seconds.

*Source: Harris and Elbourn (1992) p. 7.*

---

They suggest that this task can be set indoors or outside, and communicated verbally or using a task card. The teacher can then move around the class giving advice and assessing pupils. Pupils are given the task of observing and evaluating their partner's warm up using the following criteria:

1. Which joints are mobilised?
2. Are the joints mobilised in a controlled way?
3. Is the pulse raised gradually?
4. Do any of the mobility and pulse raising activities reflect a particular game?
5. Which main muscles are stretched?
6. Are the stretches held still for 6-10 seconds?
7. Can you guess the activity for which this warm up is designed?

(Harris and Elbourne, 1992 p. 7)

This particular example of an assessment task uses pupil prompt sheets and involves pupil personal and peer assessment. Therefore, to be able to set up assessment situations and tasks effectively, the teacher needs to be aware not only of a variety of teaching strategies and have knowledge of a range of 'entry levels' for the pupils, but she also needs to make sure that the tasks set are clearly in line with unit/lesson objectives.

The example assessment task described above involves pupils in the task of assessing themselves, and pupils can be actively involved in the whole process of assessment as SEAC (1992) have pointed out: 'Teacher assessment can help pupils to understand what they are learning and to chart their own progress. Pupils can be actively involved in their own assessment: reviewing their work and progress; setting future targets for learning; and deciding, in discussion with teachers, which pieces of work provide evidence of particular attainments'.

Pupils can be involved in the process of setting criteria, using them as personal targets and recording their own progress, with the teacher helping to moderate and give advice on the accuracy of the statements and record of assessment. The effective teacher therefore makes every effort to help pupils become more aware of what they are studying in PE and how they are progressing. Some schools re-write the statutory statements of attainment for pupils in such a language and structure that they are able to understand and use them. These are often pinned on the school PE notice-board for all to see alongside pictorial examples of the activities in the programmes of study.

Having set the assessment tasks, how does the teacher actually assess the pupils? What are the skills of collecting and recording the evidence of attainment?

## Collecting evidence and recording attainment

Teachers need to be able to collect evidence of attainment and record it in such a way that it is not: '... unwieldy or time consuming or get in the way of teaching and learning'. (SEAC, 1992)

The aim is to build up a picture of pupil progress in relation to the assessment criteria in order to be able to plan the future learning for that pupil. It is not necessary to collect evidence on everything a pupil does because this would be totally unmanageable for both teachers and pupils. As SEAC (1991) point out: 'It is only necessary to record or collect evidence of those aspects of pupil's achievements which show some significant attainment or progress'. (p. 25)

But, what counts as evidence, and how might it be collected?

The effective teacher will have at his disposal, and be prepared to use, a wide range of different approaches for producing potential evidence of attainment. These will include: written, diagrams and graphs, oral, visual and observational.

Written evidence such as descriptions, evaluations, working notes, self-assessment forms, questionnaire responses, plans (related to tactics or sequences), floor patterns, apparatus arrangements and test responses, can all provide evidence of pupil's knowledge, understanding, planning and evaluation. Evidence of planning and evaluation may also be oral as well as written, and include discussion, pupil responses to questions, pupil peer assessment and descriptions of their own work and that of their peers.

However, the most common way of collecting evidence of pupil progress in PE is as a result of direct observation, although videos, photographs, etc., may also be used.

What skills therefore, are required of the teacher in making a judgement about pupil progress and attainment based on direct observation of pupil performance? Edith Cope (1975) suggested three types of assessment situations that might occur when having to make such judgements:

- Quantifiable skills – assessed by 'measurement';
- Qualitative skills – assessed by the 'goodness of fit' model;
- Inventive and creative – assessed by aesthetic judgement.

Most observational assessment is made against a standard or 'goodness of fit' model based on the teacher's image of the movement being observed and its spatial and temporal features. Consequently, the effective teacher will have made sure that his knowledge of physical movement is broad enough to be able to have an appropriate image in his memory in readiness for making such observations and judgements. However, as Dickenson and Almond (1993) emphasise: 'For this strategy to be effective, observations need to be focussed by planned assessment objectives, and normally supported by activities or practices which enable pupils to demonstrate their ability to achieve the learning objective'. (p. 25)

Observational judgements may initially be difficult for pupils who are involved in peer assessment, and therefore the teacher may need to help them to develop their observational image of the movement being assessed by the use of task and prompt cards which will include pictures and descriptions of the movement. Unfortunately, task card images are static impressions of a movement and lack temporal and spatial features. But, pupils do need to practice their observational skills because only through practice will they learn to analyse and evaluate physical performance.

With quantifiable skills the model is much clearer and may be easily standardised in different contexts, but with qualitative skills an accurate image of the model is necessary. In the case of creative movement a model may not exist because the performance is likely to be so unique and original, therefore the teacher has to create the model at the same time as using it for assessment purposes. Such a teaching skill is likely to be acquired over years of experience of working within the area of activity concerned.

Although teachers will normally be assessing a complete physical performance, there are cases when a pupil is unsuccessful. In these instances the teacher may have to analyse and assess individual component parts of a movement or performance.

Naturally, teachers' observations are ongoing and a part of the teaching/learning process, but the teacher will need to work out a system of recording pupil progress so that a detailed comment can be made at the end of the Key Stage. As performance in PE is so 'fleeting' and transitory (unless captured on videotape), and because a pupil's performances may vary so much (e.g. effect of opponents or team members, weather conditions, etc.) it is essential that the teacher takes the opportunity to observe the pupil on several occasions over a period of time. Only by doing this can a consistent and reliable assessment of pupil performance and progress be obtained. Therefore, assessment should continue throughout the unit and key stage and not be left to the last week! Such continuous assessment throughout the unit from the first lesson allows for a more consistent observation of pupils over a longer period of time. For example, one might plan to observe a particular group of pupils working for five minutes in one lesson, and then another group for five minutes in another lesson, but all other teaching would go on regardless. All that would be different is that the teacher might record whether pupils in those groups had achieved, or were 'working towards' the appropriate learning objectives and assessment criteria.

Also, it is important that tasks are set that are progressive, thus offering pupils the opportunity to display their full range of capabilities. If a programme of progressively graduated tasks ranging from easy to difficult are set, the pupils may then be able to select those that they feel capable of completing successfully. If pupils are aware of the criteria to be used for assessment as well as the programme of progression, this will enable them to evaluate themselves more easily. This should not mean that any 'special' arrangement is made for assessment, but that assessment can be part of a differentiated plan of work normally done by the teacher.

## Involving pupils in assessment

Involving pupils in self or peer assessment does mean that a variety of teaching strategies may need to be used. Peer support and collaborative teaching strategies may be particularly appropriate for peer assessment with the teacher taking the role of consultant, adviser and moderator. Such an approach also allows the teacher to stand back and observe not only the pupil's evaluative skills, but also the development of their social skills such as cooperating and working with others. Teacher directed differentiated, 'inclusion' and 'self-check' strategies or any approach in which pupils have the opportunity to choose at which stage in a progression to enter the learning process, may all be suitable for peer assessment. However, as Latham (1992) points out, to be effective, pupils do need help: '... in focusing on the process of skill production as opposed to the end product', and, '... in observation of the key features within either the skill, tactics or the specific area to be assessed'. (p. 23)

These points were reinforced by Loose and Abrahams (1993) in their study of pupils' perceptions and attitudes towards peer assessment. They also discovered that:

- pupils needed very clear direction concerning when to do the assessment and what to look for;
- pupils were concerned about who their assessment partner would be, with same sex groupings being preferred.

Latham (1992) offers an example of a peer assessment sheet successfully implemented in schools, and this is shown in Box 23.

## Assessment of pupil's ability to plan and evaluate

One aspect of assessment within the National Curriculum that is relatively new for PE teachers is assessment of pupils' ability to plan and evaluate their own and others work. Planning health-related exercise programmes may produce pupil written work as evidence, but evidence of pupil planning of tactics in invasion games, of sequences in gymnastics or dance, may be more difficult. An example of an

# Box 23
# Example of a Peer Assessment Sheet for Tennis

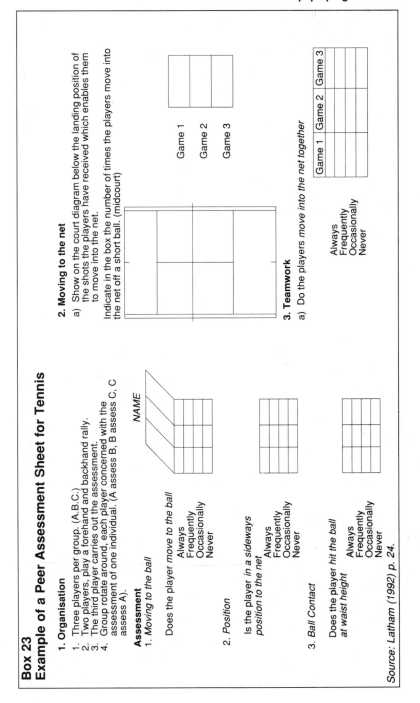

## 1. Organisation

1. Three players per group. (A.B.C.)
2. Two players, play a forehand and backhand rally.
3. The third player carries out the assessment.
4. Group rotate around, each player concerned with the assessment of one individual. (A assess B, B assess C, C assess A).

## Assessment

### 1. *Moving to the ball*

NAME

Does the player *move to the ball*

    Always
    Frequently
    Occasionally
    Never

### 2. *Position*

Is the player *in a sideways position to the net*

    Always
    Frequently
    Occasionally
    Never

### 3. *Ball Contact*

Does the player *hit the ball at waist height*

    Always
    Frequently
    Occasionally
    Never

## 2. Moving to the net

a) Show on the court diagram below the landing position of the shots the players have received which enables them to move into the net.

Indicate in the box the number of times the players move into the net off a short ball. (midcourt)

Game 1

Game 2

Game 3

## 3. Teamwork

a) Do the players *move into the net together*

| | Game 1 | Game 2 | Game 3 |
|---|---|---|---|
| Always | | | |
| Frequently | | | |
| Occasionally | | | |
| Never | | | |

*Source: Latham (1992) p. 24.*

approach to assess planning in games used in schools by Latham and Lucas (1993) included the use of the type of worksheet shown in Box 24, and Box 25 illustrates a workcard recommended by Robinson (1993) for planning/evaluating in gymnastics or dance.

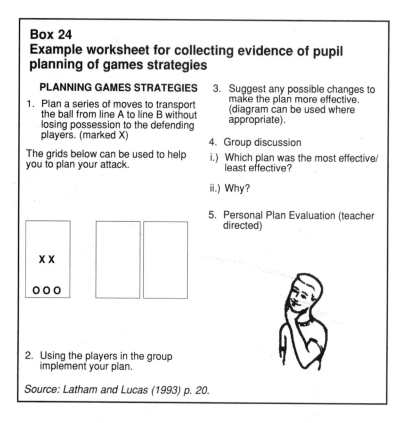

**Box 24**
**Example worksheet for collecting evidence of pupil planning of games strategies**

**PLANNING GAMES STRATEGIES**

1. Plan a series of moves to transport the ball from line A to line B without losing possession to the defending players. (marked X)

The grids below can be used to help you to plan your attack.

X X

O O O

2. Using the players in the group implement your plan.

3. Suggest any possible changes to make the plan more effective. (diagram can be used where appropriate).

4. Group discussion
i.) Which plan was the most effective/ least effective?

ii.) Why?

5. Personal Plan Evaluation (teacher directed)

*Source: Latham and Lucas (1993) p. 20.*

## Recording evidence

As far as recording evidence is concerned, a wide range of different approaches may be used, all of which should support teaching and learning and be part of everyday teaching. PE teachers have developed records of achievement, summary sheets, profiles, daily working notes and mark sheets for their own personally preferred method of recording achievement. These records might include:

- teachers' own descriptive comment, such as:
  'pupils planned different line out variations to vary tactics as part of planning in rugby'.
- notes of pupil's comment, such as:

**Box 25**
**Example worksheet for collecting evidence of pupil planning or evaluation in Gymnastics or Dance**

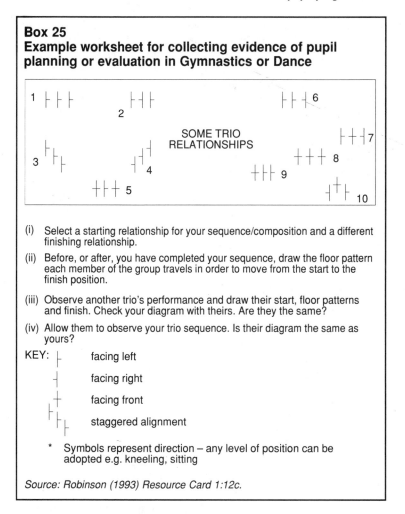

(i) Select a starting relationship for your sequence/composition and a different finishing relationship.

(ii) Before, or after, you have completed your sequence, draw the floor pattern each member of the group travels in order to move from the start to the finish position.

(iii) Observe another trio's performance and draw their start, floor patterns and finish. Check your diagram with theirs. Are they the same?

(iv) Allow them to observe your trio sequence. Is their diagram the same as yours?

KEY: ⊢ facing left

⊣ facing right

+ facing front

staggered alignment

\* Symbols represent direction – any level of position can be adopted e.g. kneeling, sitting

*Source: Robinson (1993) Resource Card 1:12c.*

'David didn't really reach up high enough to place the ball on the backboard', was a pupil comment recorded in relation to assessing and evaluating a fellow pupil when learning the lay up shot in basketball.

- notes of what happened, such as: 'completed a smooth, controlled three part movement sequence' as part of performing in gymnastics.
- pupils' written work related to planning or evaluating as shown in Boxes 24 and 25.

Evidence of pupil progress may be recorded on individual pupil record sheets, record sheets for each activity, or, more simply, as part of the class register or mark book. Almond *et al.* (1992) recommend that such individual and class record sheets should be based on the idea that pupils are either 'working towards' an objective or criteria, or have achieved it. The authors also make the point that:

'... pupils should be given credit for "being able to" – therefore it is unnecessary to differentiate, for recording purposes, between how well pupils have achieved an objective'. (p. 23)

The most important point is that the method of recording should be manageable, and naturally the question of 'when' to record is an important issue. It can be particularly problematic for PE teachers working outside in a variety of weather conditions, or in the gym or sports hall with additional safety issues to consider, and even at the end of lessons when equipment routines and showering has to be dealt with, than it is for the classroom teacher. The effective teacher of PE will therefore have planned in advance how and when she will record evidence of pupil achievement and progress, whether at the end of the lesson or during the lesson. A variety of pieces of advice were offered by HODs in the TEPE Project:

Short notes in the register will be the most meaningful. ROA's are too bulky and not easily accessible for day to day needs.

Keep it with the register – have a simple system.

Assess only a few each lesson.

Have a system of regular recording – every lesson in a mark book.

## Pupil involvement in recording progress

Several HODs mentioned the importance of involving pupils in recording their own progress: 'Always allow pupils to do self-assessment so you can see how they perceive themselves.' 'Pupils need to feel part of the assessment process.'

Pupils can be directly involved in recording their own progress using personal records of achievement, record cards, review sheets and booklets that the pupil is able to keep, or is retained by the teacher. This may take the form of specific record cards or questions related to a particular module or in the form of a teaching group wall chart.

All the records of pupil progress and attainment may be placed in a folder or portfolio and kept at the school but accessible to pupils who may have the opportunity to add to it.

The effective teacher will not only work hard to establish a positive pupil attitude towards completion of review sheets, records of achievement, and the whole process of self-assessment, but will also design the sheet in such a format that the pupil will have the opportunity to respond in different ways, as well as have appropriate spaces for pupil comments. Using different forms of presentation such as ticking lists of achievement, filling in 'bullseyes', having open boxes and open sentences (e.g. 'I need help with...), and comment banks, as recommended by Carroll (1993) and Hatfield and Phillips (1989), may be more interesting and motivating for pupils.

Care should be taken with the completion of records of achievement by pupils. As they are often seen as a negotiated record between the class teacher and the pupil, then pupils may need help from the teacher in the completion of the record. In some schools this discussion and negotiation takes place within the tutorial period. It would be inappropriate, therefore, for the completion of the record to be left as a piece of set work to be completed while the teacher is away from the class. The record should also be checked by the teacher for accuracy.

When they write about their work, pupils should have the opportunity to devise 'action plans' for the future which will be discussed with the teacher and then followed up later to see if they have been achieved. Also, pupils might be encouraged to discuss each others work and targets, as this promotes a more analytical approach. Those pupils who are less confident about writing evaluations and reviews of their work would naturally benefit from discussion about their work first of all. Review sheets might include:

- What have you achieved?
- What are your strengths and weaknesses?
- In what way have you improved?
- What are your future targets?

Whatever is included it is important to keep such records and review sheets manageable for both pupils and teachers, and constantly under review.

Departments of PE may wish to moderate individual teacher's judgements of pupils, and this can be done by observing the pupil working (either directly as part of team teaching, or on video), and other tangible evidence produced by the pupils.

The question of 'When will I have the time to do this?' is often raised by PE teachers. The answer from one HOD in the TEPE project was quite straightforward: 'PE teachers are always assessing pupils throughout the lesson – now we just have to be a little more formal about it'. What is particularly important is that the new teacher in a school familiarises himself with the school principles and policies for record keeping.

Finally it is important to keep in mind why such records of pupil progress are being kept:

- They should help with the planning of pupils' future work and in particular in identifying areas of concern so that remedial work may be planned and therefore continuity of education achieved.

- They should contribute to pupils' personal and social development through increased motivation and an awareness of their strengths and weaknesses.
- They provide the information on which reports to other teachers, parents and pupils may be made.

What ways are there for reporting pupil progress?

## Reporting pupil progress

As far as the National Curriculum is concerned, the minimum requirement is that teachers should report pupil progress against the end of key stage descriptions. This report may take the form of a general comment that describes the overall attainment of the pupil, or be specific statements related to particular aspects of the work covered, and the level of attainment achieved. Teachers do not have to report on everything they record about a pupil's work, and schools are responsible for designing the summative summary documentation.

The report of a pupil's progress is often termed a 'profile' or 'record of achievement'. This document must be of value to all parties including the pupil, and be transferable and in a style that would be recognised throughout the country by future trainers, educators or employers. It should also provide positive evidence of progress for the pupil to discuss and negotiate her future planning, and a place to comment upon personal and social attributes. It is basically a summary document or précis of the collection of evidence within the pupil's portfolio of evidence of achievement gained throughout the formative process. It should offer parents information about their child's general progress and should be part of the school's policy of assessment, recording and reporting.

As far as the use of profiles and records of achievement in PE are concerned, Robinson (1992) believes that they should serve the following purposes:

- communication of information;
- reaffirmation of educational principles;
- acknowledgement of pupil attainment/progress;
- record of pupil achievement;
- an indication of pupil/teacher involvement in the learning process.

In addition, records of achievement provide an opportunity to involve the pupil and parents in planning and reviewing the pupil's progress, thus identifying with parental help a pupil's strengths and weaknesses. This in turn enables both parents and teachers to facilitate the individual development of the pupil.

A profile or record of achievement might contain the following:

(1) Personal details of the pupil;
(2) Attendance record;
(3) Subject/course curricular aims and targets;
(4) Pupil experiences and activities covered;
(5) Pupil achievement and effort during the course
   – Pupil comments: 'My main achievements ...'
   – Teacher effort and attainment grades/marks, etc.
(6) Additional achievements by the pupil (e.g. awards, certificates, representative honours);
(7) Agreed targets;
(8) Teacher's comment;
(9) Pupil and teacher signatures.

The whole process of linking National Curriculum programmes of study, assessment criteria related to end of Key Stage descriptions, recording of pupil progress and reporting to parents, has been neatly put together into a computerised planning, assessment, recording and reporting system by Ian Spode and Peter Whitlam for Dudley teachers (Dudley Physical Education Advisory Service, 1993). The reporting format uses a statement bank based on assessment objectives which is transferred to an optical mark reader system, from which a prose report for parents is produced.

Student teachers and NQTs will have to familiarise themselves with the school and PE department procedures for recording and reporting pupil attainment and achievement, and will need to develop the skills of working with pupils in their personal review of progress and target setting. In addition, the teacher will need to be able to use a wide variety of techniques for collecting and recording evidence of pupil progress, and this will include familiarity with computerised systems.

# CHAPTER 12

# Supporting the new Physical Education teacher in school

## Introduction

With teacher training rapidly moving towards a more school-based model, the professional training in teaching skills for student teachers is increasingly becoming the responsibility of the class teacher or 'subject mentor' in the school. As Bolton (1993) points out, effective teaching necessitates, in all who undertake it: '... mentoring and training skills required in initial teacher training, the induction of new teachers, school improvement and professional development'. (p. 15)

What does the school mentoring role entail?
What are the skills and competencies required of those taking on this new role?
What specific help and guidance do new entrants to the profession of teaching PE need?

This chapter examines these issues, largely from the point of view of recent research and development work on mentoring in general, but also drawing upon the findings of research with student and newly qualified teachers of PE (NQTs) who have taken part in the TEPE Project.

The aim is to offer guidance to those PE teachers in schools who will be taking on the role of subject mentor with student PE teachers for the first time.

## The subject mentor role

There are a number of different views concerning the role of the 'mentor' in initial teacher education. Jacques (1992), for example, views the mentor's role as involving: '... being an instructor, teacher, a counsellor and assessor rather than simply a craft expert to be copied by the novice'. (p. 340)

In his school, as a coordinator of mentoring, Berrill (1992) recommends Heron's (1986) six categories of counselling intervention as being a suitable model for the various dimensions of mentoring activity. These are:

- prescriptive — telling people what they should do;
- informative — providing essential knowledge and information;
- supportive — affirming an individual's worth;
- cathartic — sensitively drawing out and dealing with emotions;
- confronting — assertively challenging false or limiting ideas;
- catalytic — empowering, by providing the means of independent development.

In an attempt to help class teachers to make the transformation in their role to one in which they are more fully involved in the initial training of teachers, Hurst and Wilkin (1992) have produced a series of 'Guidelines for Mentors and Supervisors' designed to support staff involved in the Cambridgeshire Articled Teacher Pilot Scheme (Cambridge University Department of Education, CUDE, 1990). The guidelines represent the views of teachers who have been involved in the scheme for a number of years, and therefore reflect a wealth of experience in mentoring. The guidelines make a series of recommendations for mentors related to:

- relationships with the training institution;
- relationships with the trainee;
- induction and planning a programme for the trainee;
- observing the trainee;
- conducting a debriefing discussion;
- the wider professional role of the trainee;
- the assessment of the trainee.

Naturally, the school and the training institution should make sure that there are clear and prompt lines of communication between the two 'partners' concerning all issues related to the trainee, and that each makes known to the other their professional expectations and needs. Also, it should be made clear what the school (or department) 'expects' of the trainee in terms of their professional development, and the procedures to be used in the case of a trainee having problems.

Catering for the 'wider professional role' of the trainee is an important aspect of school-based training. A number of the student and newly qualified teachers taking part in the TEPE Project mentioned how their lack of knowledge of such wider professional issues had become an area of 'concern' and an area which they felt 'unprepared for' prior to starting to teach in their new school. In addition to the subject specific role of, for example, pupil assessment, student teachers need to be aware of and involved in pastoral work, tutorial group work and the teaching of personal and social education, and have some experience of parents' evenings. They might also experience sharing teacher duties, participating in school trips, attending in-service courses or school meetings, and being aware of the work of the careers service and other outside agencies and their functions.

The 'guidelines' produced by Hurst and Wilkin (1992) recommend that the assessment of the trainee should be in the form of a profile, which should act as a continuous record of the trainees' development as a teacher, and be regarded by all parties as more of a professional learning and development aid than an evaluation exercise.

The role of planning the student teacher's training programme, observation of lessons, conducting of debriefing discussions, assessment, and the overall relationship between the mentor and trainee, are all part of the skills and competencies of being a mentor.

## The skills and competencies of being a mentor

Shaw (1992) believes that the 'generic' core skills which are essential for supporting and supervising trainee teachers include: '... needs analysis; interpersonal skills such as counselling, negotiation and conflict solving, giving positive and negative feedback; observation and assessment skills; setting targets and report writing'. (p. 86)

### (1) Needs analysis and planning a programme for the trainee

In order to be able to identify the starting point for planning a progressive programme of induction and training, the mentor needs information about the trainee's previous experience. This might include 'subject knowledge' of the areas to be taught in the school curriculum and previous teaching experience. Many of the student PE teachers in the TEPE Project mentioned 'a lack of knowledge in certain unfamiliar activities' as an area of concern prior to starting their teaching practice in school. With this background information, mentors will then be able to identify 'gaps' in the trainees' knowledge that they may need help with, as well as be able to understand the individual's background in terms of type of school attended, and their perceptions of the role of the teacher. This background knowledge will also enable the mentor to develop a programme that, as Hurst and Wilkin (1992) recommend: '... is a phased and suitably paced introduction to teaching, appropriate to the trainee's skills, confidence and interest'. (pp. 47–8)

This may initially entail the trainee assisting with classes, providing the opportunity to team teach with an experienced teacher, and planning for them to work with another student teacher. Hurst and Wilkin (1992) also suggest, that when planning a programme for a trainee teacher, it should not necessarily be expected that they should teach pupils that might be regarded as 'difficult' or of 'low ability', but that if such classes are provided, then the trainee should receive full support and appropriate guidance.

When planning a training and induction programme, mentors should also make sure that trainees are aware of the resources and facilities available (possibly during preliminary visits), the levels of attainment and behaviour patterns that they might expect of particular classes, and provide opportunities for the trainee to observe other teachers working. The latter point is essential in order to allow the trainee to appreciate the range of teaching approaches that are used within the department. As one PE student teacher taking part in the TEPE Project pointed out:

'I started teaching from day one when I knew very little of the school policy and procedure. I would have appreciated more time to observe at the school prior to my main teaching practice.'

## (2) Interpersonal skills

Many feel that the skills of counselling are crucial to being an effective mentor, as well as an effective teacher. Hill and her colleagues (Hill, Jennings and Madgwick, 1992), suggest that the effective mentor is able to develop an open and trusting working relationship with the trainee through the use of 'active listening skills' and the provision of 'relevant feedback'. As a result, a positive climate is created in which the trainee's needs, concerns and difficulties are outlined and systematically acted upon. The aim is to establish a 'supporting supervisory relationship' with the trainee in which 'personal self-reflection' and self-appraisal are central to the trainee's professional development without creating a relationship founded on dependence. Creating a 'reflective practitioner' is at the heart of the process, and the mentor will need to be able to 'reflect upon' and define the basis of this 'craft knowledge' if the trainee is to be able to do likewise.

## (3) Lesson observation and the development of teaching skills

Berrill (1992), in outlining a programme for structured mentoring in the development of teaching skills, puts forward what he terms the 'formative process'. Having identified a series of 'competence areas' concerning teaching skills (shown in Box 26), he and his group of school mentors developed a set of practical criteria for the observation and analysis of these aspects of teaching expertise.

For example, referring to the competence area 'Use of planning framework', the criteria used for observation of a lesson might include:

- How relevant is the lesson to the scheme of work (or syllabus) and lesson plan?
- Is it clear what knowledge, concepts, skills or values are to be learned?

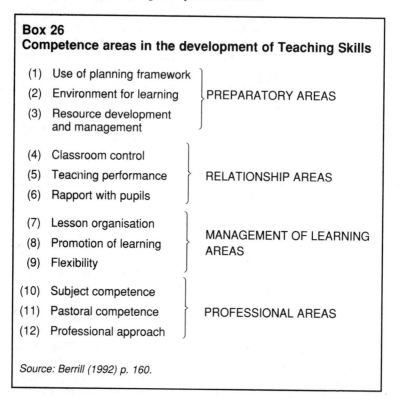

**Box 26**
**Competence areas in the development of Teaching Skills**

(1)  Use of planning framework
(2)  Environment for learning      PREPARATORY AREAS
(3)  Resource development
      and management

(4)  Classroom control
(5)  Teaching performance      RELATIONSHIP AREAS
(6)  Rapport with pupils

(7)  Lesson organisation
(8)  Promotion of learning      MANAGEMENT OF LEARNING
                                 AREAS
(9)  Flexibility

(10)  Subject competence
(11)  Pastoral competence      PROFESSIONAL AREAS
(12)  Professional approach

*Source: Berrill (1992) p. 160.*

- Is the lesson content, structure and teaching approach appropriate for what has to be learned?
- Is material appropriate for the range of pupil ability? (Differentiation)
- To what extent are cross-curricular issues built into the lesson?

Naturally, a school Head of Department would need to make sure that the trainee was made aware of several items on this list, not least in relation to schemes of work and syllabus.

For the purpose of assessment these criteria would then be broken down into a five level assessment scheme.

The next stage in Berrill's formative process entails the mentor and trainee choosing a competence area to focus on, and in which the criteria could be used. A pre-observation meeting would then be arranged to discuss the criteria, and establish how they might relate to the planning, content and development of the lesson. The mentor would then discuss with the trainee which criteria would be used for the observation of the lesson, although Berrill suggests that for early lessons it might be better to see just what arises rather than have set criteria to focus upon. Alternatively, the focus of the observation might come from the trainee's own concerns and perceived difficulties. Later, the criteria would be used to ensure that the observation is undertaken in a 'disciplined, focussed and accountable manner'.

Shaw (1992) believes that this 'partnership' process (mentor and trainee) for planning lesson observation should follow a series of clearly defined stages:

Stage 1 – The focus of the observation is planned with the trainee and decisions made concerning whether the observation will be used for developmental or formal assessment purposes.

Stage 2 – A time and a place is agreed for the observation.

Stage 3 – An agreement is reached as to the actual role of the mentor/observer during the lesson, and whether the mentor should be 'inobtrusive' or a participant in the lesson.

Stage 4 – A time and a private place is agreed for debriefing.

Stage 5 – Observation stage with written record made (difficult if participating in the lesson).

Stage 6 – Mentor offers brief and positive informal feedback at the end of the observation.

Stage 7 – The formal debriefing occurs as soon as possible after the observation, with feedback based on the mentor's factual record of the observation and related to the agreed 'focus' of the lesson.

## (3) Giving feedback after observing a lesson: The debriefing session

At the formal debriefing session the mentor feeds back to the trainee what was observed, and, in the case of Berrill's criteria, the trainee should be informed of the extent to which criteria were satisfactorily fulfilled, and the 'level' achieved in the area of competence agreed beforehand. However, other aspects of teaching may also be dealt with if deemed important at the trainee's stage of development, providing it does not 'drift' too far away from the original agreed area of competence being focussed upon in the observation. This may be subject specific and relate to the preparation of the scheme of work, individual sequences of lessons and teaching material. For example:

Were the aims and objectives of the lesson appropriate? Were these related to National Curriculum end of key stage statements and criteria for assessment?
Were the activities appropriate for the range of abilities in the class?
Were the activities developed in a progressive way?

Were the activities appropriate for the facilities and equipment that were available, or the weather conditions?
Was an alternative lesson plan available?
Was a range of teaching approaches used in relation to particular lesson objectives?

The giving of feedback after a lesson can be a very delicate process and therefore it is important that the mentor develops a positive professional relationship with the trainee beforehand. Student teachers need factual and clear feedback on the development of their teaching skills. Therefore, a balance of positive and negative feedback is important, with some of the 'good' aspects dealt with first. This gives the trainee the feeling that the mentor does see something of value in their early attempts at teaching. Asking the trainee how they felt the lesson had gone is also a useful way to start the debriefing session. Student teachers can be very honest and highlight their own lesson's shortcomings. This means that the mentor may not have to raise certain negative issues, and be able to act in a more positive way by posing questions concerning how certain aspects of teaching may be improved, how particular problems may be solved, and exploring the various issues that would help the trainee to improve their teaching skills.

However, both Berrill (1992) and Shaw (1992) see the most important function of this meeting being target setting, in which tasks are set for subsequent weeks. These targets need to be realistic, yet achievable and challenging, related to agreed criteria, appropriate to the individual trainee's stage of development, and recorded in the trainee's note book or pro-forma. Ideally, no more than than three to five targets should be agreed upon.

Hurst and Wilkin (1992) recommend that the debriefing discussion should not only be a regular, formal and timetabled meeting with both parties available, but be at least a period in length, so that there can be adequate discussion of preparation and evaluation of the lesson. This meeting is also a suitable time to review the trainee's file, which should represent a complete and up-to-date record of their work at the school.

The 'Guidelines for Mentors and Supervisors' developed by the teachers in Cambridgeshire (CUDE, 1990), recommends a particular approach to conducting the debriefing discussion which should include the following (Hurst and Wilkin, 1992):

- the trainee should be encouraged to review and reflect upon their practice as a part of their progressive professional development;
- the mentor should encourage the trainee to develop a professional 'independence' that views mistakes as learning experiences;
- the mentor should not only act in a supportive manner but should also use an appropriate response style for the circumstances and be

prepared to change this if the response of the trainee is such that a change in approach is desirable;

- the mentor should see the discussion agenda as flexible and be able to take into account the specific needs of the trainee;
- the mentor should attempt to be constructive rather than critical and end the debriefing on a positive note;
- a copy of the notes taken during the lesson observation should be given to the trainee and these should form the basis of the debriefing discussion;
- the notes should also be used to provide evidence to support points made when discussing the lesson.

As the debriefing session involves the mentor in using their counselling skills, a sympathetic and positive tone of voice with sensitive use of eyes and body language are important, as is the need for a quiet room without interruptions.

According to Berrill (1992), the next stage of his 'formative process' takes place after a three week period when another agreed competence area is focussed upon with its own set of criteria used as a basis for observation. At the end of each three-week period Berrill suggests that a formative assessment is made, but earlier targets are also considered and any improvement recorded.

## (4) Assessment and report writing

If the lesson observation is for formal assessment purposes it is important that the mentor states clearly to the trainee not only the recommendation that will be made, but also 'why' it is made, and how it relates to the factual report and agreed targets.

Shaw (1992) believes that the writing of reports on the professional progress of student teachers needs to refer only to fact rather than uncorroborated subjective opinion, and should be written in a language that is 'neutral and professional'. If the school and PE Department have an agreed set of criteria concerning what they believe is 'effective teaching' (which may be based on the teacher competencies outlined in DES circular 9/92, DES, 1992b), then there exists an objective basis for the writing of reports. Naturally, all parties ought to be aware of these criteria and the meaning of them.

Hurst and Wilkin (1992) suggest that the assessment of the trainee teacher should take the form of a profile. This profile should act as a continuous record of the trainee's development as a teacher while at the school. They believe it should be open, negotiable and accessible to the trainee (in terms of both assessment procedures and the document itself), and should provide the trainee with opportunities for self-assessment. Ideally, the profile should contain sections referring to the different areas of professional skill development and experience.

One of the difficulties that may arise within the role of mentor are the tensions that can occur in the transition from being a supporter and 'critical friend', to that of being an assessor. Shaw (1992) believes that when conflicts do arise between mentor and trainee, the mentor needs to apply 'lightly developed skills of negotiation':

> ... anticipating and avoiding possible conflict, non-confrontational verbal or body language, good verbal and non-verbal communication, choosing appropriate settings for the negotiation to take place, clearly identifying and separating issues, the ability to review and summarise the other person's points, acknowledging the value of the other person's point of view and identifying issues of agreement. (p. 88)

The whole question of assessing the professional skills of student teachers does raise a number of difficulties, particularly in the context of a competency-based programme. Not only is the competency approach found wanting in terms of research support, but it is argued that competent teachers are not necessarily 'effective' teachers (McNamara, 1992). Consequently, as Berrill (1992) suggests: 'A problem therefore arises in any competency-based scheme which leads to summative forms of assessment, since technical proficiency does not necessarily equate with teaching excellence'. (p. 166)

However, although one can visualise certain difficulties with summative student teacher reports or profiles based on 'competencies', Berrill does go on to point out that in his school scheme: 'We can say with confidence, however, that teaching excellence involves high levels of proficiency in the competencies we have identified'. (p. 166)

It is therefore essential that subject mentors and University 'link' tutors agree to some extent on a 'shared technical culture', or those teaching skills and so-called 'competencies' that may be used in the assessment of student teachers. Only then will mentors, University tutors and trainees be working towards the same end product, and in turn avoid the problems that have bedevilled the teacher training scene in the United States as far as physical education is concerned (Dodds, 1989).

## The professional development of the student teacher of Physical Education: The need for an individualised approach

Those helping the student teacher of PE to gradually establish their teaching and professional skills, do need to be aware of the fact that each trainee is an individual, will progress at their own speed, and that the trainee's needs may be different to their own. For example, student teachers are initially more concerned about 'self' issues and classroom management, and how they are going to cope and 'survive' in the teaching environment, whereas the experienced teacher is more concerned about pupil learning. On the other hand, the trainee needs to appreciate that they may not be 'thinking' in the same way as the experienced teacher, and therefore must be prepared to ask the kind of questions about discipline, management, planning and motivation of pupils that will help them in their professional development.

This appreciation by mentors that student teachers have very different concerns to themselves is important in the planning and on-going modification of a programme for the development of teaching and professional skills. As far as pre-service PE teachers are concerned, research by Boggess, McBride and Griffey (1985) suggests that both University tutors and school subject mentors could improve their effectiveness by: '... empathising with the developing structures of concerns that evolve during student teaching'. (p. 212)

The first stage of student teacher concerns (prior to their first period of teaching practice) is about subject knowledge (and in particular those activities they are less familiar with), class management and control, concerns about the school and staff expectations, their ability to teach, be accepted by staff and pupils, and planning and preparation. Fuller (1969) believes that there is at this time a strong fear of failure, a need to be liked and accepted by pupils and to please supervisors.

Concern over planning lessons and schemes of work is quite understandable because the trainee is being asked to plan for a situation which they are totally unfamiliar with. Equally, concern about class control and management reflects the trainee's doubts about whether or not they will be able to control unruly children. Collaborative teaching with the mentor might help the trainee to overcome the anxiety that such a situation creates. They would then be able to observe the rules and routines and class monitoring skills that the mentor has established for efficient class management, and be aware of the clear expectations that an experienced teacher lays down for pupil work during a lesson.

Collaborative teaching may be built into the programme for the student teacher in such a way that lessons are jointly planned and jointly taught by the mentor and trainee. According to Burn (1992), such an approach allows the trainee to be involved in three kinds of learning:

(1) They learn to plan lessons jointly with an experienced teacher and become aware of issues (many unforeseen) involved in the planning process.
(2) Trainees gradually learn the skills of teaching through being responsible for a component of the lesson, yet also being able to identify with the lesson as a whole.

(3) The trainee also learns about the experienced teacher's 'craft knowledge', not only as a result of observation of the teacher working, but also because of being involved at the planning stage of the lesson and having a degree of responsibility for the teaching of the lesson.

However, those who have been involved in collaborative teaching have noted a number of problems with this approach, but also ways of overcoming them.

In some cases teachers have found this approach to be a little threatening, because it puts their practice under scrutiny. On the other hand, where mentors and trainees have worked in this way from the beginning, the 'planning and teaching together' atmosphere has helped to develop a 'colleague' relationship between the two parties.

'Role confusion' can occur during lessons of collaborative teaching, with the two parties not really knowing what the other is doing, and the pupils also being confused. It is really up to the mentor to plan the timing of the lesson so that the trainee knows when she is solely responsible for the class and their discipline. When lesson plans are prepared in collaboration with the subject mentor in the early stages of teaching, it is less likely that the trainee would have to change aspects of the plan, as might have been the case with a plan prepared without supervision.

The careful planning of a collaborative lesson is therefore essential, and it must be designed to help the trainee to develop their teaching skills gradually. Provision of appropriate times for experience of working with less able pupils, taking a class discussion, setting certain tasks according to the trainee's stage of development, are all important, as is the need to provide time for a post-lesson debriefing session. However, collaborative teaching would be inappropriate if the trainee is at the stage of needing to be involved in whole class management. It is therefore important that the changing needs and concerns of the trainee are taken into account when planning an individualised programme for student teacher professional development.

Although the Boggess study (Boggess *et al.*, 1985) showed that concerns related to class control continued throughout the first semester of teaching practice, a factor termed 'the routine tasks of teaching' emerged at mid-semester. It appears that at this stage of teaching practice, trainee PE teachers were concerned about 'the inflexibility of the teaching situation', 'working with too many pupils', 'inadequate facilities', and 'too many non-instructional duties'. These items represent the 'realities' of teaching; those everyday duties of experienced PE teachers and the various unforeseen situations and restrictions that can affect planned lessons (such as weather, loss of indoor space, equipment missing, etc.), but are totally new to those just entering the profession. Boggess and her colleagues recommend that those supervising pre-service teachers of PE need to help them to become more efficient in their use of instructional routines (with resulting 'time on task' benefits), and give trainees advice on 'correctly interpreting the actions of children and adolescents' in relation to class management and discipline.

According to Boggess *et al.* (1985), the final stages of student teacher concerns are about assessment and evaluation of their teaching performance, and whether or not they are really suited to teaching as a profession. They suggest that as far as PE trainee teachers are concerned, supervisors and mentors can alleviate the anxieties of trainees earlier in the practice by offering them regular and consistent evaluation throughout the teaching practice period.

Many of the earlier student teacher concerns prior to the first teaching practice can be alleviated by considerate and thoughtful staff who are prepared to 'give time' to help trainees to understand the school as a workplace; by giving them information about routines, policies and ways of working which are unique to their department. They need to feel a part of the school, to feel wanted and valued as a trainee professional, and to feel that there are colleagues who are interested and care about the progressive development of their teaching and professional skills. Unfortunately, several student teachers taking part in the TEPE Project did not receive this kind of support, and some of them were reluctant to ask for help. In certain cases they would have preferred more time to observe other teachers, and would have liked help with planning and organisation. They expressed a need for information about pupils' previous experience, knowledge about the school disciplinary system, advice and help with teaching unfamiliar activities, and just 'time' to talk through their concerns. Some trainees mentioned that they had 'learned to cope' by themselves, 'overcome their own difficulties', and to some extent only experience in the teaching situation had helped some of them to alleviate certain concerns. It was as if they had suddenly realised that they could 'do it', and that they had been silly to worry about, for example, 'standing in front of a class of children'. However, what is important is that the mentor 'supports' the individual trainee in a planned and individualised way, and does not leave them to 'sink or swim'. Quality support is particularly important during those first attempts at teaching.

As the TEPE Project revealed, the main difficulties experienced by student teachers of PE during those first lessons involved such issues as:

- Lesson delivery – including getting to know pupil names; the use of simple, clear and precise explanations; appropriate variation in voice tone; timing of lessons; and class positioning to monitor pupils and keep them 'on task'.
- Organisation and management of lessons – including general lesson organisation as well as specific organisation of equipment

and groups; lesson routines and transitions; issuing equipment and getting classes changed.

- Discipline and class control – including keeping control and handling problem pupils; ensuring quiet and gaining class control before talking; motivating reticent pupils and getting pupils to follow instructions.
- Knowledge – particularly in relation to a lack of confidence in having to teach unfamiliar activities as well as the depth of knowledge required to teach the broad range of activities that make up the school PE curriculum. Also the lack of knowledge of pupil abilities, skill level and previous experience to aid planning of lessons, and knowledge of school equipment for teaching.
- Planning – difficulties caused by overplanning and trying to achieve too much in a lesson; being unsure about the matching of material to pupil skill levels and ability and progression.

Certain personal difficulties also existed, largely to do with a lack of confidence and 'nerves'.

The trainees in the TEPE project generally received the help and advice they needed to overcome these difficulties, but 13% said that they did not. One trainee believed that :

Perhaps it's necessary to learn through your own mistakes and improve as a result of that!

Another trainee who had difficulties with:

... setting attainable targets, knowing what children were particulary capable of – discipline problems with some groups – and mixed lessons, catering for all skill levels.

– mentioned that:

I really learned through experience which was what the school expected.

Student teachers need a structured individual programme of support to cope with the many concerns and difficulties experienced in the early stages of teaching. They have their own individual problems and concerns, and these are not always alleviated 'through experience' or just 'getting on with it'.

School subject mentors therefore need to treat each student teacher as an individual with their own individual pathway along the road to becoming an effective teacher. Some will learn effective teaching skills and become more aware of the complexities of teaching faster than others, while others will need more time and considerable counselling. Just as there are differentiated routes to learning for pupils, there should be individualised routes to learning how to teach for trainee teachers. Although a class teacher or mentor may have an excellent trainee teacher one year, it doesn't mean that they should expect the same rapid progress from another trainee the following year.

Class teachers and subject mentors also need to beware of attempting to 'clone' a copy of themselves in their trainee – it is impossible to have the same high expectations in terms of teaching performance from a trainee's first term in teaching that one might have created in 15 years of experience. The trainee's progress should be viewed in a developmental way. Initially they may be viewed as a novice who is totally unaware of what to expect when standing in front of a group of pupils, having all the 'self' concerns regarding class management and being able to remember the tasks they have prepared. Then they may progress through a variety of stages of concern that eventually may lead to a truly 'reflective practitioner', primarily concerned with pupil learning and with many of their organisation and management teaching skills running on 'auto-pilot'. It was noticeable in the TEPE Project that student PE teachers were largely concerned about knowledge, discipline and control, teaching skills, being accepted by pupils and staff, knowledge of the school and pupils, planning and being assessed, whereas NQTs in their first term of teaching appeared to have concerns dominated by meeting new staff and pupils, finding out about new routines, their timetable and additional school duties.

The effective subject mentor will therefore not only use his counselling skills to ascertain the trainee's stage of development and concerns at different points in time during their term in his school, but will plan and modify his programme for the trainee in relation to their individual needs.

Sometimes, too much is expected of student teachers during their first term in school. For example, two HODs taking part in the TEPE Project expected student teachers to be able to do the following in terms of professional duties in their department:

... teach a wide range of sports/activities, including umpiring skills; cope with mixed ability classes of varying sizes, including SEN provision; pay special regard to safety factors; show a variety of teaching styles; be flexible and able to accommodate changes due to the weather; show willingness to become involved in extra-curricular activities.

... teach *all* aspects of PE throughout the age range, including GCSE and 'A' level.

Clearly, in the case of a lot of student PE teachers, such expectations would be too great, particularly as many of those taking part in the TEPE Project expressed concern about their ability to teach the full range of activities in the school curriculum. School subject mentors need to appreciate that, in many cases, student teachers do also have to contend with the transition from University to professional life, and the personal difficulties than can arise along the way. The trainees in the TEPE Project mentioned difficulties to do with tiredness, travelling and working late, feelings of isolation, lifestyle conflicts and a lack of time to prepare. Many simply need time to adjust to a professional working day and a full working week!

In essence, the mentor may need to view herself as not only a professional guide, facilitator and assessor, but also a bit of a personal pastoral tutor or counsellor along the way.

# REFERENCES

Abernathy, B. (1993) Attention. In R. N. Singer, M. Murphy and K. L. Tennant, (eds) *Handbook of Research on Sport Psychology*, 127–70. New York, Macmillan.

Adams, J. A. (1971) A closed-loop theory of motor learning. *Journal of Motor Behaviour*, 3, 111–50.

Almond, L., Dickenson, B. and Waring, M. (1992) *An Introduction to the Physical Education National Curriculum: A Practical Guide*. Sandwell Education Department.

Anderson, W. (1980) *Analysis of Teaching Physical Education*. St. Louis, C. V. Mosby.

Arena, L. (1979) *Descriptive and experimental studies of augmented instructional feedback in sport settings*. Unpublished Doctoral Dissertation, Ohio State University.

Armstrong, C. W. (1977) Skill analysis and Kinaesthetic experience. In R. S. Stadulis (ed.) *Research and practice in physical education*, 13–18. Champaign, Illinois, Human Kinetics.

Armstrong, C. W. (1986) Research on movement analysis: Implications for the development of pedagogical competence. In M. Pieron and G. Graham (eds) *Sport Pedagogy*. 1984 Olympic Scientific Congress Proceedings, 6, 27–32. Champaign, Illinois, Human Kinetics.

Armstrong, C. W. and Hoffman, S. J. (1979) Effects of teaching experience, knowledge of performer competence, and knowledge of performance outcome on performance 'error' identification. *Research Quarterly*, 50, 318–27.

Arrighi, M. A. and Young, J. C. (1987) Teachers perceptions about effective and successful teaching. *Journal of Teaching in Physical Education*, 6, 2, 122–35.

Ashy, M. H., Lee, A. M. and Landin, D. K. (1988) Relationships of practice using current technique to achievement in a motor skill. *Journal of Teaching in Physical Education*, 7, 115–20.

Atkinson, P. and Delamont, S. (1985) Socialisation into teaching in the research which lost its way. *British Journal of Sociology of Education*, 6, 3, 316–17.

Ausubel, D. (1960) The use of Advance Organisers in the learning and retention of meaningful verbal material. *Journal of Educational Psychology*, 51, 267–72.

Ausubel, D. P. (1968) *Educational Psychology: A Cognitive View.* New York, Holt, Rinehart & Winston.

Bakker, F. C., Whiting, H. T. A. and Van Der Brug, H. (1990) *Sport Psychology: Concepts and Applications.* Chichester, John Wiley & Sons.

Bandura, A. (1969) *Principles of behaviour modification.* New York, Holt, Rinehart & Winston.

Bandura, A. (1977) *Social Learning Theory.* Englewood Cliffs, New Jersey, Prentice Hall.

Barrett, K. (1979) Observation for teaching and coaching. *Journal of Health, Physical Education and Recreation,* 50, 1, 23–5.

Barrett, K. (1983) A hypothetical model of observing as a teaching skill. *Journal of Teaching in Physical Education*, 3, 1, 22–31.

Behets, D. (1990) Concerns of pre-service physical education teachers. *Journal of Teaching in Physical Education*, 10, 66–75.

Behets, D. (1991) Teacher enthusiasm and effective teaching in physical education. *Physical Education Review*, Spring, 50–5.

Belka, D. E., Lawson, H. and Lipnickey, S. C. (1991) An exploratory study of undergraduate recruitment into several major programs at one University. *Journal of Teaching in Physical Education*, 10, 286–306.

Bellack, A. A., Pavitz, J. R., Kliebard, A. M., Ayman, R. T. and Smith, F. L. (1966) *The Language of the Classroom.* New York, Teachers College Press, Columbia University.

Bennett, N. (1978) Recent research on teaching: A dream, a belief, and a model. *British Journal of Educational Psychology*, 48, 127–47.

Berliner, D. (1979) Tempus Educare. In P. Peterson and H. Walberg (eds) *Research on Teaching: Concepts, findings & implications.* 120–35. Berkeley, CA., McCutchan.

Berliner, D. C. and Tickunoff, W. T. (1976) California's beginning teacher evaluation study: Overview of the ethnographic study. *Journal of Teacher Education*, 27, 24–34.

Berrill, M. (1992) Structured Mentoring and the Development of Teaching Skill. In M. Wilkin (ed.) *Mentoring in Schools*, 155–72. London, Kogan Page.

Beveridge, S. K. and Gangstead, S. K. (1988) Teaching experience and training in sports skill analysis. *Journal of Teaching in Physical Education*, 7, 103–14.

Biddle, S. (1991) Motivating Achievement in Physical Education: A Psychology of Success and Failure. In N. Armstrong and A. Sparkes (eds) *Issues in Physical Education*, 91–108. London, Cassell.

Biddle, S. (1993) Attribution research and Sport Psychology. In R. N. Singer, M. Murphy and L. K. Tennant (eds) *Handbook of Research on Sport Psychology*, 437–66. New York, Macmillan.

Biddle, S. and Fox, K. (1988) Achievement Psychology. *British Journal of Physical Education*, 19, 4, 182–5.

Biddle, S. and Goudas, M. (1993) Teaching styles, class climate and motivation in Physical Education. *British Journal of Physical Education*, 24, 3, 38–9.

Bloom, B. (1984) The 2 Sigma Problem: The search for methods of group instructions as effective as one to one tutoring. *Educational Researcher*, June/July, 4–16.

Bloom, B., Englehart, M., Furst, E., Hill, W. and Krathwohl, D. (1956) *Taxonomy of educational objectives: The Classification of educational goals. Handbook One: Cognitive Domain*. New York, Longmans Green.

Boggess, T. E., McBride, R. and Griffey, D. C. (1985) The concerns of physical education student teachers: A developmental view. *Journal of Teaching in Physical Education*, 4, 202–11.

Bolton, E. (1993) Teaching Skills. In L.E.A.P. (Local Authorities in Association with Higher Education Institutions), *Developing Teaching Skills*. The Educational Broadcasting Services Trust, London, L.E.A.P.

Borko, H. and Niles, T. (1987) Descriptions of teacher planning. In V. Richardson-Koehler (ed.) *Educators Handbook: A Research Perspective*, 167–87. White Plains, N.Y., Longmans.

Borys, A. H. and Fishbourne, G. J. (1990) A comparison of pre-service and in-service teacher's conceptions of successful teaching. In M. Lirette, C. Pare, J. Dessureault and M. Pieron (eds) *Physical Education and Coaching: Present State and Outlook for the Future*. 41–6. Proceedings of the AIESEP 1987 World Convention, Quebec, Presses de l'Universite du Quebec.

Boyce, B. A. (1991) The effects of an instructional strategy with two schedules of augmented feedback upon skill acquisition of a selected shooting task. *Journal of Teaching in Physical Education*, 11, 47–58.

Branwhite, T. (1988) The PASS Survey: School based preferences of 500+ adolescent consumers. *Educational Studies*, 14, 165–76.

British Association of Advisers and Lecturers in Physical Education (BAALPE) (1989a) *Physical Education for Children with Special Educational Needs in Mainstream Education*. Leeds, White Line Press.

British Association of Advisers and Lecturers in Physical Education (BAALPE) (1989b) *Teaching and Learning Strategies in Physical Education*. Leeds, White Line Press.

*British Journal of Physical Education* (1987) Special issue: Physical Education for children and students with special educational needs, 18, 5.

*British Journal of Physical Education* (1990) Special issue on Special Educational Needs and PE, 21, 4.

*British Journal of Physical Education* (1993) Special issue on Special Educational Needs and PE, 24, 3.

Brophy, J. (1983) Classroom organisation and management. *Elementary School Journal*, 83, 265–85.

Brophy, J. and Good, T. (1986) Teacher behaviour and student achievement. In M. Wittrock (ed.) *Handbook of Research on teaching*, 3rd Edition, 328–75. New York, Macmillan.

Brown, A. (1986) *Active Games for Children with Movement problems*. London, Harper and Row.

Brown. A. and Jones. G. (1989) *Mainstreaming children with special educational needs in Physical Education*. University of Newcastle-Upon-Tyne, Department of Physical Education and Sport.

Brown, G. A. and Armstrong, S. (1984) Explaining and explanations. In E. C. Wragg (ed.) *Classroom Teaching Skills,* 121–48. London, Croom Helm.

Brown, G. A. and Edmundson, R. (1984) Asking questions. In E. C. Wragg (ed) *Classroom Teaching Skills,* 97–120. London, Croom Helm.

Brown, G. A. and Hatton, N. (1982) *Explanations and Explaining: A Teaching skills workbook*. D.E.S. Teacher Education Project Focus Books, London, Macmillan Education.

Brown, G. and Wragg, E. C. (1993) *Questioning*. London, Routledge.

Burn, K. (1992) Collaborative Teaching. In M. Wilkin (ed.) *Mentoring in Schools,* 133–43. London, Kogan Page.

Burwitz, L. (1975) Observational learning and motor performance, British Proceedings of Sports Psychology, 255–62. British Society of Sports Psychology.

Byra, M. and Coulon, S. C. (1994) The effect of planning on the instructional behaviours of pre-service teachers. *Journal of Teaching in Physical Education*, 13, 2, 123–39.

Byra, M. and Marks, M. C. (1993) The effects of two pairing techniques on specific feedback and comfort levels of learners in the reciprocal style of teaching. *Journal of Teaching in Physical Education*, 12, 3, 286–300.

Calderhead, J. (1986) *A Cognitive perspective on teaching skills*. Paper presented at the British Psychological Society Education Section Annual Conference, Nottingham.

Calderhead, J. (ed.) (1987) *Exploring Teachers Thinking*. London, Cassell.

Cambridge University Department of Education (CUDE) (1990) *Guidelines for Mentors and Supervisors*. Cambridge, CUDE.

Capel, S. (1993) Anxieties of beginning physical education teachers. *Educational Research*, 35, 3, 281–7.

Carlisle, C. and Phillips, D. A. (1984) The effects of enthusiasm training on selected teacher and student behaviours in pre-service physical education teachers. *Journal of Teaching in Physical Education*, 4, 1, 64–75.

Carr, W. (ed.) (1989) *Quality in Teaching: Arguments for a Reflective Profession*. London, Falmer Press.

Carroll, R. (1993) *Assessment in Physical Education: A 'Teachers' Guide*. London, Falmer Press.

Chamberlain, C. and Lee, D. T. (1993) Arranging practice conditions and designing instruction. In R. N. Singer, M. Murphey and L. K. Tennant (eds) *Handbook of Research on Sports Psychology*, 213–41. New York, Macmillan.

Cheffers, J. T. F. and Mancini, V. H. (1978) Teacher student interaction. In W. G. Anderson and G. Barrette (eds) What's going on in Gym: Descriptive studies of PE classes. *Motor Skills: Theory into Practice*. Monograph 1, 39–50.

Clark, C. M. and Peterson, P. L. (1986) Teachers' thought processes. In M. C. Wittrock (ed.) *Handbook of research on teaching*, 3rd Edition, 255–96. New York, Macmillan.

Clark, C. M. and Yinger, R. J. (1987) Teacher planning. In J. Calderhead (ed.) *Exploring Teachers Thinking*, 84–103. London, Cassell.

Cohen, S. (1987) Instructional alignment: Searching for the magic bullet. *Educational Researcher*, November, 16–20.

Cohen, L. and Manion, L. (1989) *A Guide to Teaching Practice*. London, Routledge.

*Collins English Dictionary* (1986) London, Collins.

Cooke, N., Heron, T. and Heward, W. (1983) *Peer Tutoring*. Columbus, OH, Special Press.

Cope, E. (1975) Evaluation of Physical Education in the Social Context. *Journal of Psycho-Social Aspects of Physical Education*, Dunfermline College of Physical Education, April, 42–52.

Cruickshank, D. R. and Kennedy, J. J. (1986) Teacher Clarity. *Teaching and Teacher Education*, 2, 43–67.

Curriculum Council for Wales (1992) *Physical Education in the National Curriculum*. Cardiff, CCW.

De Bono, E. (1983) The Direct teaching of thinking as a skill. *Phi Delta Kappan*, 64, 703–8

De Bono, E. (1985) The CoRT thinking programme. In J. Segal, S. Chipman and R. Glaser (eds), *Thinking and Learning Skills, Vol 1: Relating instruction to research*. Hillsdale NJ, Erlbaum.

De Knop, P. (1986) Relationships of specified instructional teacher behaviours to student gains in tennis. *Journal of Teaching in Physical Education*, 5, 2, 71–8.

Denham, C. and Lieberman, A. (1980) (eds) *Time to Learn*. Washington DC, National Institute of Education, US Department of Education.

Department of Education and Science (1984) *Initial Teacher Training: Approval of Courses*. Circular 3/84, London, DES.

Department of Education and Science (1985) *Education Observed, 3: Good Teachers.* London, DES.

Department of Education and Science (1988a) *The New Teacher in School.* A survey by HM Inspectors in England and Wales 1987, London, HMSO.

Department of Education and Science (1988b) *Task Group on Assessment and Testing (TGAT).* Report, London, DES.

Department of Education and Science and the Welsh Office (1988c) *Records of Achievement: Report of the evaluation of national pilot schemes.* London, HMSO.

Department of Education and Science (1989a) *National Curriculum: From Theory to Practice.* London, HMSO.

Department of Education and Science (1989b) *Discipline in Schools.* (The Elton Report). London, HMSO.

Department of Education and Science (1989c) *Report of the Records of Achievement National Steering Committee.* London, HMSO.

Department of Education and Science and the Welsh Office (1991) *Physical Education for ages 5 to 16.* Final Report of the National Curriculum Physical Education Working Group. London, HMSO.

Department of Education and Science (1992) *Reform of Initial Teacher Training: A Consultative Document.* London, DES.

Department For Education (1992) *Initial Teacher Training (Secondary Phase).* Circular 9/92, London, DFE.

Dewar, A. M. (1989) Recruitment in Physical Education teaching: Towards a Critical Approach. In T. J. Templin and P. G. Schempp (eds) *Socialisation into Physical Education: Learning to Teach,* 39–57. Indianapolis, Indiana, Benchmark Press.

Dickenson, B., and Almond, L. (1993) Assessment in Physical Education: A Practical Model for implementing National Curriculum Assessment requirements *British Journal of Physical Education,* 24, 4, 22–6.

Dierenfield, R. B. (1982) *Classroom disruption in English Comprehensive Schools.* Minnesota, Macalester College Education Department.

Dodds, P. (1989) Trainees, field experiences and socialisation into teaching. In T. J. Templin and P. G. Schempp (eds) *Socialisation into Physical Education: Learning to Teach,* 81–104. Indianapolis, Indiana, Benchmark Press.

Dodds, P., Rife, F., and Metzler, M. (1982) Academic learning time in Physical Education: Data collection, completed research, and future directions. In M. Pieron and J. Cheffers (eds) *Studying the Teaching in Physical Education* 37–52. Proceedings of the AIESEP World Convention, Boston, University of Liege, Belgium, AIESEP.

Dodds, P. and Placek, J. H. (1991) Silverman's RT-P.E. Review: Too simple a summary of a complex field. *Research Quarterly for Exercise and Sport,* 62, 4, 365–8.

Dodds, P., Placek, J. H., Doolittle, S., Pinkham, K. M., Ratcliffe, T. A. and Portman, P. A. (1991) Teacher/Coach Recruits: Background profiles, occupational decision factors, and comparisons with recruits into other Physical Education occupations. *Journal of Teaching in Physical Education*, 11, 161–76.

Doyle, W. (1977) Paradigms for research on teacher effectiveness. In L. Shulman (ed.) *Review of Research in Education*, Vol 5, 163–98. Itasca, Illinois, F. E. Peacock.

Doyle, W. (1986) Classroom organisation and management. In M. Wittrock (ed.) *Handbook of Research on Teaching*, 3rd Edition, 392–431. New York, Macmillan.

Dudley Education Services (1991) *Physical Education in Dudley: Reciprocal Teaching*. Dudley Metropolitan Borough Council.

Dudley Physical Education Advisory Service (1993) *Physical Education: Assessment, Recording and Reporting*. Dudley Metropolitan Borough Council.

Dunkin, M. J. and Biddle, B. J. (1974) *The Study of Teaching*. New York, Holt, Rinehart and Winston.

Eggleston, J. F., Galton, M. J., and Jones, M. E. (1976) *Processes and Products of Science Teaching*. Schools Council Research Studies, London, Macmillan.

Emmer, E. (1987) Classroom management and discipline. In V. Richardson-Koehler (ed.), *Educators' Handbook*, 233–58. New York, Longman.

Emmer, E., Evertson, C. and Anderson, L. (1980) Effective classroom management at the beginning of the school year. *Elementary School Journal*, 80, 219–31.

Evans, J. and Williams, T. (1989) Moving Up and Getting Out: The Classed and Gendered Career Opportunities of Physical Education Teachers. In T. J. Templin and P. G. Schempp (eds) *Socialisation into Physical Education: Learning to Teach*, 235–48. Indianapolis, Indiana, Benchmark Press.

Evertson, C. (1987) Managing classrooms: A Framework for Teachers. In D. Berliner and B. Rosenshine (eds) *Talks to Teachers*, 54–74. New York, Random House.

Evertson, C. and Emmer, E. (1982) Effective management at the beginning of the school year. *Journal of Educational Psychology*, 74, 485–98.

Feiman-Nemser, S. (1983) Learning to Teach. In L. Shulman and G. Sykes (eds) *Handbook of teaching and policy*, 150–70. New York, Longman.

Fernandez-Balboa, J. M. (1991) Beliefs, Interactive thoughts, and Actions of Physical Education Student Teachers regarding pupil misbehaviours. *Journal of Teaching in Physical Education*, 11, 1, 59–78.

Fink, J. and Siedentop, D. (1989) The development of routines, rules, and expectations at the start of the school year. *Journal of Teaching in Physical Education*, 8, 3, 198–212.

Fishburne, G. J. and Hall, C. R. (1987) Visual and Kinaesthetic Imagery Ability in Children: Implications for teaching Motor Skills. In G. T. Barrette, R. S. Fiengold, C. R. Rees, and M. Pieron (eds), *Myths, Models, and Methods in Sport Pedagogy*, 107–12. Champaign, Illinois, Human Kinetics.

Fisher, C. W., Berliner, D., Filby, N., Marliave, R., Cahen, L. and Dishaw, M. (1980) Teaching behaviours, academic learning time, and student achievement: An Overview. In C. Denham and A. Lieberman (eds), *Time to Learn*, 7–32. Washington DC, National Institute of Education, US Department of Education.

Fitts, P. and Posner, M. (1967) *Human Performance.* Belmont, California, Brooks/Cole.

Fox, K. and Biddle, S. (1988) The Childs' Perspective in Physical Education, Part II: Childrens' Participation Motives. *British Journal of Physical Education,* 19, 2, 79–82.

Fox, K. and Biddle, S. (1989) The Childs' Perspective in Physical Education Part VI: Psychology and Professional Issues. *British Journal of Physical Education*, 20, 1, 35–8.

Fuller, F. F. (1969) Concerns of teachers: A developmental conceptualisation. *American Educational Research Journal*, 70, 263–8.

Gage, N. L. and Berliner, D. C. (1975) *Educational Psychology.* Chicago, Rand McNally.

Gagne, R. M. (1974) *Essentials of Learning for Instruction.* Illinois, University of Chicago Press.

Gallagher, J. D. (1982) The effects of developmental memory differences on learning skills. *Journal of Physical Education, Recreation and Dance*, 53, 36–7.

Gallagher, J. D. (1984) Influence of developmental information procesing abilities on childrens' motor performance. In W. Straub and J. Williams (eds) *Cognitive Sports Psychology*, 153–67. Lansing, NY, Sports Science Associates.

Gallagher, J. D. and Hoffman, S. (1987) Memory developments and childrens' sport skill acquisition. In D. Gould and M. R. Weiss (eds) *Advances in Pediatric Sport Science*, 187–210. Champaign, Illinois, Human Kinetics.

Gallagher, J. D. and Thomas, J. R. (1984) Rehearsal strategy effects on developmental differences for recall of a movement series. *Research Quarterly for Exercise and Sport*, 55, 123–28.

Galton, M., Simon, B. and Croll, P. (1980) *Inside the Primary Classroom.* London, Routledge and Kegan Paul.

Gettinger, M. (1988) Methods of proactive classroom management. *School Psychology Review*, 17, 227–42.

Godbout, P., Brunelle, J. and Tousignant, M. (1987) Who benefits from passing 'through the programme? In G. T. Barrette, R. S. Feingold, R. C. Rees and M. Pieron (eds) *Myths, Models and Methods in Sport Pedagogy*, 183–98. Champaign, Illinois, Human Kinetics.

Goldberger, M. and Gerney, P. (1986) The effects of direct teaching styles on motor skill acquistion of fifth grade children. *Research Quarterly for Exercise and Sport*, 57, 215–19.

Goldberger, M. and Howarth, K. (1993) The National Curriculum in Physical Education and the Spectrum of Teaching Styles. *British Journal of Physical Education*, 24, 1, 23–8.

Goldberger, M., Gerney, P. and Chamberlain, J. (1982) The effects of three styles of teaching on the psychomotor performance and social skill development of fifth grade children. *Research Quarterly for Exercise and Sport*, 53, 116–24.

Good, T. L. and Brophy, J. E. (1991) *Looking in Classrooms*. New York, Harper Collins.

Gould, D. R. and Roberts, G. C. (1981) Modeling and motor skill acquisition. *Quest*, 33, 214–40.

Gould, D. and Weiss, M. (1981) The effects of model similarity and model talk on self-efficacy and muscular endurance. *Journal of Sports Psychology*, 3, 17–29.

Graber, K. C. (1989) Teaching tomorrow's teachers: Professional preparation as an agent of socialisation. In T. J. Templin and P. G. Schempp (eds) *Socialisation into Physical Education*, 59–78. Indianapolis, Indiana, Benchmark Press.

Graham, G., Soares, P. and Harrington, W. (1983) Experienced teachers effectiveness with intact classes: An ETU study. *Journal of Teaching in Physical Education*, 2, 2, 3–14.

Graham, G. (1992) *Teaching Children Physical Education*. Champaign, Illinois, Human Kinetics.

Grant, B. C. (1990) Assessing teacher effectiveness in Physical Education by observing the student. *British Journal of Physical Education*, Research Supplement, 8, 11–15.

Greenockle, K. M., Lee, A. M. and Lomax, R. (1990) The relationship between selected student characteristics and activity patterns in a required high school physical education class. *Research Quarterly for Exercise and Sport*, 61, 59–69.

Griffey, D. C. and Housner, L. D. (1991) Differences between experienced and inexperienced teachers' planning decisions, interactions, student engagement, and instructional climate. *Research Quarterly for Exercise and Sport*, 62, 2, 196–204.

Groisser, P. (1964) *How to use the fine art of questioning*. New York, Teachers' Practical Press.

Groves, L. (1979) *Physical Education for Special Needs*. Cambridge, Cambridge University Press.

Gustart, J. L. and Springings, E. J. (1989) Student learning as a measure of teacher effectiveness in physical education. *Journal of Teaching in Physical Education*, 8, 298–311.

Hardy, C. (1990) Pupils' understanding of teachers' instructions. *Bulletin of Physical Education*, 26, 3, 17–22.

Hardy, C. (1992) Pupil misbehaviour during physical education lessons. *Bulletin of Physical Education*, 28, 2, 59–67.

Hardy, C. (1993) What pre-service teachers and their supervisors see as salient features of non-successful teaching of swimming. *Bulletin of Physical Education*, 29, 1, 44–58.

Harris, J. and Elbourne, J. (1992) Highlighting Health-related Exercise within the National Curriculum – Part 3. *British Journal of Physical Education*, 23, 3, 4–9.

Harvey, O. J., Hunt, D. E. and Schroder, H. M. (1961) *Conceptual Systems and Personality Organisation*. New York, John Wiley and Sons.

Hastie, P. A. and Saunders, J. E. (1990) A study of monitoring in secondary school physical education classes. *Journal of Classroom Interaction*, 25, 1 & 2, 47–54.

Hatfield, S. C. and Phillips, R. (1989) *Records of Achievement in Physical Education*. Topic No 3, NWCPEA.

Hellison, D. R. (1978) *Beyond Balls and Bats*. Washington, DC, AAHPERD.

Hellison, D. R. (1985) *Goals and Strategies for Teaching Physical Education*. Champaign, Illinois, Human Kinetics.

Hellison, D. R. and Templin, T. J. (1991) *A Reflective Approach to Teaching Physical Education*. Champaign, Illinois, Human Kinetics.

Hendry, L. B. (1971) An exploratory analysis of expectations for the physical education teachers' role. Unpublished MSc Thesis, University of Bradford.

Heron, J. (1986) *Six Category Intervention Analysis*. 2nd Edition. Human Potential Research Project, University of Surrey, Guildford.

Hill, A., Jennings, M. and Madgwick, B. (1992) Initiating a Mentorship Training Programme. In M. Wilkins (ed.) *Mentoring in Schools*, 116–132. London, Kogan Page.

Hoffman, S. J. (1983) Clinical diagnosis as a pedagogical skill. In T. J. Templin and J. K. Olson (eds) *Teaching in Physical Education*, 35–45. Champaign, Illinois, Human Kinetics.

Hoffman, S. J. and Sembiante, J. L. (1975) Experience and imagery in movement analysis. British Proceedings of Sports Psychology, 288–295. British Society of Sports Psychology.

Houghton, S., Wheldall, K., Jukes, R. and Sharpe, A. (1989) The effects of limited private reprimands and increased private praise on classroom behaviour in four British secondary classes. Birmingham University Centre for Child Study.

Housner, L. (1990) Selecting master teachers : Evidence from process-product research. *Journal of Teaching in Physical Education*, 9, 3, 201–26.

Housner, L. (1991) Teacher Cognition. In T. J. Martinek (ed.) *Psycho-Social Aspects of Teaching Physical Education*, 35–55. Dubuque, IA, Brown and Benchmark.

Hurst, B. and Wilkin, M. (1992) Guidelines for Mentors. In M. Wilkin (ed.) *Mentoring in School*, 43–57. London, Kogan Page.

Imwold, C. H. and Hoffman, S. J. (1983) Visual recognition of a gymnastic skill by experienced and inexperienced instructors. *Research Quarterly for Exercise and Sport*, 54, 149–155.

Imwold, C. H., Rider, R. A., Twardy, B. M., Oliver, P. S., Griffin, M. and Arsenault, D. N. (1984) The effects of planning on the teaching behaviour of pre-service physical education teachers. *Journal of Teaching in Physical Education*, 4, 39–49.

Jacques, K. (1992) Mentoring in Initial Teacher Education. *Cambridge Journal of Education*, 22, 3, 337–50.

Jowsey, S. (1992) *Can I Play Too?* London, David Fulton.

Joyce, B. and Weil, M. (1986) *Models of Teaching*, 3rd Edition. Englewood Cliffs, N.J., Prentice Hall.

Keh, N. C. and Lee, A. M. (1994) Students use of feedback during badminton instruction. *Research Quarterly for Exercise and Sport, Abstracts of Completed Research, 65, Supplement, A–77.*

Kirk, D. (1988) *Physical Education and Curriculum Study: A Critical Introduction.* London, Croom Helm.

Kounin, J. S. (1970) *Discipline and group management in classrooms.* New York, Holt, Rinehart & Winston.

Kounin, J. S. and Gump, P. V. (1958) The ripple effect in discipline. *Elementary School Journal*, 35, 158–62.

Kyriacou, C. (1991) *Essential Teaching Skills.* London, Blackwell.

Landers, D. M. and Landers, D. M. (1973) Teachers versus peer models: Effects of model's presence and performance level on motor behaviour. *Journal of Motor Behaviour*, 5, 3, 129–39.

Latham, A. M. (1992) Pupils' self-assessment: Can teachers help? *British Journal of Physical Education*, 23, 1, 23–5.

Latham, A. M. and Lucas, T. (1993) Planning assessment and the assessment of planning in games. *British Journal of Physical Education*, 24, 4, 17–21.

Lawrence, D. (1989) *Enhancing self-esteem in the classroom.* London, Paul Chapman.

Lawson, H. (1983) Toward a model of teacher socialisation in physical education: The subjective warrant, recruitment and teacher education. *Journal of Teaching in Physical Education*, 2, 3, 3–16.

Lawson, H. (1989) From Rookie to Veteran: Workplace conditions in physical education and induction into the profession. In T. J. Templin and P. G. Schempp (eds) *Socialisation into Physical Education: Learning to Teach*, 145–163. Indianapolis, Indiana, Benchmark Press.

Lawton, J. (1989) Comparison of two teaching methods in games.

*Bulletin of Physical Education*, 25, 1, 35–8.

Lee, A. (1991) Research on teaching in physical education: Questions and comments. *Research Quarterly for Exercise and Sport*, 62, 4, 374–79.

Lee, A. M., Keh, N. C. and Magill, R. A. (1993) Instructional effects of teacher feedback in physical education. *Journal of Teaching in Physical Education*, 12, 3, 228–43.

Lirgg, C. D. and Feltz, D. L. (1991) Teacher versus peer models revisited: Effects on motor performance and self-efficacy. *Research Quarterly for Exercise and Sport*, 62, 217–24.

Locke, L. (1975) *The Ecology of the Gymnasium: What the tourists never see*. Proceedings of the Southern Association for Physical Education of College Women.

Locke, L. and Woods, S. (1982) Teacher enthusiasm. *Journal of Teaching in Physical Education*, 1, 3, 3–14.

Loose, S. and Abrahams, M. (1993) Peer assessment: Some thoughts and proposals. *British Journal of Physical Education*, 24, 4, 8–13.

Lortie, D. (1975) *Schoolteacher: A Sociological Study*. Chicago, University of Chicago Press.

McBride, R. E. (1990) Sex role stereotyping behaviours among elementary, junior and senior high school physical education specialists. *Journal of Teaching in Physical Education*, 9, 249–261.

McBride, R., Boggess, T. and Griffey, D. (1986) Concerns of in-service physical education teachers as compared with Fuller's concern model. *Journal of Teaching in Physical Education*, 5, 149–56.

McConachie-Smith, J. (1991a) Assessment of Progression in National Curriculum Physical Education. *British Journal of Physical Education*, 22, 2, 11–15.

McConachie-Smith, J. (1991b) Assessment of learning in Gymnastics. *British Journal of Physical Education*, 22, 3, 31–5.

McCullagh, P. (1986) Model status as a determinant of observational learning and performance. *Journal of Sports Psychology*, 8, 319–331.

McCullagh, P. (1987) Model similarity effects on motor performance. *Journal of Sports Psychology*, 9, 249–60.

McCullagh, P. (1993) Modeling: Learning, Developmental and Social Psychological considerations. In R. N. Singer, M. Murphey and K. L. Tennant (eds) *Handbook of Research on Sports Psychology*, 106–126. New York, Macmillan.

McKinney, C. W., Larkins, A. G., Kazelskis, R., Ford, M. J., Allen, J. A. and Davis, J. C. (1983) Some effects of teacher enthusiasm on student achievement in fourth grade social studies. *Journal of Educational Research*, 76, 4, 239–53.

McLeish, J. (1981) *Effective Teaching in Physical Education*. University of Victoria, British Columbia.

McNamara, D. (1992) (The) Reform of teacher education in England and Wales: Teacher competence, panacea or rhetoric? *Journal of Education for Teaching*, 18, 3, 278–85.

Magill, R. (1993) Augmented feedback in skill acquisition. In R. N. Singer, M. Murphey and K. L. Tennant, (eds) *Handbook of Research on Sports Psychology*, 193–212. New York, Macmillan.

Magill, R. A. and Wood, C. A. (1986) Knowledge of results as a learned variable in motor skill acquisition. *Research Quarterly for Exercise and Sport*, 57, 170–73.

Marland, M. (1975) *The Craft of the Classroom*. London, Heinemann.

Marland, M. (1992) Leading from the front. *Times Educational Supplement*, 10th January, 16.

Marteniuk, R. G. (1976) *Information Processing in Motor Skills*. New York, Holt, Rinehart & Winston.

Martinek, T. J. (1988) Confirmation of a teacher expectancy model: Student perceptions and causal attributions of teaching behaviours. *Research Quarterly for Exercise and Sport*, 59, 2, 118–26.

Martinek, T. J. (1989) The Psycho-social dynamics of the Pygmalion Phenomena in physical education and sport. In T. J. Templin and P. G. Schempp (eds) *Socialisation into Physical Education*, 199–218. Indianapolis, Indiana, Benchmark Press.

Martinek, T. J. (1991) *Psycho-Social Dynamics of Teaching Physical Education*. Dubuque, IA, Brown and Benchmark.

Martinek, T. J. and Johnson, S. (1979) Teacher expectations: Effects on dyadic interaction and self-concept in elementary age children. *Research Quarterly*, 50, 60–70.

Martinek, T. J. and Karper, W. (1984) Multivariate relationships of specific impression cues with teacher expectations and dyadic interactions in elementary physical education classes. *Research Quarterly for Exercise and Sport*, 55, 32–40.

Martinek, T. J., Crowe, P. B. and Rejeski, W. J. (1982) *Pygmalion in the Gym: Causes and Effects of Expectations in Teaching and Coaching*. West Point, New York, Leisure Press.

Maslow, A. H. (1970) *Motivation and Personality*. New York, Harper and Row.

Masser, L. (1987) The effect of refinement on student achievement in a fundamental motor skill in grades K through 6. *Journal of Teaching in Physical Education*, 6, 174–82.

Mawer, M. A. and Brown, G. A. (1982) Teacher guidance behaviour in educational gymnastics lessons with elementary age children. In M. Pieron and J. Cheffers (eds) *Studying the Teaching in Physical Education*, 123–130. University of Liege, Belgium, AIESEP.

Mawer, M. A. and Brown, G. A. (1983) Analysing teaching in Physical Education. In M. A. Mawer (ed.) *Trends in Physical Education*. Aspects of Education 29, Journal of the Institute of Education, 71–95, University of Hull.

Mellor, W. (1990) *An overview of Mosston's Spectrum of Teaching Styles*. Queens University, Kingston, Ontario.

Metzler, M. (1989) A review of research on time in sport pedagogy. *Journal of Teaching in Physical Education*, 8, 2, 87–103.

Metzler, M. (1990) *Instructional Supervision in Physical Education*. Champaign, Illinois, Human Kinetics.

Mosston, M. and Ashworth, S. (1986) *Teaching Physical Education*. Columbus, Ohio, Merrill Pub. Co.

National Curriculum Council (NCC) (1990) *Curriculum Guidance 3: The Whole Curriculum*. York, UK, NCC.

National Curriculum Council (NCC) (1992) *Physical Education Non-Statutory Guidance*. York, UK, NCC.

National Institute of Education (1975) *Teaching as Clinical Information Processing*. Report of Panel 6, National Conference on Studies in Teaching. Washington DC, National Institute of Education.

Nielson, A. B. and Beauchamp, L. (1991) The effect of training in conceptual kinesiology on feedback provision patterns. *Journal of Teaching in Physical Education*, 11, 126–38.

Newell, K. M., Morris, L. R. and Scully, D. M. (1985) Augmented information and the acquisition of skills in physical activity. In R. L. Terjung (ed.) *Exercise and Sports Science Reviews*, 235–61. New York, Macmillan.

Office for Standards in Education (OFSTED) (1993a) *Handbook for the Inspection of Schools*. London, OFSTED.

Office for Standards in Education (OFSTED) (1993b) *Working papers for the Inspection of Secondary Initial Teacher Training*. London, OFSTED.

Office for Standards in Education (OFSTED) (1993c) *The New Teacher in School*. London, OFSTED.

Olson, J. K. (1983) Catenas: Exploring meanings. In T. J. Templin and J. K. Olson (eds) *Teaching in Physical Education*, 286–97. Champaign, Illinois, Human Kinetics.

Paese, P. C. (1986) Comparison of teacher behaviour and criterion process variables in an experimental teaching unit (ETU) taught by pre-service physical education majors at the entrance and exit levels. In M. Pieron and G. Graham (eds) *Sport Pedagogy*, 207–13. Proceedings of the 1984 Olympic Scientific Congress, 6. Champaign, Illinois, Human Kinetics.

Perrott, E. (1982) *Effective Teaching: A practical guide to improving your teaching*. London, Longmans.

Peterson, P. L. and Clark, C. M. (1978) Teachers' reports of their cognitive processes during teaching. *American Educational Research Journal*, 15, 555–65.

Phillips, D. A. and Carlisle, C. (1983) A comparison of physical education teachers categorised as most and least effective. *Journal of Teaching in Physical Education*, 2, 3, 55–67.

Pieron, M. (1982) Effectiveness of teaching a psychomotor task: Study in a micro-teaching setting. In M. Pieron and J. Cheffers (eds) *Studying the Teaching in Physical Education*, 78–89. University of Liege, Belgium, AIESEP.

Pieron, M. (1983) Teacher and pupil behaviour and the interactive process in physical education classes. In R. Telema, V. Varstala, J. Tiainen, L. Laakso and T. Haajanen (eds) *Research in School Physical Education*, 13–30. University of Jyvaskyla, Finland, AIESEP.

Pieron, M. and Cheffers, J. (eds) (1988) *Research in Sport Pedagogy: Empirical Analytic Perspective.* International Council of Sport Science and Physical Education, Verlag Karl Hofman D-7060, Schorndorf.

Pieron, M. and Delmelle, V. (1982) Augmented feedback in teaching physical education: Responses from the students. In M. Pieron and J. Cheffers (eds) *Studying the Teaching in Physical Education*, 142–50. University of Liege, Belgium, AIESEP.

Pinhiero, V. E. D. and Simon, H. A. (1992) An operational model of motor skill diagnosis. *Journal of Teaching in Physical Education*, 11, 3, 288–302.

Placek, J. H. (1983) Conceptions of success in teaching: Busy, Happy and Good. In T. J. Templin and J. Olson (eds) *Teaching in Physical Education*, 47–56. Champaign, Illinois, Human Kinetics.

Placek, J. H. and Dodds, P. (1988) A critical incident study of pre-service teachers' beliefs about success and non-success. *Research Quarterly for Exercise and Sport*, 59, 4, 351–58.

Pollock, B. J. and Lee, T. D. (1992) Effects of the model's skill level on observational motor learning. *Research Quarterly for Exercise and Sport*, 63, 1, 25–29.

Posner, M. I. (1969) Short-term memory system in human information processing. In R. N. Haber (ed.) *Information-Processing Approaches to Visual Perceptions.* New York, Holt, Rinehart and Winston.

Read, B. (1993) Practical knowledge and games education at Key Stage 3. *British Journal of Physical Education*, 24, 1, 10–14.

Rikard, G. L. (1991) The short-term relationship of teacher feedback and student practice. *Journal of Teaching in Physical Education*, 10, 275–85.

Rikard, G. L. (1992) The relationship of teachers' task refinement and feedback to students' practice success. *Journal of Teaching in Physical Education*, 11, 4, 349–57.

Rink, J. E. (1985) *Teaching Physical Education for Learning.* St Louis, Miss., C. V. Mosby.

Rink, J. E. and Werner, P. (1987) Student responses as a measure of teacher effectiveness. In G. T. Barrette, R. S. Feingold, C. R. Rees and M. Pieron (eds) *Myths, Models and Methods in Sport Pedagogy*, 199–206. Champaign, Illinois, Human Kinetics.

Rink, J. E., Werner, P. H., Hohn, R. C., Ward, D. S. and Timmermans, H. M. (1986) Differential effects of three teachers over a unit of instruction. *Research Quarterly for Exercise and Sport*, 57, 132–38.

Roach, N. K. and Burwitz, L. (1986) Observational learning in motor skill acquisition: The effect of verbal directing cues. In J. Watkins, T. Reilly and L. Burwitz (eds) *Sports Science : Proceedings of the VII Commonwealth and International Conference on Sport, Physical Education, Dance, Recreation and Health*, 349–354. London, E & F Spon.

Robinson, S. (1992) *Assessment in Physical Education: A Developmental Programme*. British Association of Advisers and Lecturers in Physical Education.

Robinson, S. (1993) *Managing the Physical Education Curriculum, A Developmental Programme for Key Stages 3 and 4*. Aspects of Physical Education, Stowmarket, Suffolk.

Rogers, C. R. (1983) *Freedom to learn for the 80's*. Columbus, Charles Merrill.

Rolider, A., Siedentop, D. and Van Houten, R. (1984) Effects of enthusiasm training on subsequent teacher enthusiastic behaviour. *Journal of Teaching in Physical Education*, 3, 2, 47–59.

Rosenshine, B. (1970) Evaluation of classroom instruction. *Review of Educational Research*, 40, 279–300.

Rosenshine, B. (1976) Classroom instruction. In N. Gage (ed.) *The Psychology of Teaching Methods*, 335–71. Seventy-fifth Yearbook, National Society for the study of Education, Chicago, University of Chicago Press.

Rosenshine, B. (1979) Content, time, and direct instruction. In P. Peterson and H. Walberg (eds) *Research on Teaching: Concepts, findings and implications*, 28–56. Berkeley, CA, McCutchan.

Rosenshine, B. and Furst, N. (1973) The use of direct observation to study teaching. In R. M. W. Travers (ed.) *Second Handbook of Research on Teaching*, 122–83. Chicago, Rand McNally.

Rosenshine, B. and Stevens, R. (1986) Teaching Functions. In M. Wittrock (ed.) *Handbook of Research on Teaching*, 3rd Edition, 376–91. New York, Macmillan.

Rosenthal, R. and Jacobson, L. (1968) *Pygmalion in the Classroom*. New York, Holt, Rinehart and Winston.

Rugby Football Union (1992) *Skills practices for all*. London, RFU.

Schempp, P. G. (1989) Apprenticeship-of-observation and the development of physical education teachers. In T. J. Templin and P. G. Schempp (eds) *Socialisation into Physical Education: Learning to Teach*, 13–37. Indiana, Benchmark Press.

Schon, D. (1983) *The Reflective Practitioner*. London, Temple Smith.

Schon, D. (1987) *Educating the Reflective Practitioner*. London, Jossey-Bass.

School Curriculum and Assessment Authority (SCAA) (1994a) *Physical Education in the National Curriculum*, Draft Proposals. London, SCAA.

School Curriculum and Assessment Authority (SCAA) (1994b) *Physical Education in the National Curriculum*, National Curriculum Draft Orders. London, SCAA.

Schools Examination and Assessment Council (SEAC) (1991) *Teacher Assessment in Practice*. London, SEAC.

Schools Examination and Assessment Council (SEAC) (1992) *Teacher Assessment at Key Stage 3*. London, SEAC.

Schroder, H. M., Driver, M. J. and Streufert, S. (1967) *Human Information Procesing: Individual and Group Functioning in Complex Social Situations*. New York, Holt, Rinehart & Winston.

Schwab, J. J. (1969) The Practical: A Language for Curriculum. *School Review*, 78, 1–23.

Scraton, S. (1993) Equality, co-education and physical education in secondary schools. In J. Evans (ed) *Equality, Education and Physical Education*, 130–53. London, Falmer Press.

Scully, D. M. (1988) Visual perception of human movement: The use of demonstrations in teaching motor skills. *British Journal of Physical Education*, Research Supplement, 4.

Shaw, R. (1992) Can mentoring raise achievement in schools? In M. Wilkin (ed.) *Mentoring in Schools*, 82–96. London, Kogan Page.

Shearsmith, K. and Laws, C. (1988) *Change of Focus in Teaching Games: What we say and what we do*. Crofton School and West Sussex Institute of Higher Education.

Shulman, L. S. (1987) Knowledge and Teaching: Foundations of the new reform. *Harvard Educational Review*, 57, 1, 1–22.

Shute, S., Dodds, P., Placek, J., Rife, F. and Silverman, S. (1982) Academic learning time in elementary school movement education: A descriptive analytical study. *Journal of Teaching in Physical Education*, 1, 2, 3–14.

Siedentop, D. (1989) The effective elementary specialist study. *Journal of Teaching in Physical Education*, 8, 3, Monograph.

Siedentop, D. (1991) *Developing Teaching Skills in Physical Education*, 3rd Edition. California, Mayfield Pub. Co.

Siedentop, D., Tousignant, M. and Parker, M. (1982) *Academic Learning Time – Physical Education. 1982 Revision Coding Manual*. School of Health, PE and Recreation, Ohio State University.

Silverman, S. (1985) Relationship of engagement and practice trials to student achievement. *Journal of Teaching in Physical Education*, 5, 13–21.

Silverman, S. (1988) Relationships of selected presage and context variables to achievement. *Research Quarterly for Exercise and Sport*, 59, 35–41.

Silverman, S. (1991) Research on teaching in physical education. *Research Quarterly for Exercise and Sport*, 62, 4, 352–64.

Silverman, S., Tyson, L. A. and Krampitz, J. (1992) Teacher feedback and achievement in physical education: Interaction with student practice. *Teaching and Teacher Education*, 8, 333–44.

Smith, M. D. (1990) Enhancing self-responsibility through a humanistic approach to physical education. *Bulletin of Physical Education*, 26, 3, 27–31.

Smith, L. and Geoffrey, W. (1969) *The Complexities of an Urban Classroom*. New York, Holt, Rinehart & Winston.

Spackman, L. (ed.) (1983) *Teaching Games for Understanding*. Curriculum Development Centre for Physical Education, The College of St Paul and St Mary, Cheltenham.

Standing Conference on Physical Education (SCOPE) (1985) *Teaching Quality and Physical Education*. Annual Conference Proceedings, Nottingham, Sheffield City Polytechnic, PAVIC Publications.

Stenhouse, L. (1975) *An Introduction to Curriculum Research and Development*. London, Heinemann Education.

Stodolsky, S. S., Ferguson, T. L. and Wimpelberg, K. (1981) The recitation persists: But what does it look like? *Journal of Curriculum Studies*, 13, 121–30.

Strasser, B. (1967) A conceptual model of instruction. *Journal of Teacher Education*, 18, 1, 63–74.

Stroot, S. A. and Morton, P. J. (1989) Blueprints for learning. *Journal of Teaching in Physical Education*, 8, 213–22.

Suffolk Education Department (1987) *In the Light of Torches: Teacher Appraisal*. London, Industrial Society.

Taba, H. and Elzey, F. F. (1964) Teaching strategies and thought processes. *Teacher College Record*, 65, 524–34.

Talbot, M. (1990) Equal opportunities and physical education. In N. Armstrong (ed.) *New Directions in Physical Education*, 1, 101–20. Champaign, Illinois, Human Kinetics.

Talbot, M. (1993) A gendered physical education: Equality and Sexism. In J. Evans (ed.) *Equality, Education and Physical Education*, 74–89. London, Falmer Press.

Taylor, P. H. (1970) *How Teachers Plan their Courses*. Slough, Bucks, National Foundation for Educational Research.

Templin, T. J. and Schempp, P. G. (1989) An introduction to socialisation into physical education. In T. J. Templin and P. G. Schempp (eds) *Socialisation into Physical Education: Learning to Teach*, 1–10. Indianapolis, Indiana, Benchmark Press.

Thomas, J. R. (1980) Acquisition of motor skills: Information processing differences between children and adults. *Research Quarterly*, 51, 158–73.

Thomas, S. (1991) Equality in Physical Education: A consideration of key issues, concepts and strategies. In N. Armstrong and A. Sparkes (eds) *Issues in Physical Education*, 56–73. London, Cassell.

Thorpe, R., Bunker, D. and Almond, L. (1986) *Rethinking Games Teaching*. Department of Physical Education and Sports Science, Loughborough University.

Tobin, K. (1987) The role of wait time in higher cognitive learning. *Review of Educational Research*, 57, 69–95.

Tom, A. (1988) Teaching as a Moral Craft. In R. Dale, R. Ferguson and A. Robinson (eds) *Frameworks for Teaching: Readings for the Intending Secondary Teacher*, 33–52. London, Hodder & Stoughton for the Open University.

Tousignant, M. (1982) Analysis of the task structures in secondary physical education classes. Unpublished Doctoral Dissertation, Ohio State University.

Tousignant, M. and Brunelle, J. (1982) What have we learned from students and how can we use it to improve curriculum and teaching. In M. Pieron and J. Cheffers (eds) *Studying the Teaching in Physical Education*, 3–26. University of Liege, Belgium, AIESEP.

Tousignant, M. and Siedentop, D. (1983) A qualitative analysis of task structures in required secondary physical education classes. *Journal of Teaching in Physical Education*, 3, 47–57.

Turner, A. P. and Martinek, T. J. (1993) A comparative analysis of two models for teaching games. *International Journal of Physical Education*, 30, 1, 15–31.

Turvey, J. and Laws, C. (1988) Are girls losing out? The effects of mixed sex grouping on girls' performance in physical education. *British Journal of Physical Education*, 19, 6, 253–55.

Tyler, R. W. (1950) *Basic Principles of Curriculum and Instruction*. Chicago, Illinois, University of Chicago Press.

Underwood, M. (1991) *Aspects of Gymnastics and Independent Learning Experiences (AGILE)*. Exeter University School of Education, London, Thomas Nelson and Son.

Underwood, M. and Williams, A. (1991) Personal and Social Education through Gymnastics. *British Journal of Physical Education*, 22, 3, 15–19.

Watkins, C. and Wagner, P. (1987) *School Discipline: A Whole School Approach*. Oxford, Basil Blackwell.

Weiss, R. M. and Klint, K. A. (1987) 'Show and Tell' in the Gymnasium: An investigation of developmental differences in modelling and verbal rehearsal of motor skills. *Research Quarterly for Exercise and Sport*, 58, 2, 234–41.

Wendt, J. C. and Bain, L. L. (1989) Concerns of pre-service and in-service physical educators. *Journal of Teaching in Physical Education*, 8, 177–80.

Werner, P. and Rink, J. (1989) Case studies of teacher effectiveness in second grade physical education. *Journal of Teaching in Physical Education*, 8, 280–97.

Werner, P., Rink, J. and Hinricks, R. (1984) Effects of intervention in the teaching process on jumping and landing abilities of second grade children. Paper presented at the 1984 Olympic Scientific Congress, Eugene, Oregon.

Wheldall, K. and Merrett, F. (1987) Training teachers to use the behavioural approach to classroom management in the development of BATPACK. In K. Wheldall (ed.) *The Behaviourist in the Classroom*, 130–68. London, Allen & Unwin.

Wheldall, K. and Merrett, F. (1988) Packages for training teachers in classroom behaviour management: BATPACK, BATSAC and the Positive Teaching packages. *Support for Learning*, 3, 86–92.

Wheldall, K. and Merrett, F. (1989) *Positive Teaching in the Secondary School*. London, Paul Chapman.

White, A. and Coakley, J. T. (1986) *Making decisions: The response of young people in the Medway towns to the 'Ever thought of Sport?' Campaign*. Greater London and S.E. Regional Sports Council.

Williams, A. (1993) Aspects of teaching and learning in Gymnastics. *British Journal of Physical Education*, 24, 1, 29–32.

Williams, J. G. (1986) Perceiving human movement: A review of research with implications for the use of the demonstration during motor learning. *Physical Education Review*, 9, 53–58.

Wilson, S. M., Shulman, L. S. and Richert, A. E. (1987) 150 Different ways of knowing: Representations of Knowledge in Teaching. In J. Calderhead (ed.) *Exploring Teachers' Thinking*, 104–24. London, Cassell.

Witkin, H. A., Moore, C. A., Goodenhough, D. R. and Cox, P. W. (1977) Field dependent and field independent cognitive styles and their educational implications. *Review of Educational Research*, 47, 1–64.

Woods, P. (1990) *Teacher Skills and Strategies*. London, Falmer Press.

Wragg, E. C. (ed.) (1984) *Classroom Teaching Skills*. London, Croom Helm.

Wragg, E. C. (1993) *Classroom Management*. London, Routledge.

Wragg, E. C. and Dooley, P. A. (1984) Class management during teaching practice. In E. C. Wragg. (ed.) *Classroom Teaching Skills*, 21–46. London, Croom Helm

Wragg, E. C. and Wood, E. K. (1984a) Teachers' first encounters with their classes. In E. C. Wragg (ed.) *Classroom Teaching Skills*, 47–78. London, Croom Helm.

Wragg, E. C. and Wood, E. K. (1984b) Pupil appraisals of teaching. In E. C. Wragg (ed.) *Classroom Teaching Skills*, 79–96. London, Croom Helm.

Yerg, B. J. (1981) The impact of selected presage and process behaviours on the refinement of a motor skill. *Journal of Teaching in Physical Education*, 1, 1, 38–46.

Yerg, B. J. and Twardy, B. M. (1982) Relationship of specified instructional teacher behaviours to pupil gains on a motor skill task. In M. Pieron and J. Cheffers (eds) *Studying the Teaching in Physical Education*, 61–8. University of Liege, Belgium, AIESEP.

Zahorik, J. A. (1975) Teachers' planning models. *Educational Leadership*, 33, 134–9.

Zeichner, K. and Tabachnick, B. (1981) Are the effects of university teacher education 'washed out' by school experiences? *Journal of Teacher Education*, 32, 3, 7–11.

# I N D E X